*Will You Still
Need Me,
Will You Still
Feed Me,
When I'm 84?*

Will You Still Need Me, Will You Still Feed Me, When I'm 84?

DORIS FRANCIS

Indiana University Press • Bloomington

LIBRARY OF CONGRESS CATALOGING IN PUBLICATION DATA

Francis, Doris
Will you still need me, will you still feed me,
when I'm 84?

Bibliography: p.
Includes index.
1. Jewish aged—Ohio—Cleveland. 2. Jews—Ohio—
Cleveland—Social conditions. 3. Jewish aged—England—
Leeds (West Yorkshire) 4. Jews—England—Leeds (West
Yorkshire)—Social conditions. 5. Cleveland (Ohio)—
Social conditions. 6. Leeds (West Yorkshire)—Social
conditions. I. Title.
HV1471.C58F7 1984   305.2'6'089924077132   82-49351
ISBN 0-253-36545-7
1 2 3 4 5 88 87 86 85 84

*To my beloved mother
and in loving memory of my father*

Contents

Illustrations

Maps

Figures

Acknowledgments

First, let me thank these members of the Case Western Reserve University faculty for their support and encouragement of this research project: Eugene Uyeki, John Glasson, Norbert Dannheauser, George Rosenberg, and Charles Callender. I owe special appreciation to my good friend and mentor, Sutti Ortiz, who graciously offered unstinting time, patience, and direction.

Judah Rubinstein, Research Director of the Jewish Community Federation, and Dr. John Grabowski of the Western Reserve Historical Society answered many questions on the history of the Jews in Cleveland. Ellie Gerson, Mila Stein, and Lillian Greenberg provided encouragement and introduced me to people in the neighborhood and to others helpful to my study. I especially appreciate attending Lillian's weekly discussion group at the Jewish Center and benefited from our conversations at lunch afterward. Belle Likover and the staff of the Nutrition Program at the Jewish Center provided a comfortable atmosphere where I could meet many elderly people. To the mailmen, Mr. Spencer and Mr. Green, I owe great thanks, for it was they who introduced me to my informants. And I discussed many of my research findings with Rabbi Marvin Spiegelman and Ceal Friedberg.

But most of all, I want to thank my many Cornell neighbors for their friendship and generous sharing of time and information. I enjoyed our long visits.

I want to express my appreciation to the many people in Leeds who helped me professionally and personally: Heinz Skyte, Mr. and Mrs. John Solk and their family, David Lester, Pauline Sliw, Max and Barbara Usher, Nigel Grizzard, Pippa Landey, Mrs. King, and my many friends on the Knightsdale Estate. All provided needed information and friendly conversation. Their gifts of time and warm hospitality made my year in England memorable indeed.

Appreciation also is expressed to the Battelle Memorial Institute, The Memorial Foundation for Jewish Culture, and Case Western Reserve University, whose financial assistance made this study possible.

The following individuals must also be thanked for their generous sharing of expertise and experience in critiquing the manuscript: Anna V. Brown, Sidney Spector, and Jean Luppens. Thanks to lexicographer and friend, David Guralnik, who prepared the Glossary of Yiddish terms. Transcriptions follow YIVO convention. Appreciation, also, to Virginia Benade, who typed the manuscript, and to Sandy Siebenschuh, who edited it. But it is to my dear husband Louis, and to my kin, neighbors, and friends, especially fellow dissertation writers Nancy, Cindy, and Connie, that I am grateful for support and encouragement.

*Will you Still
Need Me,
Will You Still
Feed Me,
When I'm 84?*

Introduction

THIS BOOK EXPLORES HOW TWO GROUPS of elderly Jews—one in Cleveland, Ohio, and the other in Leeds, England—have adapted to the role of being aged. These two groups have several things in common: they are, for the most part, poor; they are Jews in predominantly Gentile cultures; their childhoods were spent in Eastern European environments; and they are now old in Western industrial countries. But their roles and ability to cope with growing old are different indeed. What these roles are and why they are so different are the subjects of this book.

The underlying argument in the book is based on several assumptions.

1. Kinship roles are ambiguous and are not explicitly stated in Western industrial society. In such societies, roles are defined on the basis of class, ethnicity, occupation, and age and sex differences as much as they are on kinship. But the importance of these defining factors varies throughout the life cycle. Kinship responsibilities, for example, are heightened for the parents of young children, but as children grow older, parents' roles are defined more by other social factors, such as occupation and class. When men and women retire, they rely again on kinship ties to define their position, particularly if they are poor and have not assumed prestigious positions or participated in religious activities.

2. The kinship role of retired fathers and mothers is even less clearly specified than are kinship obligations in society as a whole. When people retire, they must make a transition from a composite role structure defined by occupation, class, kinship obligations, religious precepts, and ethnic ideology to one where occupation is irrelevant, where low income evens out class differences, and where age/sex components and family relations again assume importance. But the kinship obligations of elderly retired mothers and fathers are seldom specifically stated. No clear legal, economic, or religious framework helps delimit kinship roles for aged parents. Ethnic ideology is varied or vague, and religious precepts are not always appropriate. Instead, elderly parents have to think out, negotiate,

1

and operationalize their new roles, mostly on the basis of kinship rights and obligations.

3. This process of self-definition cannot be done in the abstract. To some extent, ideological statements and public expressions of norms can help—religious teachings about moral responsibilities, legal rules for and obligations of family members, and cultural statements about idealized parents and elderly people in newspapers or other mass media. But such abstractions are almost always unrealistic models. Older people who must rely on such cultural and religious models have great difficulty adjusting to the realities of aging.

4. The elderly define their own roles through exchanges with other older parents who are their friends and kinsmen, as well as with their children and grandchildren. While rites of passage are helpful in some situations (for example, marriage and the death of a loved one), in industrial society such rites are hardly relevant for the elderly. The transition to the status of retired elder is only indirectly acknowledged through their marginal participation in others' rites of passage or in retirement or widowhood. Without specific rites to help them adjust to a new social position and an altered role, the elderly must negotiate their rights and duties with others in their social environment.

Four factors help the aged adjust to their new roles. The first three are the quality of earlier family relationships; the shared life styles of aged parents and adult children; and the presence of lifelong, intimate friends. Although it is difficult to weigh the relative importance of these inter-related factors for each individual, it seems clear that the number of close friendships people are able to sustain throughout their lives is crucial in their adjustment to new roles in old age. And it is the one factor social policy can still affect by building housing for the elderly and offering relevant programs at day centers. The fourth factor is, then, the quality of the residential environment where the elderly settle, and the peer relations within these residential settings.

Kinship and friendship are part of a set of ongoing social exchanges. Both affect the attitudes of the elderly toward interaction with children and their ability to participate in and adjust to relations with peers. I believe that kinship must be analyzed as part of a total set of social relations. We must focus on exchanges that engender relations and define boundaries between people rather than on sanctions that back jural definitions of roles. The friendship rules of equivalency, confidentiality, and intimacy concern only the individuals who share the relationship and transact their own bargain.[1] Friendship can be associated with kinship, but we must distinguish their separate components. As we will see, the Cleveland and the Leeds people I studied differ greatly in both their kinship and their friendship networks.

Cleveland and Leeds elderly contrast in their adjustments to old age in terms of their residential housing as well. Much anthropological work in culture and aging has been done in response to an emerging social and economic problem—providing for the health and welfare of the burgeoning number of aged persons in modern industrial society. Advocates of age-segregated housing report "greater social activity, more help in emergency, and higher morale in settings where old people are available as potential friends and neighbors."[2] Several recent studies deal with the significance of age as a principle of social organization and ask under what conditions and through what processes age provides a basis for community creation.[3] Among the factors necessary for the development of shared social relationships and a "we feeling" are a common territory, social and cultural homogeneity, small size, and residents with leadership skills.

Of the two communities discussed in this book, only in the housing estate in Leeds has a sense of community based on age emerged. The Cleveland high-rise (Carroll Arms) has failed to create a sense of interdependence and identification, probably because many of the elderly residents are frightened by and dependent on management (and thus unable to participate in social activities), and because many residents have not established a workable self-definition through previous exchanges with kin and friends. Preexisting social relationships with friends and children are crucial in determining how people will adjust to new roles and be able to form a new community. Yet recent studies on the subculture of the elderly focus almost exclusively on effective ties within the new residence; in so doing, they view kinship and friendship as separate, nonconflicting, and psychologically complementary relationships.[4] Surely this is an untenable theoretical position.

In this study we compare two groups of elderly people who handle old age differently. The people in Cleveland, Ohio, are lonely and uncertain about their role in their families. They are afraid that they are no longer needed and are reluctant to ask for favors from adult children. They conduct social relationships with caution, using their friends to bolster their self-images. The elderly in Leeds, England, are less anxious and more accepting of family and old friends, whose regular companionship they enjoy. Their lives closely mesh ideal values and actual behavior. This

book will attempt to explain these different reactions to old age by explor-
ing the economic, social, and kinship experiences of these two groups of
elderly.[5]

We begin with a comparison of two types of urban structures—the
small and stable society of Leeds and the larger, more mobile and dis-
persed Jewish population of Cleveland. Almost everyone in the study
began life in Eastern Europe around the turn of the century. As we
compare their experiences as immigrants, their patterns of residential mobility, the quality of their neighborhood lives, and their kinship relations,
we will see patterns emerging that can help explain their later differences
in adjustments.

CORNELL: THE NEIGHBORHOOD AND ITS RESOURCES

The first sample of informants are among the Cleveland elderly who
live in an inner-core suburb. Their neighborhood is called Cornell.*
There have been Jewish residents in Cornell since the neighborhood was
first developed in 1910. The present occupants, however, moved there
about twenty years ago from older Jewish areas in the inner city. They did
not grow up in Cornell, nor did they raise their children there.

The elderly residents of Cornell, who are in their mid-seventies and
early eighties, came to the neighborhood when they were over sixty years
old, after having moved many other times during their lives. Many are
widows, divorcees, or single women. Although most live alone, a few
have unmarried children still at home, and one shares an apartment with a
single brother. But most residents have neither children nor kin in the
neighborhood.

Cornell Jews were born in Eastern Europe—in Russia, Poland,
Lithuania, or Latvia—and emigrated to America before 1914. They left
behind parents and siblings who did not survive the Nazi holocaust. Many
are practicing Orthodox Jews. Yiddish is still the preferred language
among friends and is occasionally heard in neighborhood shops. Few
received any formal education after arriving in the United States. Most are
women. Their husbands were furriers, tailors, dry cleaners, and painters;
only a few owned their own businesses. Today, these Cornell elderly live
on a limited income from Social Security. The women seem physically
frail, and many suffer from heart conditions or glaucoma.

In the early 1960s, older Jews found Cornell a desirable place to live.

*I have changed the name of the neighborhood to ensure the confidentiality of my infor-
mants.

Apartment buildings in Cornell.

The Carroll Arms in Cornell. (Photo by Sandy Glendinning)

Rents were comparatively low and a variety of housing was available in the large three-storied apartment buildings on the side streets or above the shops along the avenue. Public transportation, a *shul* (an Orthodox Jewish synagogue), and kosher meat and poultry markets were within walking distance. Cornell was a "Jewish neighborhood" with Jewish people and Jewish shops.

In the mid-1960s, however, conditions began to change. Few neighborhood residents had extra cash, and local businesses had difficulty surviving. Many of the merchants were old, and most of the small markets closed. Now the bakeries, fresh produce stores, and fish shops are all gone. Only two kosher butchers remain.

At the same time, university students began to move into this "gray, shabby" neighborhood, as one resident described it. Many students found the large suites with low rents suitable for a communal life style. Landlords discovered that they could ask higher rents without making repairs. "Head shops" catering to a young clientele and selling leather goods, candles, incense, and so forth, replaced the older Jewish stores.

When low-income housing for the elderly was built in other parts of Cleveland, some older Cornell residents seized the opportunity to escape. As the neighborhood became known as a place for hippies and drugs, the more affluent older Jews moved to better areas further east. The *shul* was sold. Other old people passed away. Gradually the number of elderly residents in Cornell declined. By the early 1970s, only a handful of old people remained in each apartment building (see census map).

In 1974 the Cornell neighborhood was slated for urban renewal and a low-income, high-rise apartment structure was built for the elderly. For many residents, this new building seemed to offer a solution to their problems. They could move into a clean, new apartment in the area they knew, and many were eligible for rent supplements. Fifty percent of the initial applicants to the high rise were Cornell residents. Elderly people living in other parts of Cleveland also decided to move to the Carroll Arms. Currently 75 percent of the occupants of the new building are Jewish, and this part of Cornell resembles a "Jewish area" again.

LEEDS: GENERAL DESCRIPTION OF THE COMMUNITY AND ITS RESOURCES

After completing my study of the Cornell elderly, I was given the opportunity to do research with a similar group of older Jewish people in a large, industrial British city comparable to Cleveland. Leeds, Manchester,

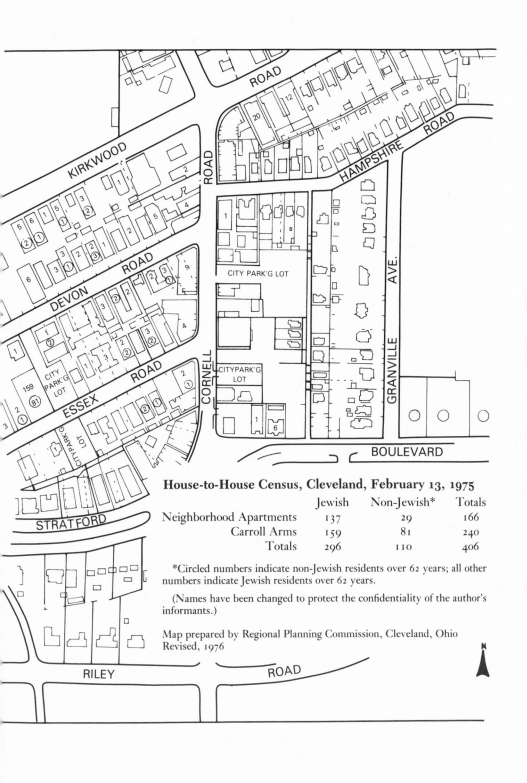

House-to-House Census, Cleveland, February 13, 1975

	Jewish	Non-Jewish*	Totals
Neighborhood Apartments	137	29	166
Carroll Arms	159	81	240
Totals	296	110	406

*Circled numbers indicate non-Jewish residents over 62 years; all other numbers indicate Jewish residents over 62 years.

(Names have been changed to protect the confidentiality of the author's informants.)

Map prepared by Regional Planning Commission, Cleveland, Ohio
Revised, 1976

and Glasgow were possible sites, but Leeds offered the most valuable field situation. Urban renewal programs had begun there earlier than in other metropolitan centers. In 1956, the Leeds Jewish community, anxious to prevent the dispersal of aged Jews, built a Housing Estate that offered homes to elderly, working-class people at rents comparable to those in public housing. Thus many of the elderly, working-class Jews in Leeds had been living on the Estate for almost twenty years when I began my study. In contrast to Leeds, the older Jewish neighborhoods in Manchester and Glasgow had only recently broken up. The elderly had scattered to different areas and were just beginning to adjust to new neighbors. Leeds offered the continuity I needed for a comparison with Cornell.

In 1950 the members of the Leeds Jewish Welfare Board had proposed a Jewish Housing Estate. Their aim was to provide accommodations for the members of the Jewish community still living in the older sections of the city, where housing was dilapidated and a number of families had to share outdoor toilet facilities. With a grant from the Leeds Corporation, the Board constructed new units, and the Jewish Estate opened in 1959.

The Knightsdale Housing Estate is located in a section of Leeds known as Medina.* In the 1950s this was a new and desirable area; it is still in the heart of the Jewish community. Here are located the synagogues, Jewish religious schools, social clubs, and kosher butchers. While a few well-to-do Jews have moved farther out, "most of the Jewish community of Leeds lives within a one-mile radius of [Medina] corner."[6]

Over the years the number of units on the Knightsdale Estate has grown. Today there are over 200 flats, housing 310 residents. Rents have risen because the Estate is classified as a Housing Association and must meet government fair-rent standards. Many residents, however, are eligible for rent supplements and receive other benefits to help pay heating bills. The initial aim of the Estate was to rehouse "people of necessitous means" who lived in deplorable conditions, and this goal has largely been met. Applications are now coming from elderly people who live in areas isolated from other Jews and from those who have sold homes but still lack adequate capital to purchase a new flat. Originally several families with young children lived on the Estate, but these youngsters have grown up and moved away. In most cases, their parents still occupy their family homes. Many husbands have passed away. The character of the Estate has, therefore, gradually changed over the past twenty years and now

---

*The names of the Housing Estate and its location have been changed to protect the confidentiality of my informants.

Informants lived in row houses before moving to the Knightsdale Estate.

Flats on the Knightsdale Estate are like the row houses where informants used to live.

houses many elderly widows who live alone. Recently, however, there has
been an effort to diversify the population, and a few young families are
moving in.

METHODOLOGY[7]

Stage One: Learning the Neighborhood

I began my anthropological field research on how the elderly adjust to
an aged role in suburban Cleveland. But because of the suspicion and
reserve of older Cornell people, it was not possible to use random-
sampling techniques in selecting a group of informants. Initially, the staff
at the Jewish Center introduced me to a few neighborhood residents. But
it was only through the help of two mailmen, who had had routes in the
neighborhood for twenty years, that I was able to locate elderly residents
systematically and to be introduced to them by someone whom they knew
and trusted. On the days that Social Security checks were delivered and
the elderly were certain to be home, I accompanied the mailmen on their
routes and was introduced as a friend doing a research project about the
neighborhood and its older residents. For the next several months, I got to
know people informally and conducted a census and survey interviews.

Stage Two: Focused Research on Social Supports

From this initial group, twenty aged residents were selected for intensive study. In choosing a sample, I was guided by the Townsend report
statistics on family structure in the United States.[8] However, for this
study I analyzed only the life histories of individuals who at the time had
at least one adult child living in Cleveland.

In conducting this second stage of research, which lasted almost two
years, I continued to use a combination of participant observation and
interviewing techniques, focusing on my chosen informants and their
social networks. I accompanied these elderly to many activities—social
clubs, the Nutrition Program at the Jewish Center, temple sisterhood
groups—and also joined them for afternoon coffee at the local deli. I often
met informants while shopping and banking in the neighborhood, where I
also lived. They, in turn, introduced me to friends, neighbors, and family
members. I spent many additional hours with each informant, both visiting informally and conducting intensive interviews about their social support systems. Here I used open-ended questions developed and refined
through my first months of research. (See Appendix A for a copy of this

aide-mémoire.) All material, both observed behavior and informants' statements, and in some cases the discrepancies between them, was recorded daily in detailed field notes. Because participant observation was so intensive, the size of my in-depth sample is limited. However, I gathered a great deal of additional qualitative information from other elderly Cornell residents in my informants' networks.

I organized the data about each in-depth informant into charts showing life history and receipt of services from kin, neighbors, friends, and social service agencies (see Appendix B). I have changed the names to maintain confidentiality.

After about six months of field research, the high-rise apartment building for low-income elderly was completed in the Cornell neighborhood. Since 50 percent of the initial tenants were Cornell residents, I observed the effects of this project on their lives and the neighborhood. About half of my previously selected informants and their neighbors chose to move into this high-rise. This allowed me to compare their social relationships over time—before, during, and after their move—and to contrast their adjustment with that of others who chose to remain in their own apartments.

Stage Three: Systematization, Measurement, and Cross-National Comparison

As I collected more focused data, I returned to the theoretical literature to help me translate the patterns I was observing into a more general explanatory hypothesis. Additional information was collected on life histories, residential moves, and urban ecology. I used this data to construct network profiles, which in turn helped me interpret the behavior and attitudes of informants. Additional research measures were also devised to evaluate my model, but the Leeds sample provided significant comparative data.

My ten-month study in Leeds benefited from the previous lengthy period of field work in Cornell. Research there was more focused, and a second sample functioned as a check on my Cornell findings. In selecting a sample from the Leeds Jewish Housing Estate, I tried to match characteristics with those of the aged informants in Cornell. Again because of the reserve of the elderly, I sought assistance from the secretaries of both the Housing Association and the Tenants' Association, and they suggested potential informants. After getting to know these people informally at club meetings and Estate activities, I chose ten individuals to interview in depth. All were elderly people who had been married and raised families and who had lived on the Estate for over fifteen years. Like the Cornell informants, most are widows in their mid-seventies and early eighties who were born in Russia, Poland, Lithuania, or Latvia. But unlike Cornell people, who left their parents in Europe, these informants came to England as young children with their parents and were educated in Leeds.

Leeds was the center of the British clothing industry, and many immigrants came from Eastern Europe with the specific goal of finding work in the West Riding. Both parents and spouses of my informants were employed in the tailoring trades. Neighborhoods in Leeds are relatively stable, and many informants lived near parents and siblings after they were married. Most had lived in the same area for twenty-five years or more. As in Cornell, I participated with and observed these people in many activities and also met their families, neighbors, and friends. Interestingly, Leeds informants seemed more willing to trust and confide in me, perhaps knowing I was in Leeds for a limited time and could not live directly on the Estate. Personal and family data and information on services have been recorded on a chart for each in-depth informant (see Appendix B).

Stage Four: Final Data Analysis

When I returned to America and completed the indexing and analyzing of my field notes in preparation for writing up my research, I found my Cornell informants glad to see me. A few now shared deeper confidences that before they had avoided. In Cornell, people are initially cautious, requiring intense contact over time to develop trust. I have maintained my friendship with these elderly and telephone and visit regularly. Until recently, I continued to live in the neighborhood. Time and again in talking with my informants and observing their behavior, I discover that my research findings and conclusions are reconfirmed. In the summer of 1981, I returned to Leeds to visit my friends on the Knightsdale Estate and again found that my hypotheses were reverified.

I

Opportunities and Constraints

THE ELDERLY DO NOT LIVE IN A vacuum. They must relate to particular events in their environment—in this case, to Cornell and Leeds. Their social, cultural, and economic environments have changed dramatically over the years, and are changing still. Their ability to cope with existing opportunities is varied, and it changes, too, as they grow older. To understand the present, we must examine the past.

CLEVELAND—JEWISH SOCIAL AND ECONOMIC HISTORY

The Eastern European Jews who settled in Cleveland in the first decades of the twentieth century found an already established German Jewish community.[1] Until the 1880s, the Jews who came to Cleveland were primarily from Bavaria and Bohemia. Cleveland Jewry remained strongly Germanic for many years. These Jews kept their foreign family names, spoke German, and were mainly involved in grocery or meat businesses or peddling. By 1839 there were enough Jews to form a religious congregation and have their own cemetery grounds. But the early history of this first Jewish congregation abounds in ideological conflicts. Theological and ritual differences kept the members divided, and soon a second synagogue was founded. These two congregations, both of which boasted growing and prosperous memberships, dominated Cleveland Jewish religious and communal life for many years.

Meanwhile, the city was developing commercially and economically. The Ohio Canal had been opened to the Ohio River, which connected Cleveland with the interior of the state. Cleveland became the outlet for Ohio's agricultural and mineral products. This prosperity attracted new settlers—the census of 1840 records a population of 7,600 people. With the discovery of iron ore in the Lake Superior region, Cleveland's position was further enhanced. It became the natural meeting place for ore from the Superior region and coal from Ohio, Pennsylvania, and West Vir-

13

ginia. Thus Cleveland soon became a center of heavy industry, with oil refineries, iron and steel mills, foundries, and machine shops sprawled about the city. Cleveland's population increased rapidly, and Jews were among the new residents.

While iron, steel, oil, and machinery were the primary reasons for Cleveland's prosperity, they were not the businesses that attracted Jews with capital resources. Near these large industries were the modest factories where German Jews produced soft goods. They dominated the clothing trades, manufacturing and selling cloaks, shirts, suits, and knitwear.[2]

By the second decade of the twentieth century, the manufacture of women's and men's clothing, hosiery, and knit goods ranked among Cleveland's foremost industries. Many of these firms had been founded in the 1870s or later, and entrepreneurship remained predominantly Jewish. Profits from the large factories, department stores, and the clothing industry were invested in banking, merchandizing, and streetcars. The entrepreneurs behind these businesses formed a well-established Jewish mercantile group, the pillar of civic and Jewish life. And they were not the only successful Jews. Others involved in dry goods, liquor, and tobacco were equally prosperous, along with professional men, journalists, and bankers.

Newly arrived German Jews usually began their careers as peddlers and small merchants. A stint at peddling seems to have been necessary for many newcomers. Soon, however, many became shopkeepers, and innumerable small stores checkered the Jewish area. Many retailed what they bought wholesale. Bakers or dairymen sold what they produced themselves. Most were marginal businesses, however, set up from accumulated savings; many were opened and subsequently abandoned.[3]

Although highly stratified and divided, the German Jewish community in the middle of the nineteenth century was also socially self-involved. At first its locus was in the neighborhood near the east Central Market district. Many German Jews lived southeast of Huron Road and East 6th Street along the axes of Woodland, Scovill, and Central avenues to about East 30th Street. Here they were close to the German-speaking population (which was not necessarily Jewish) and to the markets where many earned their livelihood. As the Jewish community grew in size and wealth, it began to scatter eastward. By the mid-1880s prominent Jews lived along Woodland and Case avenues. The Excelsior Club, an exclusive Jewish men's organization, opened at East 37th and Woodland Avenue in

1887.[4] This was the summit of Jewish clubs and the scene of prosperous social affairs. But when these wealthy German Jews tried to move to a new building near Western Reserve University, they faced opposition from their Christian neighbors. After thus learning that wealth and civic activity were not enough to admit Jews to upper-class Christian society, they generally followed a policy of self-exclusion.[5]

Jews lower down on the social ladder also experienced hostility. In the mid-nineteenth century, Jewish peddlers were often molested, and gangs of boys occasionally assaulted worshipers on the High Holidays. Some Jews were denied houses to rent. Those who sought education, housing, or social life outside the Jewish quarter were often disappointed.

During the administration of Progressive Mayor Tom Johnson (1901–1909), however, Jews became prominent in official governmental circles. These American-educated sons and grandsons of the early immigrants believed that civic bodies have an obligation to act on the problems of poverty and immigration. Consequently, when Eastern European Jewish immigrants arrived at the turn of the century, they found an established Jewish community with a sense of social responsibility, a well-established system of charitable institutions, and experience and connections throughout the city. They were the only immigrant group with a native wing that could furnish social and philanthropic leadership. "For the East European immigrants, the example of their predecessors provided a model—for many *the* model—of the way to be an American and a Jew."[6]

After 1881, Jewish immigrants began to come to Cleveland from Eastern Europe. According to one interpretation, these European Jews emigrated mainly for economic reasons: "It was the fivefold increase of East European Jewry during the nineteenth century, and the failure of the economy to keep pace with this multiplication, which must be considered the most deeply rooted cause. Repressive Russian laws restricted economic opportunities still further, and drove Jews to a feeling of hopelessness about their future in Russia."[7] Most of these Jews had been confined to the Russian Pale of Settlement or to the provinces of Russia and Poland, where they ran small businesses and worked in traditional crafts. Jews were barred from the land and the newer Russian industrial cities. Pogroms and edicts lent urgency to their exodus.

The first response of the Cleveland German Jews to the plight of their East European brethren was to hold mass meetings urging generosity and charity. After 1890, more active and sustained interest resulted in collections of clothing and household goods and the establishment of a Russian

Refugee Society. These charitable efforts reveal, however, a mixture of altruism and enlightened self-interest: "We want to teach them the customs of the land and to prepare them for citizenship, and to conduct themselves as citizens. It is a well-known fact, no matter what one Jew does, all Jews are blamed for it."[8]

The great influx of Eastern European Jews to Cleveland came between 1905 and World War I. The Russo-Japanese War, the revolution of 1905, the counterrevolutionary pogroms, and the economic depression of 1906–1907 drove Jews out of Russia. In 1900, Jews constituted 5 percent of Cleveland's population; by 1920, the figure had reached 9 percent—an increase in population from 25,000 to 75,000.[9] At the same time, the Cleveland economy was expanding in fields where Jews sought their livelihood.

As Jews immigrated to Cleveland, so, too, did other ethnic groups. Poles, Rumanians, Slovaks, Italians, Magyars, and Greeks settled in Cleveland and changed the ethnic composition of the city. In 1900, 32.6 percent of the population were foreign-born; 42.9 percent more were native-born with one or two foreign-born parents. The population of Cleveland still reveals these ethnic concentrations: of the total 1980 population of 2,064,194, 7 percent are foreign-born and 19 percent are native-born with one or two foreign-born parents.

During the late 1890s, a substantial number of Eastern European Jews, Italians, and some Slovaks began to settle in the old areas of early German Jewish settlement. This district was contiguous to Broadway and included Hill, Orange, Cross, and Berg streets and lower Woodland Avenue. These immigrants settled near the northwest tip of the area, and many remaining German Jews fled eastward along Woodland Avenue. The evacuation of the German Jewish population was very rapid during this period of heavy immigration.[10]

> During the ten years from 1896 to 1906, the neighborhood experienced a 92 percent population shift. Only 8 percent of the 1896 population of 3,175 adults remained within its boundaries in 1906, and only 5 percent of the total remained at the same address during the period. Some of the movement, particularly in the case of the German Jews, was to east of the E. 35th Street boundary, and hence still within a mile or two. . . . The bulk of the movement was to distant and scattered parts of the city.[11]

The few German Jews who remained were skilled or white-collar workers—carpenters, machinists, salesmen, and clerks—and garment workers, cigarmakers, and peddlers.[12]

Employment

Like the earlier German Jews, the new Eastern European immigrant found peddling a prime occupation. A trade requiring little capital investment or special training, it was the first rung on the occupational ladder. Physical assault was a problem, however, and police protection was minimal until 180 peddlers formed their own Peddlers' Protective Association. Later, Jews were taught the correct methods of peddling at the Council Educational Alliance, and there were fewer arrests for violation of peddling ordinances. A quotation from Morgenstern's memoirs reveals the kind of physical and psychological stamina required for peddling:

> I went to a *landsman* with whom my Uncle Leybe lived. . . . In a few days we had already bought a horse and wagon and with high hopes gone out to trade—or, as it was called, peddling. But instead of heading toward the isolated farms away from the city, where the farmers were eager to receive peddlers amicably, my uncle, who was the manager of our business, rode out only a mile or so from our house. He began to "huckster" on the top of his voice: "Paper! Rags! Paper! Rags!" But the only immediate response to this announcement were the jeering cries of the street-urchins: "God-damn-Jew-Sheeny!" These insults cut me to the heart and their bitter taste was more than I could bear.
>
> Even more bitter for me was to observe how my uncle, as he left the yard of a house where he had hoped to buy something, would pick up whatever came to his hand and throw it into the wagon. It made me miserable to see him do it. And no matter how much I argued with him, "Uncle, how can you do this, it's plain stealing!" he had only one answer: "That's business! That's the business of peddling! Everything goes into the wagon. If you're too finicky you'll never make a living!"[13]

Newly arrived immigrants could also find work in cigar factories, tailoring shops, and workshops. These immigrant occupations were suited to a sweatshop or loft-room production system, and a number of them were located within the Jewish neighborhood or on its periphery. They offered few amenities: health, sanitation, and quality of the goods produced were poor. The following quotations from documents of factory inspectors describe conditions in a tailoring shop and the Brudno Stogie Cigar Factory:

> *34 Croton St.* Tailor shop. No. in shop, 16; No. of women, 7; Girl 18 yrs. old working for $3.00 a week with no certificate; one water closet; no cloak room; no ventilation; floor filthy and garments thrown around on it; work from 7:30 to 6:00, with 1 hr. for dinner, for from $6.00 to $8.00.

Brudno Stogie Factory. No. in shop, 1st room, 19 women; second room, 16 women, 4 men; third floor, 47 men. The ventilation of the entire building very bad. Fire escape extends to the window of third floor and is not fastened to the walls; swings out from building fully an arm's length. No means of collecting the scraps from cigars; simply thrown on floor, walked over, swept up and sold to other firms to make the cheap scrap tobacco and clippings which are in very many cases used for chewing tobacco as well as smoking. While I was standing in the room an old man who was wrapping cigars took a violent fit of coughing and sat there spitting on the floor, right into the scraps of tobacco. Not one person in the place used a knife to trim the cigars. They all bit off the ends, and either swallowed the saliva or spat it out on the floor. The mouths and faces of both men and women were stained with the juice. . . . Every face wore the same blank expression. They looked and acted like machines. Did not notice a single person smile in the place. One window in the rear of second floor was open, but the air from the alley was so filled with the odor of decaying fruit and vegetables that it was impossible to leave it up for long.[14]

Thus, while Cleveland Jewish immigrants were employed in a wide variety of jobs, they were concentrated in a few occupations. Predominant were garment workers, independent peddlers and the kindred trades of rag and metal junk dealers and sorters, as well as carpenters, grocers, teamsters, and drivers.[15]

Cleveland's garment industry, unlike the one in Leeds, employed people of various ethnic backgrounds, and ethnic and religious attachment were not primary in organizing workers into unions or in reinforcing connecting ties. Also unlike Leeds, women's garments tended to be made in substantial, modern Cleveland factories, well-capitalized and employing modern methods and machinery. (Men's clothing was produced in small workshops.) Yet unionism in the years before World War I was generally ineffective. In 1911, for example, the International Ladies Garment Workers Union called a general strike of 5,000 workers, but the large manufacturers, who were well-organized and willing to absorb large losses, kept out the union. The ILGWU organizer continued to try to organize nationality branches for Jewish and other workers, but garment workers generally feared and avoided unionism. In 1918, wartime prosperity and rapid inflation encouraged union organizers to strike again for recognition and large wage increases. But once more, the large, well-financed clothing manufacturers refused any dealings with trade unions. Federal authorities intervened, however, and workers were awarded a large wage increase. These contracts marked a new era in labor relations within Cleveland's ladies' garment industry.

While ethnic diversity and trade-union ideals made ethnic and religious attachment a secondary matter in the Cleveland clothing industry, other trades were strongly Jewish in membership and self-definition. Those Jews who were employed in small, mainly Jewish trades organized readily; and Jewish bakers, drivers and bottlers of seltzer, carpenters, and joiners formed entirely Jewish, though small, unions.

Housing and Demography

Not all Jews worked in modern factories or were unionized. As we have mentioned, many Eastern European Jewish immigrants worked under deplorable conditions in neighborhood workshops, and large numbers lived in overcrowded housing. The recent work of John Grabowski of the Western Reserve Historical Society provides insight into the nature of the Jewish immigrant neighborhoods and the dynamics of social relationships.[16] As we have noted, the first area of immigrant settlement was the market region. As Eastern European Jews moved into this neighborhood and German Jews moved out, the region changed. There was a tremendous growth in the number of people; total population rose over 48 percent during the ten-year period from 1896 to 1906. The single-family homes of one- or two-story frame construction were altered by subdivisions or rear additions. These changes made it possible for more family units to occupy each house and thus led to overcrowding. An average of 3.29 working adults lived in each building, and some houses had as many as six different surnames listed among the inhabitants.[17]

Confirming statistics of overcrowded Jewish immigrant neighborhoods come from a 1908 government report. In 1908 the United States Commission on Immigration visited Cleveland to study housing and labor conditions among immigrants. In the East 26th Street area they found 70.9 percent of the residents to be Russian Jews. They reported an average of 5.7 persons per household paying $8.95 a month for an average of 4.17 rooms. Five years later, in 1913, the square mile near East 26th Street was found to be inhabited by 3,397 families comprising 21,480 persons, mainly Italians and Russian Jews. This area contained "some of the worst housing conditions of the city."[18]

Grabowski correlates this overcrowding with the limited economic resources of the new residents. Their jobs "brought small economic return and subsequently forced their practitioners to economize by sharing rents with other families."[19]

In their overcrowded and impoverished neighborhoods, immigrants assisted one another by forming mutual aid societies, which reflected the informal helping networks in Eastern Europe. Chesed Shel Emeth [True Kindness] Cemetery Association was founded in 1903 to serve its dues-paying membership and to provide burial for the indigent. One informant's father, the owner of a second-hand furniture store on East 55th Street, served as the first president of Chesed Shel Emeth for twenty-five years. Other mutual benefit societies protected immigrants against the high costs of illness. A Hebrew Shelter Home offered free lodging to homeless newcomers for three days. The numerous small immigrant synagogues organized on the basis of old-country ties; the various political, social, and charitable groups; and the trade unions among bakers, bricklayers, and carpenters all brought neighbors into closer contact. These associations allowed many self-respecting immigrants to escape the onus of charity and the patronizing of their elite German brethren.

Parallel to the Eastern European mutual aid societies were the communal and charitable endeavors of the more established German Jews. These activities were not new to the Russian immigrants; the German Jews had already organized the Council Educational Alliance in the heart of the immigrant neighborhood. This was not a settlement house where the more educated members of the native Jewish community came to live among the newcomers. Rather, it was a "contribution to the welfare of immigrant Jews from their benevolent brethren."[20] Chartered in 1899, the C.E.A. was organized to "engage in educational and philanthropic work" and to be a "cultural and inspirational center for the people of the neighborhood." Free Sabbath school, Hebrew classes, legal aid, gymnasium, playground, public baths, and child care were offered. Each month, more than 850 adult immigrant students attended the English classes, and many more used the branch library located at the Council. Sewing and dressmaking classes trained girls to work in the needle trades. Young men took part in the debating and social clubs and attended public forums and lectures.

Meanwhile, the demographic makeup of the surrounding area was changing, and the immigrants had to struggle with a shifting population and deteriorating conditions. Movement into and through this old Jewish neighborhood continued at a rapid pace. In 1906 Italian and Slavic groups partially populated the border areas of the Jewish neighborhood; by 1910 they had advanced to the core of the Jewish region. Ethnic conflict became more frequent. Many Jews moved to the areas between East 37th and East 55th streets, the new center of the city's Jewish population. The result was an almost 50 percent decrease in the number of Jews in the East 26th Street area between 1906 and 1916. As Italians moved in to replace them, the percentage of Italians and Jews in the neighborhood almost equalized: "By 1916, only 3.39 percent of the inhabitants present in 1906 remained at their same address, and only 5 percent of the people present in 1906 even remained within the neighborhood's confines."[21]

These statistics speak of rapid neighborhood migration and the resulting mixture of ethnic groups. In a ten-year period, the West Central district area "had experienced an almost complete population turnover. . . ."[22] As the more prosperous moved away, conditions deteriorated for those who remained. There was severe overcrowding; lack of adequate ventilation, plumbing, light, and heat; and a prevalence of communicable diseases, mainly tuberculosis. Economic opportunities were limited and welfare needs increased. The Hebrew Relief Association, which collected funds for food, fuel, clothing, and medical supplies for indigent Jews, reported a growing casework load.

It was to this overcrowded, impoverished, and ethnically mixed neighborhood that the Jews of this study came when they first arrived in Cleveland. They were young teenagers, and many lived with relatives, finding employment in clothing factories or neighborhood workshops and businesses. There were few opportunities for economic advancement. The socioeconomic composition of the neighborhood had changed and could no longer support the marginal businesses set up from shopkeepers' accumulated savings. The more well-to-do Jews had left the area, and newcomers were forced to rely on the unwilling patronage of other ethnic groups. It was difficult to get a toehold on the economic ladder. One informant recalls that her dark-haired husband was frequently mistaken for an Italian when he took his vegetable cart through the neighborhood. A description from the published memoirs of an Eastern European immigrant who lived in this area as a child further documents the neighborhood's altered economic situation:

> Our neighborhood on Orange Avenue was changing. The Orthodox Russian, Polish, and Lithuanian Jews were originally a small enclave who had emigrated to Cleveland years before and had built the Shul which was then within walking distance of their homes. But the second generation was being crowded out by the influx of the Italians and the Negroes who formerly lived at the foot of the Broadway hill and had begun to come up in numbers. In addition, the area was becoming a wholesale food and meat market and business buildings had also begun to infiltrate and occupy more and more of the neighborhood.

Orange Street was becoming run down, a street of shacks and open markets. Housing history was repeating itself. Numbers of Pop's customers in the area began to move farther east on Woodland and its tree-lined side streets. The moving occurred not only because the neighborhood was becoming shabby, but as their economic situation improved, the residents looked for finer homes in more attractive areas.

The friendly family atmosphere that had prevailed was disappearing. When I walked the short distance to Mrs. Seidman's store for molasses cakes or licorice sticks, I was no longer greeted by friends both young and old. It was sad when Mrs. Seidman sold her business to an Italian grocer. To start over at her late age and try to compete to satisfy the tastes of the changing neighborhood was too much. Week after week we heard of more and more Orthodox families who had "fled." And when another saloon or poolroom appeared on the block, my mother announced that this was the last straw. We've got to move. . . .[23]

Between 1916 and 1919 numbers of southern blacks moved into Cleveland. Many settled on and around Central Avenue, filtering south to Scovill, Woodland, and Orange avenues. "By 1929, this region had become predominantly black, with the Jewish population decreasing to 55 percent of the total population."[24]

Through Grabowski's statistical analysis of the early Jewish immigrant neighborhoods, one can suggest continuing demographic trends. Because we have no published material on the history of the Russian Jewish community in Cleveland, detailed accounts of the social, occupational, and interethnic composition of neighborhoods are unavailable. My informants, however, have suggested the general outline of these patterns.

First is the rapid and frequent migration of people through neighborhoods and the resulting dispersion of the Jewish community. As soon as Jews were able to accumulate money, "they quickly moved to more commodious quarters."[25] Neighborhoods became economically segregated and ethnically mixed. The poorer Jews were the last to move in and the last to leave. They were forced to cope with an ever-increasing number of neighbors of different ethnic and racial groups. Because their residence in a neighborhood was short and precarious, poor Jews rarely established friendships with these strangers. One informant, for example, recalls that her family was friendly only with other Jews whom they recognized and trusted. They visited Jewish friends on weekends and kept to themselves the rest of the week.

These trends of frequent migration and residential dispersion continued throughout the war years and are continuing even now. In the 1920s, the

Jewish population of Cleveland—86,400 people—remained relatively stable. Jews constituted more than 9 percent of the total population.[26] But within Cleveland, population movements kept altering the face of neighborhoods. In the prewar years, the center of Jewish life was largely in the 55th Street-Woodland Avenue district. But by 1918, East/55th Street had become the main thoroughfare of a declining Jewish neighborhood. By 1924 the area around 55th Street, which extended from East 46th to East 66th streets and from Cedar to Grand avenues, housed only 17,000 Jews. Three years later, in 1927, only 8,000 Jews remained. By the end of the 1920s, East 55th Street was only a poor backwater of a once-thriving area.

During these years, the East 105th-Glenville and Superior Through sections and the Mount Pleasant-Kinsman district were the growing Jewish neighborhoods. They were the principal successors of the East 55th Street district. East 105th was a relatively cosmopolitan area, adjacent to the University Circle complex of academic and cultural institutions. In the late 1920s, 32,000 Jews lived in this district, which was "the heart of the Jewish community life of Cleveland. It consists of many groups and classes . . . ; there is a strata of artisans, small shopkeepers, and communally unattached and unorganized individuals. . . . No miraculous transformation has occurred in their lives by the simple act of moving from 55th Street to the 105th Street district. Some of them may be slightly better off economically. . . ."[27]

Even newer than the 105th Street area of settlement was the Mount Pleasant-Kinsman district, which held 22,000 Jewish residents by 1927. Many of the informants in my study rented homes there. Jews in Kinsman lived alongside other ethnic groups, mainly Italians and Czechs. In the mid-1920s Mount Pleasant-Kinsman was "a growing Jewish community of about twelve to fifteen thousand persons of working class status who are beginning to own their own homes and enjoy the beginnings of a better competence in life. They came originally from the Fifty-fifth Street area. The section is newly built, several Orthodox synagogues have already been erected, and organized life along labor, fraternal, religious, and philanthropic lines has begun to spring up."[28]

Thus in the twenties, Jews in Cleveland lived in neighborhoods dictated by their economic means. Movement to new neighborhoods was one sign of continued economic mobility within the Jewish community. While there was a variety of housing suited to their different economic levels, most Jews preferred to live in two-family homes and apartments: "One third of all Jewish families . . . lived in two-family dwellings, up and

down, as contrasted with 36 percent of all families living in such accommodations. The 26 percent living in large apartment houses may be contrasted with the 13 percent [among non-Jews] . . . and the 20 percent
living in one-family dwellings with the 26 percent of all families in one-
family dwellings."[29]

The period between 1930 and 1940 marked a demographic slowdown.
During the Depression unemployment reached new heights, and few
could move to new neighborhoods. By 1945, there were still heavy concentrations of Jews in the Glenville-East 105th Street area and the Mount
Pleasant-Kinsman district. At that time, the Glenville-East 105th Street
area was ⅖ Jewish, ⅖ non-Jewish white, and ⅕ black.

But the suburban movement, which had started with a trickle in the
1920s and which would eventually sweep Cleveland Jewry beyond the
city's limits, gained momentum in the 1940s. "The suburbs . . . attracted
the younger, native Jews, who occupied higher economic brackets and
were more mobile than their aging foreign parents."[30] The more prosperous Jews again began moving further east to better and more expensive
homes. In the 1940s, Cleveland Heights ranked second as a Jewish neighborhood, and the Cornell district was a desirable Jewish section. By the
time my informants moved to Cornell in the 1960s, this district had
already begun to decline.

The number of Jews living in Cleveland in 1971 was estimated to be in
the range of 75,000 to 80,000. The figure constitutes approximately 3 to 4
percent of the general population of the Greater Cleveland area. In terms
of municipal populations, nearly 50 percent of the residents of Cleveland
Heights were Jewish, as were 40 percent of the residents of Shaker
Heights, 80 percent of those residing in University Heights, 90 percent of
the inhabitants of Beachwood, and 30 percent of the residents of South
Euclid (see map). From the 1920s until the present, the patterns have
continued: rapid migration, residential dispersion, changing ethnic populations within neighborhoods, and Jews dwelling together on the basis of
their economic means.

The occupational and economic changes begun in the ghetto areas during the 1910s and 1920s also continued. Many children of immigrant
parents sought to leave the old immigrant trades of peddling, tailoring,
and carpentry. There were growing numbers of merchants, grocers, druggists, contractors, clerks, and managers. These young and mobile Jews
moved to the suburbs, where they joined Conservative and Reform congregations. No longer content with the older, slow-moving *shuls* wedded

THE JEWISH MIGRATION

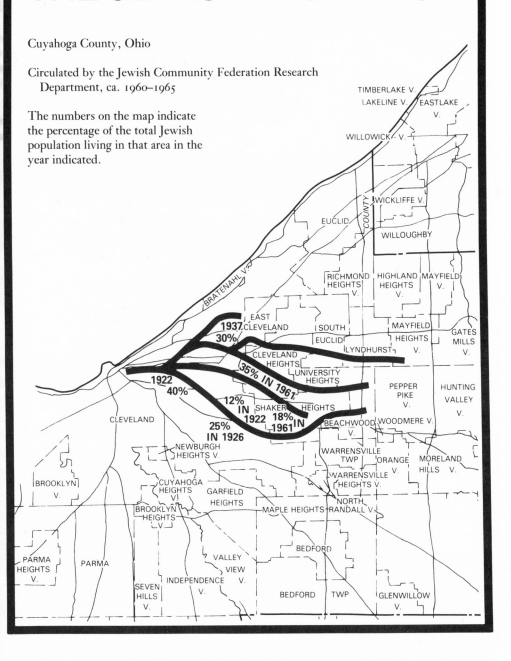

Cuyahoga County, Ohio

Circulated by the Jewish Community Federation Research
Department, ca. 1960–1965

The numbers on the map indicate
the percentage of the total Jewish
population living in that area in the
year indicated.

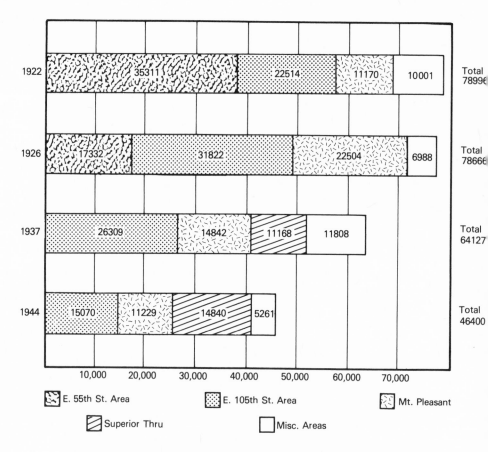

JEWISH POPULATION IN THE CITY OF CLEVELAND BY AREAS, 1922–1944

Jewish Community Center Papers, Western Reserve Historical Society.

to Yiddish and Eastern European ways, they left these Orthodox synagogues to their aging, foreign-born parents.

During the postwar years, occupational shifts continued. Jews entered
the service industries, light manufacturing, and banking. Children and
grandchildren of the earlier immigrants became independent businessmen
and salaried or self-employed professionals. The gap between the life-
styles of the older immigrant Jews and their children and grandchildren
broadened: "Striking shifts were observed between first and third generation groups in identification and membership from Orthodox to Conserva-

tive and Reform, as well as declines in regular synagogue attendance, observance of kashrut, Jewish organization and use of Yiddish as a spoken language."[31]

The poor and aged Orthodox Jews were left to live in declining, ethnically mixed neighborhoods. In the 1960s the lives of the aging, immigrant Jews of Cornell bore witness to these demographic trends. These elderly parents inherited a life in older Jewish neighborhoods that had already been abandoned by their prosperous children and grandchildren.

LEEDS—JEWISH SOCIAL AND ECONOMIC HISTORY

The history of the Jews in Leeds is closely connected with the development of the Leeds clothing industry, which has been that city's staple industry for a hundred years.[32] In 1856 John Barran opened a small factory for the manufacture of ready-made clothing. (Previously, clothes had been made from a prescribed piece of material for a particular customer.) Barran used the newly invented Singer sewing machine, mechanized clothes cutting, and, with his partner Herman Friend, a Jewish subcontractor, developed a method of dividing the work into many operations. The artisan tailor was replaced by the machine and the machine operator. Less-skilled labor could be substituted for skilled workers, and costs and prices could be reduced. From this beginning, the ready-made clothing industry grew rapidly in Leeds.

During this critical initial period of the Leeds clothing industry, there was an influx of cheap, hard-working Jewish immigrant labor. To escape persecution in Russia and Poland during the three decades before 1914, many Jews came to Britain. There they found employment in the expanding clothing industry. In Leeds, the growth of the Jewish population was strikingly rapid and sudden. The immigrants settled in the district known as the Leylands, where they established a Jewish quarter with Jewish schools, shops, and places of worship.

Employment

These immigrant Jews from Russia and Poland who settled in the Leylands were of similar socioeconomic backgrounds. They followed the traditional artisan trades of tailoring, capmaking, cabinetmaking, slippermaking, and retail selling. For many, the earliest contact between the Jewish immigrant and the clothing trade in Leeds was in Herman Friend's workshop. Labor was divided between unskilled female English machinists and skilled male Jewish tailors, a distinction that has persisted in Leeds until the present. The Jews took work home to finish. Gradually, because they needed to hire people to help with this work, they themselves became small masters. A system of subcontracting and home work was established, made possible by the "deadly ease" of sewing at home. As Jewish immigration quickened and labor became cheaper and more plentiful, opportunities for independence increased. Several of the best-known Jewish clothing firms in Leeds were started by former employees of Friend.

The immigrant newcomer started on the route to entrepreneurship when he became an apprentice in a Jewish workshop. Here he worked without pay during the training period and usually learned only a single process of the subdivisional system. During his apprenticeship, he was supported by relatives and friends already settled in Leeds. But a prudent apprentice could save money quickly, and even with rudimentary training, he could soon acquire a tailoring shop and the title of "master tailor." The entrepreneur would then obtain subcontracts from the large firms, acting as a subcontractor himself. "Then he would take the work away, quickly obtain within the community the services of machinists, finishers, and pressers, and complete the work in three days. The warehouses normally paid for outside work upon its return so that the small master required working capital to cover operations for only three days."[33] Many small shops opened, some employing only four or five people in the bedroom of a cottage or in the front of a house. The average shop employed twenty-seven workers.

The rapid growth in their numbers led to severe competition among these master tailors for orders from the large firms and warehouses. They bribed foremen, voluntarily reduced prices, and accepted suggested price reductions—anything to keep an order from going to a competitor. This left little for wages or profits.

Working conditions and schedules were equally poor. Jewish masters anxious for work took orders late in the week and drove employees all through Thursday and Friday nights. Also the prevalence of day rates prompted the masters to extract the maximum of concentrated output. Promising employees more work in the afternoons, they drove them hard in the morning; when the work was done, at midday, they sent the workers home with half a day's pay. The master then dashed to the factory to pick up orders for the next day's work, lest they be taken by a competitor. Thus subcontractors had to work extremely hard for very long hours for six cold months in order not to starve in the warmer months when there were few orders.

This severe competition resulted in employees working under exploitative conditions for a bare subsistence wage. During the busy season many worked from 7 A.M. until 9 P.M., and then again into the night. Jews worked Saturdays, Sundays, and holidays. When wages fell, competition among workers increased. They earned nothing during slack seasons; and when they were working, such amenities as adequate work space, cleanliness, warmth, and sanitary facilities were virtually unknown. People working under these conditions were often ill; many died young. The system of sweated labor has been described like this: "Sweating—the effort of an uneconomic system to extract from the misery of the unorganized, ill-equipped worker the equivalent of organized, well-paid, well-equipped industry. It was the competition of flesh and blood with machinery."[34]

By 1914 this competition had produced a broad class structure in Leeds. At the top of the scale were well-established tailors and subcontractors— "the nobility of Leeds Jewry"; at the bottom was a subclass of less fortunate tailors and artisans. Landlordism also presented an opportunity for ascent on the economic scale, and profits from manufacturing and master tailoring were often invested in property. Much of the property occupied by Jews in the Leylands was bought up by Jewish buyers, who then charged high rents to their tenants. Thus workers were dependent on Jewish masters for both shelter and employment. (Between 1934 and 1939, when the Leeds Corporation bought sections of the Jewish slum area in the Leylands for demolition, 50 percent of the houses were purchased from Jewish landlords, who made sizeable profits from the sales.)

It was in the workshops that the first signs of trades union activity were seen in Leeds. Industrial conflict was widespread; hundreds of small firms had very small profit margins; and conditions of intense competition prevailed. Leeds Jews were in the vanguard of organized Jewish labor in Britain: "The first recorded strike by Jewish industrial workers took place spontaneously in Leeds in 1885."[35] The first official strike, organized by a Jewish trade union, was a general strike of Leeds Jewish clothing workers in May 1888. Workers demanded a reduction of hours, from 62 to 58 per week, without a reduction of wages. This strike clearly demonstrated the depth of the divisions between master and employee within the Jewish community. The tailors struck against the "sweating" system and against the masters, who owned the sweatshops and acted as middlemen between the factories and the tailors. In an attempt to discredit the tailors, the masters deliberately tried to stir up anti-Semitic feelings by accusing them of trying to oust Gentile female workers from the workshop section of the Leeds tailoring trade.[36] By 1900, there were 1,200 members of the Amalgamated Jewish Tailors', Machinists', and Pressers' Trades Union. Although this union improved conditions in some of the Jewish workshops, not until 1911 did a large strike prove successful. Negotiations after the strike, in which 13,000 workers in fifty-eight firms participated, brought direct wage increases and a reduction of the hours of the work week to 49½.

In the years before the First World War, the Leeds wholesale clothing trade expanded rapidly. Export trade flourished, quality improved, and for the first time Leeds manufacturers set up their own retail shops. The most important innovation, however, was a new method of tailoring—an individual bespoke an order, which was executed in a factory by large-scale divisional methods. (For a bespoke suit, measurements were taken in the shop and the order was executed in a factory. Thus the garment was factory-made, but to the customer's own measurements.)

In 1900 Montague Burton, a man whose name is synonymous with the clothing industry in Leeds, entered the clothing trade. Burton, an idealist, deplored the squalid conditions in the clothing factories and believed that making clothes to measure would be a means of raising the prestige of the common man. He based his business on the conviction that "the majority of males in the British Isles were very conscious of their uniqueness, and thus very loath to consider themselves as average men, even for the purpose of buying clothes."[37] In 1906 Burton entered the bespoke trade and opened shops designed to take orders for men's clothes that would be made in a small factory.

With the end of World War I, the new classes of lower-paid workers and the new middle-income group of clerks, professionals, and civil servants increasingly demanded ready-made clothes. Between 1921 and 1938, the number of Leeds workers employed by the large manufacturers increased 100 percent. Many small tailors left their workshops for employment in the large factories, and there were new agreements for wage increases, shorter working hours, and paid holidays. In 1938 Burton's factory in Leeds employed over 10,000 workers; one-fifth of the men in

England wore Montague Burton suits. Even during the Depression, the tailoring industry grew rapidly. Both productivity and real wages increased. It was largely due to the tailoring industry that the Depression was less severe in Leeds than in other parts of Great Britain.

By the thirties, the traditional division between Jewish and non-Jewish industries had become blurred. Several old, established, ready-made firms ceased to subcontract, and the large Jewish firms, which had been subcontractors, became clothiers in their own right. With the development of wholesale bespoke tailoring, Jewish workers left the small workshops for modern factories, where they earned more regular wages under more congenial conditions. "But even today, the imprint of the mass immigration into Leeds at the end of the last century is still very clear. Leeds still has it Jewish quarter, with its own shopping centers and its own social life."[38]

In the 1970s, however, few Jews entered the tailoring industry as workers. Of the 3,000 workers in Burton's firm, which once employed thousands of Jews, now only 200 are Jews.[39] Most Jews are in the clothing, furniture, and retailing trades, and many work in clerical jobs or as shop assistants. Children are entering the professions. Leeds Jews have become active in government and are important in the economic life of the city. But, although they have climbed the economic ladder, they are not into upper-class social life. During the First and Second World Wars, Jews were denied entry to certain restaurants, bars, and clubs, and often had to cope with overt anti-Semitism. Many now believe that the West Indians and Pakistanis have "'drawn the fire' on the nonspecific, scapegoating, anti-stranger hostility previously directed against Jews."[40] Today Jews in Leeds are afraid that Fascist or anti-immigrant movements might shift their attacks to other minority groups.

Before 1880, only about 1,000 Jews lived in Leeds. By 1900, because of Russian persecution, the number of Jewish immigrants had risen to between 15,000 and 20,000.[41] The Aliens Act of 1905 placed restrictions on immigration, and by 1914 the arrival of new immigrant Jews had almost ceased. The Leeds Jewish community is thus almost exclusively a product of Russian and Polish immigration. Unlike Cleveland, where Orthodox Jews were preceded by Reform German Jews, Leeds had no established Reform or Sephardic community and thus no group to act as examples of "English Jews." Thus Leeds, the city of "working class Jews," was populated by immigrant workmen of similar artisan trades—a homogeneous group with a common ancestry, religion, and culture. In Leeds, Jews were linked by ties of kinship, by obligations incurred upon arrival, by tenantship, by labor obligations, and by mutual concerns.

Housing and Demography

Immigrant Jews in Leeds clustered together in the confined district of the Leylands, so-called because it lies in a valley. Neighbors, relatives, and friends with similar occupations worked and lived closely together in this small district near the center of the city. The Leylands was an area of small back-to-back houses built closely together, narrow streets, and alleyways and courtyards. A porter would meet immigrants at the station, ascertain what district in the old country they hailed from, and take them to the street in the Leylands where their countrymen were living. Here the new arrivals would be given lodging for a week or two, and a collection would be taken to help the new household get started.

The cramped, working-class nature of the district, its small back-to-back houses, and the clustering of people greatly affected the community's social and economic life. Leeds Jews adjusted to crowded conditions by creating an atmosphere of openness. Houses were left unlocked, and neighbors came in without knocking. Children called their parents' neighbors and *landslayt* by kin terms, even though they were not blood relatives.[42] Neighbors cared for the children of women who worked. As in the small towns of Eastern Europe, charity was informal. The costs and burdens—care for the sick, the unemployed, and the old; trousseaux for needy brides; and accommodations for strangers—were shared. *Landslayt* from the same region or town in Eastern Europe joined together to form small synagogues out of a desire to recreate a small part of their lives in the homeland. One of those, the Vilna Shul, still exists.

These ties of mutual support and assistance extended to help with employment. Friendly Societies were usually founded by a group of men who lived on the same street or were employed in the same workshop or trade. As friends joined, they grew into networks whose members made weekly contributions and drew benefits in times of sickness, bereavement, unemployment, or other hardships. These Friendly Societies, for example, provided financial aid for the seven days of ritual confinement when an Orthodox Jew had to "sit *shive*" following the death of a family member. Funeral expenses might also be covered. Other societies divided and distributed funds at the Jewish New Year and Passover. These groups also offered such social attractions as fortnightly meetings, social and cultural events, and outings.

Friendly Societies furnished an alternative to accepting charity from the more well-to-do members of the community. Jewish workers often felt exploited by Jewish employers and landlords. From the beginning of the Jewish settlement in Leeds, wealth, English ways, and length of residence were criteria for social distinctions. Rifts developed between the groups based on degree of Anglicization and economic differences. The needy were reluctant to ask for relief, believing that receiving assistance from a friend was acceptable, but that applying to a formal organization smacked of pauperism. When the elite members of the Belgrave Synagogue formed the Board of Guardians "to give organized assistance and interest-free loans to new immigrants," many avoided it, preferring membership in a Friendly Society: "These Friendly Societies were of great significance in the social organization of the Jewish working class . . . for they represented a determined effort at mutual aid and self-help in order to be independent of the richer, more anglicized, longer established 'elite' of the Jewish community and its paternalism. They provided even the poorest individual with a sense of equality."[43]

Another working-class group that allowed independence from established institutions was the Leeds Jewish Workers' Burial Trading Society: "The end of the nineteenth century found Leeds Jewry with many working men, who could not afford to pay synagogue subscriptions, and whenever one of them died, relatives were dependent on the patronage of presidents of synagogues, who took turns in burying their dead. In 1899, Leeds Jewish workers decided to become independent. . . ."[44] This workers' cooperative provided burials for members and their families, and also supplied kosher meat at the cheapest possible price. The inscription on the Society's butcher shop—"Leeds Jewish Workers' Burial Society. Fresh Supplies Daily"—has become part of the local folklore.[45]

Thus the Jewish immigrant community of Leeds was bound together by many ties. Relationships overlapped and reinforced one another. People lived in close propinquity with kinsman and *landslayt*. On the Sabbath and High Holidays, they prayed together. Neighbors and friends worked together and belonged to the same Friendly Societies and trades unions. They shared a common fate: insecure economic circumstances, long hours of work, seasonal employment, and low wages. They were exploited by Jewish employers and landlords, men who had come from the same background but "who were no better, just luckier."[46]

Part of their cohesiveness and mutual support must also be attributed to external pressures. Living so closely together, wearing Eastern European-style clothing and speaking Yiddish, the Jews formed a visibly different

LEEDS JEWISH POPULATION

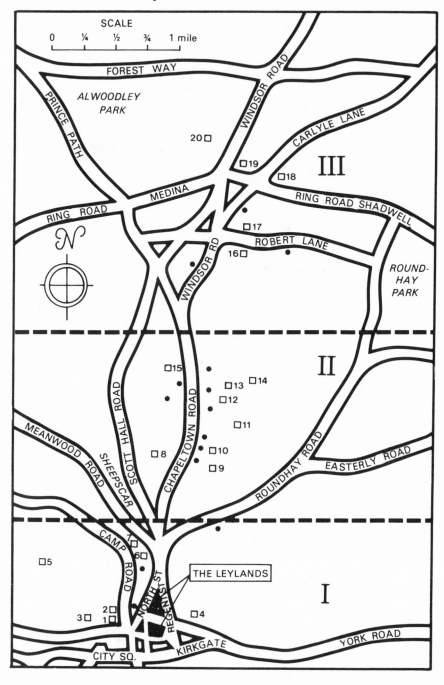

group. The Irish, who lived in a section of the Leylands directly adjoining the Jewish quarter, felt frustration and competition in housing and employment. In 1889, 621 of the 1,300 houses in the Leylands were occupied by Jews; by 1892, Jews occupied 900 of these houses, and the Wesleyan Chapel and the Roman Catholic church had been sold to Jewish buyers.[47] The secretary of the Leeds Trades and Labour Council claimed that rents had risen in the Leylands because "Jewish capitalists" had acquired property there.[48] Non-Jewish merchants bitterly resented the competition from the many Jewish stores in the Leylands, and their bitterness was fueled by exclusive Jewish trading patterns. A 1906 *Leeds Mercury* newspaper article

Key to Leeds Jewish Population Map

   I   The early areas of settlement
  II   Most heavily Jewish populated areas during and after the Second World War
 III   Newest Jewish populated areas
  ●   Location of synagogues in 1958
  □   Location of main Jewish institutions in 1958 (see list below)

  1   Clive Behrens Branch of the British Legion
  2   Jewish Board of Guardians
  3   Kosher Kitchen for Hospitals
  4   Kosher Poultry Slaughter Yard
  5   Hillel House
  6   Jewish Trades Union Institute
  7   *Mikve* (ritual bath)
  8   The Jewish Institute (Jubilee Hall)
  9   Herzl-Moser Hospital
 10   Communal Offices
 11   The Talmud Torah (Hebrew Education Board)
 12   L.J.W. Co-operative Society
 13   Mizrachi Youth Centre
 14   The Leeds Talmudical College
 15   Zionist Offices
 16   The Jewish Blind Institute
 17   The Judean Club
 18   The Old Age Home
 19   Selig Brodetsky Jewish Day-School
 20   Moor Allerton Golf Club

Reprinted with permission from Ernest Krausz, *Leeds Jewry* (Cambridge: Heffer, 1964), pp. xviii–xix. Some names have been changed to protect the confidentiality of the author's informants.

described the Jewish merchants as " 'locusts settling on vegetation,' [who] had settled down and driven out the English tradesmen."[49] The press carried other complaints about diseases and schools overcrowded with alien children who could not speak English.

There was also antagonism to Jews in the trades unions. The native-born work force saw them as competitors, prepared to work for little pay and to be hired as strikebreakers during industrial disputes.[50] Many believed that the Jews, who worked for low wages on mass-production machines, were responsible for ruining the older craft system and putting the apprentice-trained craftsmen out of work. The Jewish workers in the tailoring industry were sensitive to the reputation they were earning among Gentile trades unionists. They tried repeatedly to remedy this situation, both by organizing among themselves and by showing solidarity and support for Gentile unions. Despite these efforts, antialien feeling mounted against the "alien invasion." It culminated in the Aliens Act of 1905.

After 1910, the old ghetto in the Leylands began to break up. Migration was not as rapid as in Cleveland, however, nor were Leeds neighborhoods as economically segregated or ethnically mixed. "In the first decade of the twentieth century, the Jewish community began to move out of the Leylands. By 1937 the Ghetto of the Leylands was almost completely deserted. In that year the main concentrations were to be found on the fringes of the old Ghetto, that is, in North Street and Sheepscar, Camp Road having a large concentration, and the Chapeltown-Rounday area gaining fast. By 1947 Chapeltown became by far the most heavily Jewish populated area in the city. [During the fifties] the rapid movements of the Jewish population have taken place out of the Chapeltown area, [Medina] and Alwoodley becoming predominantly Jewish districts."[51] Instead of all of the working-class Jews being concentrated in one area of the city, several neighborhoods with distinctly Jewish composition sprang up in various districts of northeast Leeds. The older areas' shops and workshops provided employment for the residents of the area. Families no longer lived entirely among Jews, who formed only a portion of the neighborhood.

Following World War II, there was an influx of Polish and Ukrainian immigrants into Chapeltown, an area with big houses that had been abandoned or sold by their owners, who could no longer afford the servants they required. The large houses were partitioned and occupied by the Polish and Ukrainian immigrants. "This influx hastened the departure of

. . . Jews from Chapeltown so that the Jewish residential move out of the area was more rapid than it might otherwise have been."[52] The recent settlement of West Indians and Pakistanis in Chapeltown, and the large amount of slum clearance around Sheepscar and Lower Chapeltown Road, have reduced still further the number of Jewish residents in the area.

According to a recent study, the great majority of the Jewish families in Leeds now live within one mile of Medina Corner, in either Medina or Alwoodley (known as "Al-Yeedley").[53] In these modern ghettos, people still live in areas of high Jewish concentration, belong to Jewish clubs, have Jewish friends, and shop in Jewish stores. A comprehensive network of welfare services and charities is run by and for the members of the community. Social standing rests partly on involvement and participation in Jewish charitable organizations. Gossip and ostracism are still powerful social sanctions. In 1966 the Leeds Jewish population numbered between 18,000 and 20,000 people—3.5 percent of the general population. Leeds has the highest percentage of Jews of any city in Great Britain, and is the third largest Jewish community there. Although neighborhood, housing, and life style are important social criteria,[54] in comparison to Cleveland it remains a homogeneous community with a comparatively stable and uniform population.

2

Kinship

IN THIS CHAPTER WE WILL EXAMINE how the organization and social networks of their communities have affected the kinship relationships of the elderly living in Cornell and Leeds. We shall consider our informants' families of orientation and procreation, the ongoing reciprocal exchanges of services and support between aged parents and their adult children, and the parents' attitudes toward these transactions. As we shall see, the kinds of interaction that informants had with their own parents influence those they now have with their adult children.

CORNELL

Family of Orientation

Over half of the Cornell informants emigrated to the United States in the years just before World War I, when they were in their teens and early twenties. The families they left in Europe were often impoverished, and many had lost one or both parents before they were twelve. If the family had accumulated any money, it was quickly used up when the breadwinner passed away. Fathers made a meager livelihood as Torah scribes and suitcase makers or by laying parquet floors and selling liquor. Mothers worked as seamstresses or sold goods in the market to support their young offspring. Older siblings and cousins often helped raise orphaned children.[1]

A definite emphasis toward maternal kin permeates the genealogies of Cornell residents. Their families in Europe had close ties with their mothers' siblings, who often lived in the same town or came to visit frequently.[2] Although most informants remember the names of their maternal grandparents, only two can name those on their fathers' sides—and they were both prosperous and influential men. They recall little information about the generation before their parents.[3]

Contact with the mothers' kin continued in America. When they first arrived in Cleveland, most of the new immigrants went to the home of a

Cleveland hospital food tastes better when it is lovingly served by a close relative.

maternal relative—an aunt, uncle, or half-sister of the same mother. Often the same age as their cousins, they formed cordial relationships. Today these informants are still invited to family functions and are acquainted with grandnieces, grandnephews, and more distant cousins.[4] Their children are also friendly with these relatives.

In all but one case, the full siblings of Cornell informants remained in Europe.[5] They lost contact during World War I, and many family members were later killed in the Holocaust. Two women have brothers who survived by emigrating to Israel, and these ties have been renewed by visits. Only Mrs. Samuels still corresponds with a sibling in Europe, a sister in Odessa to whom she writes every month and to whom she used to send money every Passover. Although her Russian sister wants her to bring her grandniece to America so she can find a husband, Mrs. Samuels feels she is now too old to care for the girl. Also, her daughter-in-law discourages her interest in her Russian family.

When one parent died in Europe, the surviving spouse often remarried and started a second family.[6] From these unions, a number of informants have half-brothers and sisters, but they did not grow up together because of their age differences. Today they correspond only with those half-siblings who came to America.

Although the Cornell elderly left parents, sisters, and brothers in Europe, their memories remain vivid, albeit lonely and unshared. Many still have photographs of family members. Mrs. Nathan, who saw an old woman kissing a photograph as she threw it into the trash, explained that she, too, will someday destroy pictures of her relatives because her children do not recognize them. Her memories are undeveloped, frozen at the time she left. At Yom Kippur, the Jewish Day of Atonement, she lights memorial candles for each of her family members killed during World War II.

Only four Cornell people had parents who had lived in America. Two women were born after their families settled in the United States (Mrs. Eisner and Mrs. Levi); the two others came as young children (Mrs. Levitt and Mrs. Wexler). The two families who emigrated before 1880 experienced the economic and social conditions of the financially successful Cleveland Jews outlined in Chapter 1. Mrs. Levi's mother and father settled in Toronto, where the family prospered in the clothing trade. Sisters and brothers entered the business, and today many family members are clothiers. Her father was active in philanthropic endeavors and headed the Free Loan Association. After her marriage to a Cleveland doctor, Mrs. Levi returned often to spend the Jewish holidays with her family in Toronto. Mrs. Eisner's parents also emigrated in the 1880s. Her father started as a huckster but soon purchased a second-hand furniture store with a partner. By the time he retired, he owned three store fronts and a two-family home off 105th Street. For twenty-five years he served as president of both Chesed Shel Emeth Burial Society and the Hebrew Free Loan Association.

While economic opportunities were available for those who came before the mass waves of Jewish immigration, conditions were less favorable for those who arrived later. Mrs. Levitt and Mrs. Wexler came with their parents after 1910. Their families did not prosper, and their fathers remained tailors. It is useful to examine the family networks of these few informants, as that is the only detailed data available on kinship relations within the family of orientation.

Informants' relations with their own elderly parents do not support the myth of three generations living in harmony under one roof. Only Mrs. Levitt had a parent stay with her, and then only temporarily; she and her sister took turns housing their widowed mother for fifteen years. The old woman would not live with a daughter-in-law, but her sons contributed money toward her support. It was difficult for the mother to stay at Mrs. Levitt's house because the young children's cries kept her awake at night. But she made favorite family dishes, and Mrs. Levitt's husband showed her his salary check to hide nothing from her.

When her mother moved to the home of Mrs. Levitt's sister, however, the situation was less comfortable. Knowing that his wife would not argue with him in front of her mother, the husband took advantage of her presence to get his own way. Tensions mounted, and the sister begged Mrs. Levitt to take the mother back. Finally the elderly woman became very ill, and the sisters nursed her continually until her death six weeks later. Mrs. Levitt is proud that her mother never had to go to the hospital, which she dreaded. She describes how neighbors helped the family during the crisis because they knew how close they were.

The other two women with parents in Cleveland (Mrs. Eisner and Mrs. Wexler) were divorced. After their marriages ended, they moved to their parents' homes. But these arrangements soon proved unsatisfactory, and they moved out again. Although the daughters, who were busy working and bringing up children, had no time to care for their aged parents, they felt a sense of responsibility. They gave money to their fathers and visited them weekly. There were strains in these relationships, however. Mrs. Eisner feels that her father, who died in his nineties, may have outlived his children's love and concern. She is fearful that this may also happen to her. Mrs. Wexler feels that her father grew meaner as he got older. Today both women try to avoid similar tensions with their own children and make few financial or social demands.

One male informant, Mr. Isenberg, brought his mother over from Russia after he was married and had children. Frequently Mr. Isenberg had to intervene in arguments between his wife and his mother, who interfered with the way his wife ran the house. Eventually the old woman returned to Russia, where she died.

Relationships between informants and their aged parents were tense and strained. Many informants feel guilty about unmet responsibilities and unresolved conflicts between the needs of their spouses and children and the needs of their aged parents.

Sibling ties among the American brothers and sisters who do not live in Cleveland remain warm and supportive. They correspond, call each other on birthdays, and occasionally visit. When informants were younger and stronger, they visited siblings a few times each year, offering financial help or moral support. These relationships are now less intense. Mrs. Levi is saddened that she no longer receives an annual invitation to visit her sisters in Toronto. Interest and energy are centered more on children and grandchildren and less on siblings. When they move, siblings live near one of their own children rather than their sisters or brothers. Differences in socioeconomic status also separate informants from their more well-to-do siblings.[7]

Only Mrs. Eisner has a sister who lives in Cleveland. After both women were divorced, the sister helped raise Mrs. Eisner's children and took care of them while she worked. Her sense of devotion still strong, Mrs. Eisner visits her sister each week in a nursing home, taking fruit, books, and an occasional new dress, which the sister pays for. Mrs. Eisner gives three reasons for her sense of loyalty: (1) compensation for a feeling that she was not good to her elderly father, (2) fear that she may be in the same position someday, and (3) admiration for her sister, who remains independent and tries not to complain.

Two patterns emerge from informants' kin relationships with their families of orientation. For the majority of Cornell people,[8] emigration to America severed their contact with parents. Not having known their own parents as they grew old, they lost a possible role model for their own old age. They were also denied the experience of interacting with elderly parents and of using that experience with their own adult children. As we have seen, Cornell people who did have parents living in America endured relationships marked by tension and strain. Because of guilt and unresolved conflict, these informants avoid imposing on children and try to make few social or financial demands.

Family of Procreation

Spouses' Kin. Many of the husbands of Cornell informants also emigrated to America when they were in their teens and twenties. They came during the later phase of Eastern European Jewish migration, and only a few had parents who had lived in the United States. When they married, these men left their kin and settled in Cleveland. The young couple thus lived without close family members nearby. Husbands worked as hucksters, painters, subway drivers, tailors, furriers, or milkmen. Few owned their own homes or were able to establish or maintain their own businesses.

Children. Each of the Cornell informants has two or three children, at least one of whom lives in the Cleveland area. These children, now adults in their middle forties and fifties, are well-to-do and live in the Jewish suburbs east of Cornell. Most sons have their own businesses; a few are professional men. Many of the daughters work, and both daughters and daughters-in-law are active in Jewish organizations and are involved in volunteer work. The kinship relationship between informants and their adult children is overtly defined by a code of independence.

All of the informants currently live in their own apartments. Only one woman, Mrs. Weiner, has an adult son who lives with her. Although over the past fifteen years eight parents have shared a home with a child, they now reject this arrangement. Mrs. Wexler felt confined and hampered in her daughter's home, compelled to do things when she did not want to. Mrs. Moskowitz was lonely in her daughter's suburban home. The family was gone all day, and since the maid did the cooking and cleaning, there was nothing left for her to do. None of her friends lived close by, and public transportation did not reach her daughter's suburb. A determined widow in her seventies, Mrs. Moskowitz left her daughter's home, found her first job, and located a low-rent apartment in Cornell. Suburban life, even in her daughter's beautiful new home, did not suit her.

Even after they were widowed, two other women declined their children's invitations to come to live with them. Mrs. Nathan feared that an argument with a child—always a possibility for people living under one roof—might have lasting repercussions. "I would never move with kids, I would try to live by myself, or with somebody, or in a home. If you fight with a stranger, it goes by; but with kids, it's for life. One hour before my husband died, he said, 'Don't go to the kids.'" After "sitting *shive*" for one week in her son's home, Mrs. Samuels also decided not to remain there permanently. She knew that her children did not keep kosher and enjoyed a life-style different from hers. She feared she would often be left alone when the family went out:

"My son once said, 'Ma, you come to live with me. I got so many bedrooms.' I don't want to hurt him or her. My daughter-in-law is an active person. . . . She would like it, I should be there every day dressed, my best clothes, and sit, her company's going to come. Whom the hell are they? Excuse me, they were poor once upon a time. This dress—it's old-fashioned. They don't wear that. . . . Every day pay thirteen and fifteen dollars for a little cotton dress, excuse me, I don't believe in that. I don't approve of that. I don't argue with her. And if I want to call, why can't I call my friends and do what I want, you know? . . . He's a member from the Masons, he goes away, they got dances. The little girl's got her friends, and the boys got their friends, what am I going to sit by myself there? I don't feel good . . . I lay down on my couch. I can't lay down there. There I'm afraid. I'll lay down in the family room, you know, maybe somebody comes. . . . He'll fix me up. So what! They're going to fix me in the basement, my stove with my refrigerator and you could cook yourself, do yourself, I says, 'No, mine *kind*.' I says, 'You want to help me, to pay my rent. I want to stay by myself. . . .'"

Informants are also afraid that living with their children and their spouses would put their children in a difficult position. They fear the potential conflict between the demands of the mother and the wishes of the child's spouse. Mrs. Levitt does not want her daughter to try to satisfy both her mother and her husband. She remembers a friend whose son-in-law developed a heart condition from the tension of such a situation and eventually had to ask the mother to move. When a parent lives with children, they are not free to talk openly or to argue, and this is an added strain on the marriage. "There is a tendency to give too much advice when you live so closely," Mrs. Wexler said.

While Cornell parents do not wish to live with their children, they feel it is suitable for parents to give children a place to live. But even this norm has a time limit, usually a few months to a year. "The older person wants privacy, independence, and a life of one's own" (Mrs. Eisner).

This decision to live independently is dictated by a recognition of different life-styles, of their own and their children's need for privacy, and, most importantly, by the acknowledgment that there is often not a place for them in their children's homes. "You're not wanted around, and you know it" (Mrs. Eisner). "They wouldn't want me. I would fool myself. No children really want a mother to live with them. . . . I don't want my children to feel uncomfortable, like my sister did; and today, children don't want you anyways. Mollie Goulder tells me and I believe her" (Mrs. Levitt).

Independence is an affirmed value of members of the generation that left its own parents and siblings in Europe and struggled through the Depression. This code is most often articulated in terms of the needs of the informants' children for independence and the fear that their children will not love them if they are not self-reliant. The theme permeating informants' discussions of their own independence is: Parents must not demand. To be demanding or dependent is to jeopardize children's love and devotion. "They love me because I don't bother them, and they come" (Mrs. Brodsky).

Cornell parents, then, perceive a message that reinforces their own wish

Eating a meals-on-wheels dinner alone in the kitchen in Cornell.

for independence—but they interpret this message negatively. They feel rejected, afraid that if they complain their children will not want to be with them or help them. They feel they have no choice but to accept an independent life-style. Their acceptance is marked by uneasiness and resentment, however. One woman expressed this feeling in response to a discussion concerning visits from her son. "You know how it is in business, you can't expect that he should live with me, he has to have his life, too. Sometimes he's busy and has to entertain in business" (Mrs. Nathan). Others complain, "My daughter's busy with everyone but me, my daughter volunteers all the time" (Mrs. Levi).

Also contributing to these feelings of rejection and uncertainty is the belief that adult children's primary obligation is to their own children, rather than to their parents. Informants reject the philosophy, "I did for them and now they must do for me." Mrs. Samuels, for example, told a story about a duck carrying his babies across a river. The father asked the first duckling, "When I am old, will you carry me across?" The young duck answered, "Yes," and the father threw him into the water. The second son replied the same way and was also drowned. But the third duckling answered, "When you'll be old, I'll be grown up and I'll have my own family to carry." The father was satisfied and carried him across. This story expresses both an affirmation of self-reliance and an uncertainty about an elderly parent's ultimate fate. In the conflict of generations, the elderly feel they should yield to their grandchildren.

This code of independence is reinforced in conversations with and observations of peers. Mrs. Levitt described a friend who complained all the time and made demands on her children. Eventually her daughter and son-in-law moved away from Cleveland and she lost them both. After relating the story, Mrs. Levitt said, "An Americanized woman knows her place."

Thus informants feel they are part of a conflict for their children, who must be committed to business, their own family, and their community on the one hand and to their aged parents on the other. Cornell informants raised their children to succeed in business and to serve the Jewish community. They must now struggle with the implications of their success. They feel uncertain and rejected but also proud of their children's accomplishments and successes. This feeling that they must be self-reliant and resourceful colors all their decisions, and even where they live.

Services Received from Kin

Housing. Cornell elderly parents can manage within a limited income. "Rents are so expensive, and I can't afford to pay a lot of money, rent," said Mrs. Wexler. They do not want to accept rent money from their children and so remain in the Cornell area despite run-down conditions. "I didn't want my children to help me. This was the reason I stayed. I did not want to have them have to help me with the rent. It is one thing if they give me a gift or help me. . . . I try to get along," Mrs. Levitt explained. Parents are concerned that accepting money continually may become a source of annoyance. One woman whose son and daughter do not get along says that she does not take rent money because she knows that one can afford to give more than the other and she does not want to increase their dissension (Mrs. Levitt). Informants remain in Cornell; they do not "go high."

Mrs. Eisner, who can afford to pay more money for an apartment, has a different reason for remaining in Cornell. By living in an apartment above the drapery store and not having her hair done,[10] she saves enough money to pay her own way when she goes out with her daughter-in-law. "I can do my fair share," she says; because of this her relationship with her daughter-in-law has improved: "She realizes I don't make demands."

Another economic advantage of Cornell is that the neighborhood social patterns enable informants to share expenses. If the rent is too high for one person to live alone, he or she can take in a roomer or become a boarder. "I try to live my own way. I rented out. I was left with some money, but not an income. I was very sick, so it took the money and there was left little. . . . It was the lowest I could do. I had a boarder on Cornell Avenue who paid me $30 and I paid the rest of $75. This is the reason. I did not want to put pressure on my children to help, not to pressure my children" (Mrs. Levitt). This woman explained her strategy to take in a boarder in terms of her children's limited resources. Her daughter and son-in-law, who do not have much money, are still skimping. They bought a used camper and a second-hand boat—"They're not yet on top." She does not want to impose on them or to drain their resources.

Over the years, many informants have lived in Cornell as boarders or landladies. Two were still roomers when I did my field study (Mrs. Moskowitz and Mr. Isenberg). This arrangement saves money and, with luck, can be a source of companionship. Women living together shop for each other and give each other medication when necessary. They do not have to rely on their children. On the other hand, many have endured unpleasant incidents and a lack of privacy by living with someone who was incompatible. If there is only one bedroom, it must be given to the boarder. A woman who rents to a male roomer leaves herself open to gossip.

Mr. Isenberg, who is eighty-nine years old, finds a boarding arrangement a mixed blessing. He does not have to make his own bed, buy furniture, or clean the apartment. However, his landlady, whom he describes as a "witch," does not allow him to turn on lights or use the electricity to shave. He is forced to live as a "street person." At 6:00 A.M. Mr. Isenberg eats breakfast at the local Donut Shop. By 8:30 he is at the Jewish Center, where he showers and shaves. He eats lunch at the JC Nutrition Program and spends the rest of the day playing cards. By 4:30 P.M. he is at home and has eaten the soup his daughter brings each week. He walks around the neighborhood until 8:00, when it is time to go to sleep. A retired painter, Mr. Isenberg goes to the Painters' Union to play cards on Saturday and Jewish holidays. On Sunday the Jewish Center is open again, and he spends the day there. He pays his landlady $50 a month, plus one dollar for use of the refrigerator and another dollar for electricity. She pays $95 a month and sleeps in the living room; he has the bedroom. They quarrel often.

Even when Cornell parents decided to move to the new Carroll Arms building, where rents are $133 a month, they did not ask their children for assistance. Instead they applied for rent supplements and food stamps.[11] These benefits enable them to live in the new building at rates comparable to what they formerly paid as renters or boarders. Only Mrs. Feingold accepts rent money from her son, who lives in Florida.

Money. When they were younger, informants gave financial assistance to their children to use in business or for the down payment on a house. This money was usually not repaid, and they did not expect it to be.[12] Today Cornell parents believe they should not give money to their children if it is all they have to live on. This would only make them dependent. "When I had, they wouldn't take from me, and now they try to help me. . . . If they take my money and then can't return it, then where shall I go?" (Mrs. Levitt). Mrs. Levitt feels her children understand and will not take her savings. When she was seriously ill, they transferred her money to their bank account, but as soon as she recovered, they returned the funds.

Informants accept limited financial help when they need it. Children may pay for weekly groceries, buy furniture for a new apartment, or provide a little extra spending money. They also give their parents cash for birthdays and Mother's Day. Informants believe that it is all right to accept small amounts of money if children can afford to give it, but never to be a *khazer* (a pig). When Mrs. Wexler moved into the Carroll Arms and qualified for a rent supplement and food stamps, she immediately refused the money her daughters used to give her. She no longer needed it, she said. A few women secretly send part of the money they receive from well-to-do sons to other children who are less well off.

Some informants use money to reinforce a weak relationship, or as a reward for a kinship responsibility carried out with devotion. For example, Mrs. Eisner feels she can ask her daughter-in-law to take her to see her sister in the nursing home because her sister gave her daughter-in-law a generous check and family heirlooms when she married. Mrs. Levitt believes that children ask a mother to live with them only when they will benefit from the arrangement. One son-in-law she knows receives federal funds for keeping his mother-in-law; another woman cooked, baked, and cleaned so her daughter could go out to work. When the elderly mother was no longer physically able to care for the house, her children arranged for her to have her own apartment at the Carroll Arms.

Some Cornell parents also use money to reward children who treat them particularly well. Mr. Isenberg keeps a separate bank account for his daughter in appreciation of the many meals she has prepared for him. Mrs. Eisner feels she has received more time and care from her daughter than from her son, and she has changed the terms of her will accordingly.

Thus informants refuse money from adult children, except in small amounts that symbolize devotion and a desire to help. This money they use to buy groceries or to meet extra expenses. Mrs. Nathan, whose son bought her furniture and paid for a trip to Israel, maintains a pretense of adhering to this code. She gave her son part of the money and insisted on knowing the exact amount in the hope she can pay it all back.

Shopping. Informants' self-reliance extends to the routines of everyday life. In the Cornell neighborhood, the services that the elderly require for independent living are readily accessible. "I have my transportation, the bank, the Pick-'n-Pay, and for me it's O.K. I don't have to depend on my children, I can do things myself," says Mrs. Levitt. With a supermarket that has a kosher food section, two kosher meat markets, a poultry shop, a bank, a drug store with delivery service, and three bus lines, many elderly can manage on their own. They carry home small quantities of groceries, some people shopping two or three times a day to get what they need. Others pull shopping carts. Although they are limited in how much they can carry, neighbors often buy a few small items for one another.

Only a few kin help informants with shopping. Mrs. Samuels, who is legally blind, allows her daughter-in-law to shop for her. One frail lady, Mrs. Feingold, used to rely on her son; another (Mrs. Nathan) was dependent on her daughter-in-law. But these arrangements were discontinued because of family strains. The Jewish Family Service now provides them with a shopper, who drives them to the market and pushes their carts. With this assistance, both women can do marketing without having to bother their children.[13]

Clothing. Only "hippy-style" clothing can be purchased on Cornell Avenue. Although a bus goes directly to a nearby shopping mall, the Cornell elderly buy very few new garments. They receive most of their clothing as gifts for birthdays and Mother's or Father's Day. These presents range from socks and underwear to dresses, coats, and handbags.[14] Again, informants accept these presents as symbols of affection, not support. The daughters of a few women help them select special outfits.

Transportation. Cornell has good public transportation facilities, and senior citizens can ride the bus for 25¢ until four o'clock in the afternoon.[15] Almost all informants travel by themselves on the bus.[16] Getting to a

A Cornell street scene in the morning hours of a weekday when it is quiet
and the elderly do their grocery shopping and banking. There is a diur-
nal rhythm with young people shopping and strolling in the late
afternoons and on weekends.

doctor's appointment presents difficulties, however. There is a medical
center next to the shopping mall, but many doctors have moved to the
more prestigious buildings in the wealthier, eastern suburbs. These offices
are designed for people who drive automobiles—they are located on major
highways. To get there by public transporation from Cornell often entails
taking three buses and allowing a minimum of three hours each way.
Taking a taxi may well cost over $10 one way.

Cornell parents handle this problem in a variety of ways. The children
of six informants (Mrs. Margolis, Mrs. Samuels, Mrs. Levi, Mr. Isenberg,
Mrs. Weiner, and Mrs. Levitt) drive their parents to the doctor. Two
others (Mrs. Wexler and Mrs. Feingold), whose doctors have not moved,
go on the bus. The rest face a conflict. For her first appointment with an
eye doctor, Mrs. Brodsky asked her daughter-in-law to drive her. For her
second visit she decided to take a cab and happily discovered that after a
certain street, the doctor pays the additional cost. Mrs. Eisner, in contrast, chose to switch doctors rather than trouble her children. She located
a physician whose office is nearby. Only one woman (Mrs. Nathan), who
has poor relations with her daughter-in-law, stopped making appoint-

ments altogether. Eventually she found a volunteer driver, but her appointment was long overdue.

Help during Illness. Illness, too, creates a situation of dependence. When they are ill for an extended time, most call their children, who shop for groceries or pick up prescriptions. Some daughters bring prepared food. But for most short-term illnesses, such as a cold or the flu, most parents do not call their children. They manage with groceries stored in the cabinet, or a neighbor buys bread and orange juice. Only two informants (Mr. Isenberg and Mrs. Levi) are regularly taken to their children's homes when they do not feel well.

When elderly parents are seriously ill or recovering from an operation, the children give more extensive care. Most informants have convalesced at their children's homes for two or more weeks. Mrs. Eisner, however, chose not to return to her daughter's house, preferring to recuperate from her second operation at a convalescent home instead. My notes give her explanation:

"She then thought over how it was when she convalesced at her daughter's house, and how she noted them looking longingly out the window at the other couples outside, and how she felt that they must feel 'obligated to sit with me.' She told me how she had bought a bed for the first floor, and had even had a phone installed in the dining room where she was staying, as she could not do the stairs. She was there for six weeks. She said then that she saw it was 'an imposition,' that her daughter had no privacy to talk with her husband when he returned from work. 'Never again, I said to myself.' She also described her granddaughter, who was then only eight months old, and how she asked for part of her breakfast and other food, then either spilling it or wetting on her down comforter and messing up where she was staying. 'I had no life . . . I can't glorify it.'"

While they do not object to asking children for help when they are ill, informants are not comfortable accepting long-term care in their children's homes. Mrs. Nathan and others give reasons similar to Mrs. Eisner's for electing to go to the Jewish Convalescent Home. Mrs. Wexler stayed in her own apartment while recovering from a stroke. Every day her daughter brought soup and TV dinners and straightened up the apartment.

Only one parent nursed a sick adult child. Mrs. Wexler flew to California, where she spent three months caring for her daughter, who had had a nervous breakdown. The other informants do not help their adult children when they are ill, and the children do not ask their parents to help.

Contact. Although the Cornell elderly live alone and manage their daily routines without assistance, they maintain contact with their adult children. This is especially true of elderly women and their daughters. Five informants talk to their daughters daily, often two or three times a day (Mrs. Levitt, Mrs. Eisner, Mrs. Levi, Mrs. Wexler, and Mrs. Moskowitz). Usually the children call to make sure their parents are well. In return, the mother may telephone to "find out what's new," to talk over or "clarify" a problem, or simply to tell the daughter she is going out and not to worry if she does not answer the telephone. Most Cornell parents do not talk to their sons every week; rather, they phone their daughters-in-law. If mother-in-law and daughter-in-law get along well, they talk daily (Mrs. Samuels). If the relationship is moderately comfortable, they speak two times a week (Mrs. Eisner); but if relations are strained, they phone only if something out of the ordinary arises (Mrs. Nathan and Mrs. Feingold).

The telephone is the communication link between informants and their children who do not live in Cleveland. Parents usually receive a call from out-of-town children every week or two, and also on birthdays and Jewish holidays.

Cornell parents usually see their children weekly. Two women (Mrs. Brodsky and Mrs. Eisner) meet their daughters for lunch at a restaurant. Mrs. Levitt's daughter knows her routine and comes to the Jewish Center or the mall to take her out for coffee and a quick chat. Only three informants' children visit them in their apartments; these visits last about half an hour (Mrs. Nathan, Mrs. Wexler, and Mrs. Levi).[17]

Children do not seem to enjoy coming to their parents' homes. The walk-up apartments, the long, dark corridors, and the dirty sidewalks contrast too sharply with their own suburban neighborhoods. Mrs. Levitt, in particular, voiced her fear that her children do not like coming to Cornell where there are "hippies." She hoped that when she moved to the Carroll Arms her daughter and son-in-law would feel more comfortable and would come to visit more often. Only Mrs. Levi goes to her daughters' homes for Sabbath meals.

Saturday and Sunday used to be the usual days for visiting with family, but most Cornell informants and their children have modified or abandoned this custom. Mrs. Eisner notices that since her granddaughters have become teenagers, there is no longer room for her in the car and she is not included on Sunday excursions. She must seek companionship from her peers. Another informant (Mrs. Brodsky) wants to let her working daughter sleep on Sunday mornings and so joins friends at the Jewish

Center, where most informants now spend Sundays.[18] Cornell parents do not usually go to visit their children in their homes. Even when invited to spend the day, some decline the invitation: "My son, he works a whole week and he's tired. . . . He loves to watch the ball game. . . . I cannot make him to stay a couple of hours to take us home because we're tired. We want to lay down, we're elderly people, so, you know, sometimes I refuse which I don't like to refuse. . . . And she works in the garden, you don't sit down and talk to your children and have something . . ." (Mrs. Samuels).

Parents complain of lack of attention, conversation, and comfort when they are in their children's homes. Their attitude is ambivalent, however. They want to be invited, yet they are discontented when they go.

Advice. When children come to visit, they often take care of financial concerns. Three informants (Mr. Isenberg, Mrs. Moskowitz, and Mrs. Samuels) have arranged for their Social Security checks to be sent to their children's homes. The children cash the checks and take their parents the money. Adult children may also pay their parents' rent or bills by check, and the parents reimburse them. Often informants ask for assistance in reading mail or in filling out Medicaid or Medicare forms. Parents talk things over with their adult children, although not all the children welcome their parents' counsel.

Holiday Visits. The majority of Cornell parents and their children conform to the tradition of getting together on holidays. Informants usually go to their children's homes for Thanksgiving. But Passover is handled differently. The year of this study, only five informants celebrated Passover at their children's homes. Mrs. Levi stayed at her daughter's house for the whole nine days and helped with the traditional cooking. Mrs. Samuels and Mrs. Levitt took chicken soup and matzo balls for both *sdorim*. (The *seyder* is the ceremonial Passover dinner. Orthodox and Conservative Jews have *sdorim* on the evenings preceding the first and second nights of Passover.) The other two parents, Mrs. Feingold and Mrs. Moskowitz, went to their children's just for the holiday meal, which was a prepared kosher dinner purchased from a Jewish caterer. The rest of the informants declined their children's invitations. Mrs. Nathan will not travel on holy days, and she did not wish to stay for three days at her son's home, "like in a prison."[19] Mrs. Brodsky also refused, saying that she "did not want to be in the middle" of her son and his wife's family.

Passover and family parties are also the time when informants usually see their *mekhutonim*, the parents of their children's spouses. While relationships are cordial, Cornell informants are not emotionally close to these relatives through marriage. Many parents-in-law have also passed away.

In-Laws. Compatibility with a child's spouse greatly affects kinship relations and influences the amount of contact and services offered an elderly parent. This is particularly true for informants with only one son living in Cleveland. Of the four Cornell parents who must rely on daughters-in-law, only Mrs. Samuels is on good terms with the woman who shops weekly for her, cashes her Social Security checks, and calls her each morning. A second informant, Mrs. Eisner, enjoys moderately comfortable relations with her daughter-in-law. She tries not to be demanding, nor to interfere. She encouraged her son to buy a larger house and to hire full-time help for his wife. She no longer has direct contact with this son, however, and must approach him through his wife. Mrs. Eisner feels her daughter-in-law, who is an only child and maintains close ties with her own parents, does not really want to become involved with her. Mrs. Nathan and Mrs. Feingold, the other two women with sons in Cleveland, have antagonistic relationships with their daughters-in-law. Their sons are busy with business and rarely help their mothers. As noted earlier, Mrs. Nathan and Mrs. Feingold rely on volunteers to take them grocery shopping and to the doctor. Mrs. Nathan's daughter-in-law offered to shop and to help her select clothing, but Mrs. Nathan's constant criticism made the relationship difficult for both her daughter-in-law and her son, who felt he had to arbitrate. Although most informants say that they do not complain because "they [the couple] are happy," the relations between mothers and daughters-in-law are tense. Parents often feel they have no control over their daughters-in-law, who are morally bound to their own mothers, not to them.

Kinship—An Ultimate Resource

Despite some uncertainty, Cornell informants ultimately believe that their sons and daughters will be there if they need them. In an emergency, they call their children first, and family members do respond. Informants describe how their children drove to the emergency ward at four o'clock in the morning, how they postponed vacations or returned early when parents were ill, how the children rallied round in a crisis. Kinship relations for Cornell elderly are the ultimate resource in time of emergency. One Cornell woman's story poignantly underscores this need. When she was very ill, she telephoned her son to help her. He told her to call someone else, and a neighbor had to take her to the hospital. She has never talked to her son again. "I have no son," she says: "That was it. . . . If there is an emergency, you should be able to call on your own son to come. If he can't do this, what's the use of having him at all? . . . My son didn't care if I died, my own flesh and blood."

Cornell informants know her story. Feeling that they must not abuse the privilege, they often wait long hours before finally calling their children. "In a need, he will show; but it damn well has to be an emergency," says Mrs. Eisner.

Many parents say that they plan to go to an old-age home when they become too ill or too old to care for themselves. Again, they do not want to impose upon children; they are afraid that their children may not want to care for them. "When you have kids, it is not even a guarantee you'll be taken care of" (Mrs. Nathan). "I do not want to think of it . . . I'm afraid to think of it; the first month maybe yes . . . but the sixth month, it might be no" (Mrs. Eisner). Nonetheless, Cornell parents maintain hope that their children will take care of them. Mrs. Eisner, for example, spoke about her friend, who has many insurance policies in case she needs care. This woman has no children, she explained.

When I returned from field work in Great Britain, I discovered that several informants had aged very rapidly or had become too ill to care for themselves, and that their families had made new arrangements for their care. No parent was abandoned; some informants were justified in hoping that their children would look after them; others had correctly feared that they would be placed in an old-age home. When Mrs. Levi's apartment building was turned into a condominium, she went to live with a daughter. When Mr. Isenberg left the hospital, he moved into his son's home, which his divorced granddaughter and great-grandson had left. Since his son and daughter-in-law had a place for him, he did not have to return to his rented room on Cornell. He continues to go to the Jewish Center every day, however. Mrs. Levitt's son nursed her in her own apartment following her long illness, sleeping sitting up in a chair in case his mother needed him. He told me, however, that his sister did not visit because she felt their mother, now eighty-five, had lived long enough. Both Mrs. Samuels' and Mrs. Nathan's sons hired companions to take care of their mothers in their own apartments. Mrs. Nathan's condition deteriorated, however, and she is now living unhappily in the old-age home she dreaded.

Summary: Cornell Kinship Relationships
The kinship relationships between Cornell informants and their adult children are governed by a code of independence, which is marked by

ambivalence and uncertainty. Parents are self-reliant and independent partly because they are afraid of imposing on their children and jeopardizing their love.

Most studies of the ambivalence in kinship relations have concentrated on the attitudes of the younger generation. (See Chapter 7 for a discussion of this literature.) Impatient sons chafe under the domination of their elderly fathers. Religious and social sanctions attempt to control hostility and to encourage respect toward the aged. But Cornell informants show that older parents feel equally ambivalent about their adult offspring. Parents want love, attention, and respect from their children, yet they are frequently uncertain and displeased with their behavior. They are uncomfortable in their children's homes. Although they view their children as an ultimate resource in a crisis, they are reluctant to ask for time and care, even when they are ill. Because Cornell parents have no religious or economic sanctions to support them, they must rely on the general social norms that children have an obligation to care for aged parents. Cornell informants have abandoned many of the previous reciprocal exchanges that characterized earlier relationships with their adult children. They have little power to initiate new exchanges or to transact renegotiations that might help bring children's behavior more into line with their expectations.

Generally, Cornell parents' views of what kinship relations should be are unrealistic, or at least out of date, in twentieth-century America. Because they left their own parents in Europe, they were denied the experience of learning from their mothers and fathers as they grew old. They have had no realistic role model for behavior in old age. Their unrealized expectations are based on a biblically enjoined tradition: "And you shall honor the face of the elder" (Lev. 19.32); "Cast me not off in time of old age; when my strength fails, forsake me not" (Ps. 71.9). Undoubtedly, many informants mythologize about what their relations with their own parents might have been, wishing their children would conform to this ideal. But this family-centered pattern of care for the aged was shattered by the process of immigration. "It is not like we were with our parents . . . a duty, not really from the heart—they are so cold now. Children are not really the way I was used to when I was a daughter" (Mrs. Green).

Relations among informants and their elderly parents who had lived in America were a source of tension and guilt. They were never able to meet satisfactorily their own, their young families', and their aged parents' needs. Informants' concepts of relationships between elderly parents and adult children are abstract and unrealistic, too.

Because Cornell informants were never able to negotiate satisfactory relationships with their own aged parents, they cannot bring successful experiences to bear on transactions with their adult children. Kinship relations remain a source of disappointment, uncertainty, and ambivalence.

LEEDS

Family of Orientation

Like the people in Cornell, most Leeds informants were born in Russia, Lithuania, or Latvia just before the turn of the century. But, unlike the Cornell immigrants, who arrived in Cleveland in 1912 as teenagers without parents or siblings, the English informants went to Leeds as young children with their families. From the start, their experiences contrast sharply with those of the Cornell informants. The experience of growing up within the family unit and of watching their parents age is their most significant advantage, for it positively affects their adjustment to an aged role.

Parents. The parents of the English group went to Leeds because employment was available, because kinsmen had already settled there, and because they did not have to work on the Jewish Sabbath.[20] In Europe, the fathers had earned a livelihood in selling, manufacturing, and a variety of other jobs. In Leeds many became tailors and pressers; a few turned to traveling and huckstering. One woman describes her father, who had come to England without a trade: "He was a delicate man. . . . Someone suggested, at that time it was popular to go with a cart with vegetables and fruit in the street and sell from the cart. That's what he did for a couple of years, and mother went with him" (Mrs. Gottlieb).

There were close relationships between the new immigrant families and their kinsmen, who had arrived earlier. Many families went to Leeds because a mother's brother or sister, or a father's sister, was already there. Kinsmen settled near one another, visited often, and enjoyed close relationships. Many grew up with their cousins. "We were always together in each other's houses," explains Mrs. Caplan. Even relatives living in different towns visited each other frequently. Mrs. Perlman recalls going to her aunt's home in Hull for holidays: "It was our second home when we were little. We had nowhere else to go. We had no money for holidays, so we

A photograph of an informant's beloved family in Eastern Europe.

used to make our holidays there." Often more prosperous relatives would help their less well-to-do kin financially. There was always emotional support.

Over time, however, aunts and uncles died and cousins moved away. Socioeconomic distinctions and physical illness now separate cousins who were close when they were young. Nonetheless, they try to attend one another's *simkhes* (festive, happy occasions) and funerals, and to include each other in family gatherings. Mrs. Aronson convinced her son to invite the cousins, whom they rarely see, to a family *bar mitsve:* "It's all wrong, they should visit you. It's not far in a car. . . . We never see them, yet you can't make a *simkhe* without people."

Two important themes emerge from discussions with Leeds informants about their parents. First, they remember their mothers' strength, tenacity, and devotion to their children. A number of women believe their mothers' lives are models of how to deal with their own life circumstances. Second, the informants and their siblings gave unstinting care and attention to their aged parents. They describe this as correct and admirable behavior toward elderly mothers or fathers—their just due for the love and devotion they gave their children.

Theme I: Mothers. Many elderly Leeds informants lost their fathers when they were children. As the family finances dwindled, their mothers had to struggle. When informants talk about their mothers, they emphasize their perseverance and determination in hard times. Mrs. Gottlieb, for example, describes her mother's difficulties: "When father died, the wholesalers organized my mother a benefit and opened her a shop. She took a big house in Meanwood Road and made a grocery shop in the front. She kept the books in Yiddish. She took people on the books who were supposed to pay back at the end of the week, but they never paid. And so she gave up the shop, and then she went to work at the *mikve* [Jewish ritual bath]."

Mrs. Perlman's widowed mother went to the clothing factory every day to bring home work, for she was skilled at tailoring and finishing trousers: "She had to learn that trade to bring us up."[21] Despite her poverty, Mrs. Perlman's mother maintained her religious beliefs, kept her pride, and cared for her children. She prepared a hot meal every day at noon, never worked on the Sabbath, and would not accept charity: "She did not take in work after Friday morning. She worked hard, but it weren't big money. She were a wonderful woman, to bake and cook and do. . . . She didn't ask for any help. Half a crown they used to give 'em then. Well, my mother never went for half a crown because she weren't used to it."

This image of courageous, hard-working, loving mothers helped Leeds informants prepare for their own lives, which have also been filled with illness and financial difficulties. "I came out of a good family; we had a hard life. . . . She brought us up with a foundation and to know we would have good [times] and hard times," says Mrs. Perlman, who keeps her mother's photograph on top of her television set and talks to it every night. "You can see from her picture the kind of family I come out of, and so I can't mix up with a lot who aren't nice." She admires her mother's pride and courage and has tried to emulate these traits: "She never went to ask, so I didn't. . . . I never made myself lower down. Although I didn't have as much, but I made people understand I did. I got my mother. She were the most wonderful person in the world. She were thirty-eight years old with five children [when she was widowed] and she went through her life smiling and singing. She died at sixty-four. And I've done the same. . . . I'm more like my mother than any of them in nature. I've gone through my life smiling, what's the use of crying. . . ."

Many other informants spontaneously showed me photographs of their mothers while discussing family genealogies.[22] In their descriptions, informants chose attributes they themselves have come to possess. Here the maternal image serves as inspiration and example. It is also noteworthy that these Leeds people keep photographs of their parents in their living rooms, whereas Cornell elderly keep family pictures in boxes or privately display them on the bedroom dresser.

Theme II: Care and Attention. As young teenagers, the Leeds informants tried to help the family financially. Many left school at thirteen, seeking work as trousers machinists in the tailoring industry. They worked from 8 A.M. until 9 P.M., with time at noon for lunch. "We used to pin our hair up in case the inspector came in, because we weren't allowed to work so late," said Mrs. Gottlieb. Some informants did piecework, for which they were paid by the dozen.[23]

Commitment to family is also shown by the care that informants and their siblings provided for their frail and ailing parents. In speaking of those days, Leeds people often paint nostalgic pictures of the past. Mrs. Caplan, for example, moved her parents' beds downstairs, where she slept on a cot between them and nursed them both during the night. Parents were also cared for at home when they were widowed and ill.[24] "He never went into a home, we never let him. God, no, after having six children and being so good to us, we'd never put him in a home," said Mrs. Pincus. Only Mrs. Gottlieb took her mother to her own home, however.[25] Most informants shared nursing responsibilities with siblings. They speak proudly of the sacrifices they made in fulfilling kinship obligations. A feeling of devotion and a sense of responsibility emerge from their descriptions, as opposed to those of Cornell informants, who emphasize conflict, tension, and unmet obligations.

Siblings. Having been raised together and often still living in the same neighborhoods, Leeds siblings remain, and feel strongly that they should remain, emotionally close. Many sisters and brothers have died—"You lose them as you get older"—but a number of informants still have siblings in Leeds. They exchange emotional support and physical assistance. Mrs. Gottlieb, for example, visited her ill sister two or three times a day, taking hot meals and caring for her. Another woman is grateful to her sister, who shopped and cooked to help her through a bout with the flu. Leeds elderly value their siblings' help even when children live close by.

Even when siblings are too old to help each other, they try to stay in contact. Saturday afternoon is the usual family visiting time. Economic distinctions rarely separate these sisters and brothers, who still confide in each other:[26] "With us, there's no secret between us. . . . You tell them anything and they do not repeat. In our family, there's no secrets to keep,

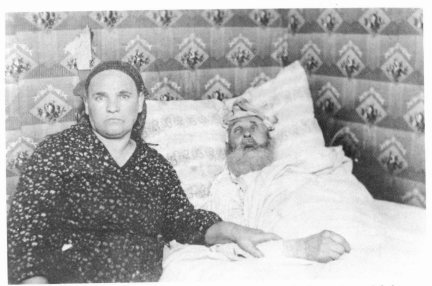

An informant remembers her mother's dedicated care for her own aged father.

not in ours. We've been very, very close . . . but now, they're further away. We're all getting older, so we can't do for one another. But really, we're very close, we love each other" (Mrs. Perlman).

Mrs. Aronson is the only exception. Her sisters and brothers, to whom she is not close, were raised by their widowed mother in Glasgow, while Mrs. Aronson was raised by an aunt in Leeds. She believes it is unwise to separate a child from the rest of the family: "We grew up strangers." Socioeconomic differences are now another barrier between her and her siblings. Frequently annoyed with her wealthy sisters, she says that she prefers "plain Janes, people who put on no airs and graces." Nonetheless, she and her family now share a common concern for a Glaswegian sister, whom they plan to take to Leeds.

When siblings do not live in Leeds, they communicate by telephone, visits, and a letter every two weeks. Mrs. Pincus exemplifies this close contact with siblings. She talks weekly with each of her five sisters in Sheffield.[27] When her husband became ill, her sisters set up a curtain business for her in the markets and supplied merchandise at cost, from their own shop.[28] Her sisters also came often during this crisis period, and they stayed with her for two weeks after her husband passed away. "Our

Sarah was very good. She left the family, her son was only ten. She stayed with me about a fortnight, the whole *shive* week and the week after. She did errands for me." When Mrs. Pincus herself had a stroke, she went to Sheffield for three months to recuperate; when she returned to Leeds her son and daughter-in-law cared for her. Every year she goes to Sheffield for Passover. "Since David's married, they don't let me stay alone."

Informants recognize that sisters and brothers provide emotional support, physical assistance, and advice. Many feel that their sisters can be counted on in an emergency. "If I was very sick, God forbid, our Sarah would come" (Mrs. Pincus). Only one informant would not impose on her sister, "who has enough of her own family to look after" (Mrs. Silverman).

Cornell informants do not have this kind of relationship with their siblings. Only one woman has a sister in Cleveland, and she is in a nursing home. Others are separated from their siblings; and illness, age, and concern with their own families keep them apart. Many Cornell informants and their spouses came to America without parents or siblings. They enjoyed close relationships with aunts, uncles, and cousins but lacked support and advice from immediate family members. Thus they had no models for aging within a close-knit family group.

Family of Procreation

Spouses' Kin. Not only Leeds informants themselves benefited from growing up within family units, but so too did their spouses. Their husbands were born in the late 1890s, usually in Leeds. Most were employed by the large tailoring firms; only two had their own tailoring shops. When the husbands' parents grew ill, their sisters, rather than they, took care of them. Thus no informant nursed an ailing mother-in-law. Relationships between informants and their parents-in-law were generally good. Only Mrs. Perlman found her husband's mother selfish and difficult to get along with. Mrs. Perlman never criticized, however, and she feels that this experience taught her how to be a good mother-in-law—"to keep quiet about what you see and just grieve."

Close family ties extended to the husband's kin, who also visited and exchanged help and advice. These friendships with brothers- and sisters-in-law were maintained even after the connecting spouse passed away. "We are still in your family; I feel I am still in the family," said Mrs. Caplan. Mrs. Gottlieb writes weekly to her sisters-in-law in London; after one had an eye operation, she went to care for her for a month.[29] She also gives them money.[30] Mrs. Caplan now looks in on her eighty-six-year-old

Friends and neighbors wishing one another a good holiday and good health.

brother-in-law, occasionally marketing for him and arranging for him to get meals-on-wheels.[31]

Children. All informants have at least one child living in Leeds. Most are sons; only two are daughters. Like the Cornell children, they are in their late forties and early fifties. Almost all live in the Jewish section of Leeds, either within walking distance or a short bus ride away from their parents. Leeds sons are employed in tailoring, dry-cleaning, government work, or personal service businesses. Only one son has his own tailoring business, which he inherited from his father. Almost all the sons' wives work or help their husbands in their businesses. The disparities in wealth and life-style that separate Cornell parents from their children are lacking in Leeds. Leeds sons have also maintained the Orthodox Jewish way of life, and many continue the *shul* affiliations begun by their fathers. The kinship relations between Leeds informants and their children are marked by both independence and interdependence, involvement, and mutual respect.

All the people interviewed in Leeds have chosen to live independently from their children. When questioned about this decision, they do not, like Cornell parents, fear being a burden, nor do they feel unwanted. Instead, they assess their unique relationships with their children and their children's spouses, and they consider their own desire for independence: "She's a bit sharp. She's too quick and I'm getting old, and I can't take it. Then when the daughter comes, there's a bit of something, and I'd have to sit there and watch it all. . . . I told her. She says straight away, 'Come and live with me. Give it up.' I said, 'Look darling, you keep your key and I'll keep mine'" (Mrs. Perlman).

Some informants admit that they could not get along with their daughters-in-law, that their life-styles are different. Just as their husbands' mothers did not come to live with them, they do not wish to live with their sons and their wives.[32] "I don't think any mother should live with a child if they can help it. I don't think you can get on with your daughter-in-law . . . I wouldn't live with Libby. She's good in every way. But I shouldn't want to live with her. Different ways from I am. Different ways. . . . A daughter-in-law is not a daughter" (Mrs. Pincus).

Underlying these statements is a desire for independence—to be on their own and to do things for themselves:

"I would live with my Barney, if I had a separate apartment, my own apartment. For instance, they have their own house and I could have my own apartment. And not to be watched-at all the time" (Mrs. Gottlieb).

"But suppose. Now I can keep myself clean. But if you get older and suppose you pass water. Or you wet. They won't like it. They'll soon give you into a home. It's all right as long as you can keep youself like that, but when a mother gets right old . . . they won't have you, love, they won't put up with it. . . . I know I'm not feeling good, I feel dizzy, and I'm lonely, but I push all that back . . . because I'd have to be sent to a home just the same, as I might as well stop here. . . . While I can be nice, why shouldn't I stay in my own home?" (Mrs. Perlman).

Leeds parents do not seem to feel unwanted, rejected, or ambivalent, as do Cornell elderly, who are often uncomfortable in their children's homes and fearful of being a burden or causing tension. They believe that their children treat them well; they simply do not wish to live with them.[33]

Independence, symbolized by having and maintaining one's own home, is important to Leeds informants. Even when old or ill, they fight to keep going. "I won't let myself go" (Mrs. Perlman). "If you don't keep work up, you get peculiar, it keeps you going" (Mrs. Caplan). Neighbors who live independently provide example, encouragement, and assistance. Leeds women have always taken care of their own homes, and they want to continue. "I've been a try-er and I'm a try-er up to this day. I've got to fight to keep up here" (Mrs. Perlman).

Services Received from Kin

Housing. Informants moved to the Knightsdale Estate in Leeds when they were in their late fifties and early sixties. At the time, most spouses were still living, although many were ill and needed a small home on one floor. The Estate was constructed and partially financed[34] by the Jewish Welfare Board, which wanted both to provide better housing for people who were living in the old, deteriorated sections of Leeds and to strengthen Jewish family life by enabling elderly parents to live near their married children. Informants found the Estate a desirable place to retire. Although the rent was slightly higher than they had previously paid, they were willing to meet the extra cost to have a new flat and to be near their families. Today, many receive supplementary government assistance for rent and heat, but none take rent money from their children.

The Jewish Welfare Board followed a comprehensive physical and social service plan when it constructed the new Knightsdale Estate. Flats were built in units of four, with two tenants sharing an entrance. Like the row houses informants left, these flats have small gardens, and neighbors live close by. There is also enough room to entertain children or even to accommodate weekend guests. A small group of shops, including a greengrocer and a kosher butcher, have been on the Estate premises from the beginning. Social service personnel employed by the Jewish Welfare Board selected prospective tenants according to need. They visited all applicants in their homes and helped them move and, if necessary, helped buy new furniture or household goods. The first tenants were also chosen because of their leadership capabilities and were encouraged by the Welfare Board to form committees and a tenants' union. They organized a *shul*, conducted their own religious services, and arranged social activities and outings. The Welfare Board, social service personnel, and a group of volunteers continue to oversee the management of the Estate, helping the tenants live independently. Since the original construction, many new groups of flats and a communal hall—where the *shul* and a day center are now located—have been added. There is a long list of people waiting to move into the Knightsdale Estate.

The Estate itself has a feeling of community. Residents tell about the first days on the new Estate, describing how neighbors met one another and became friendly. They remember gathering wildflowers in vacant lots nearby, and struggling together to found the *shul*.

Money. Unlike Cornell parents, most Leeds informants did not give money to their children to help them purchase a home or start a business. Often they had not accumulated enough money to spare. The two families who did own businesses—a market stall and a tailoring shop—gave them to their sons, who have continued to operate them.[35] "We saw he had a business, we bought him a car. I gave him plenty. I gave him the central heating. . . ." When they had extra money, Leeds informants helped their children with gifts, such as Cornell parents did.

Leeds elderly seem more willing to accept financial assistance from their children than do Cornell residents: "My son keeps me," says one.[36] They accept this help within a context of family generosity, and in the same spirit as their own efforts to clothe and educate their children. One informant, whose son is not wealthy and cannot give her large gifts, chooses to emphasize the kindness and support his assistance signifies. Leeds parents whose children can offer monetary help accept it in this same spirit:

"If he were a big, rich businessman, it would have been different . . . but he works very hard for his money. It's kindness I want, otherwise I'm one of them who's used to managing, so I manage now. . . . They do, he got me my fridge, and I needed a clock. It isn't because he pays, it's the kindness that they get it for you. Oh, I can fall back on him. . . . He's no rich man, but he wouldn't let me down" (Mrs. Perlman).

"If I run short, I know where to go. Me son would see me" (Mrs. Pincus).

Leeds parents, who have managed on limited budgets all their lives, are frugal and wish to maintain their independence. "No, I wouldn't take from the children if I've got it. I've always been a *baleboste* all my life. I've always cut my cloth according to what I had. . . . I tried a lot. I worked very hard, I didn't go for many charities, or I didn't take anything from anybody, and I went out to work" (Mrs. Stein).

These feelings of acceptance and mutual help are different from the reservations that Cornell parents express about accepting assistance. One explanation might be that Leeds informants receive financial help from sons, whereas Cornell people must rely on daughters and sons-in-law. Leeds informants are also less afraid that regularly accepting aid will pressure children or detract from their chances of getting ahead.

Shopping. Most Leeds people try to do their own food shopping as long as they are physically able. The Estate has a few small shops where they can buy kosher meat, fresh fish, and green vegetables. There is also a variety of shops at Medina Corner, a ten-minute walk or a short bus ride away. A few informants go to Leeds Market once a week. After a trip to the market, conversation centers around the price differences among Estate shops, Medina Corner, and the market. At Leeds Market, informants examine chickens and fish and go from stall to stall until they find the best fruits and vegetables for the lowest price.

Neighbors and family offer assistance when informants are not well or can no longer manage on their own. One woman's next-door neighbor not only buys all her greengrocery, fish, and chicken, she even cleans the fish and koshers the chickens before giving them to her. Another lady's son takes her to the market each week.[37] Mrs. Perlman's daughter-in-law asked her own parents to shop for her "mom-in-law," which they did until the father became ill. Then her home-help and neighbors took over. Although children buy a few heavy items or pick up things on special sale, most informants do their own grocery shopping.

Leeds people also make an effort to fetch their own pension checks. Even if they must go with a neighbor or a home-help, they try to go themselves. Mrs. Aronson makes it a social event: "If I go to the post office, from here to Medina Corner, it takes me nearly two hours to get up and down because people stop me. . . ."

Clothing. Leeds children buy coats, dresses, cardigan sweaters, scarves, and handbags for their parents, often when the parent goes to visit another child living out of town. One male informant finds that the one vest and trousers he left at his daughter's home in Nottingham have become three vests and three pair of pants when he returns for another visit. A few women with extra savings refuse help from their children. "I don't expect anything from David; he'd insult me if he offered," said Mrs. Pincus. One informant, Mrs. Stein, exploits her divorced husband's family connections to buy clothing at discount prices: "I take the coat and I ring David up, and I say, 'David, I've got a coat and it costs so much and so much, that's on the label.' And he'll say, 'All right, Anna, I'll have a look . . . and when you go next week to the shop, they'll tell you what's what.'"

Although children help with heavy laundry, many informants wash small items at home. A visitor often has to make her way through a line of brightly colored knickers and cardigans, hung on a line outside the door to dry. Others give laundry to children to wash at home in their automatic machines or to take to the laundry. Informants usually try to reimburse children, but "They don't tell me the real price, they lower it" (Mrs. Silverman).

Transportation. Although Leeds children would take their parents to the doctor, most informants choose not to ask them. The British system of socialized medicine provides rides to the hospital for physical therapy. English physicians make house calls, and many doctors have offices at Medina Corner or on a direct bus route. Thus the problem Cornell informants find so difficult is not a factor in Leeds.

Instead, Leeds children take parents for social visits to family and friends who live away.[38] Many women remember their children bringing their older friends to visit them in the hospital. Leeds children also take their parents for drives through the park or to their own homes for tea. Nevertheless, some informants would prefer to go more often and express resentment when they are not included:

"Mostly, he takes me to his place. They used to take me about more, but now they've been out on Sunday and they never bothered. But I don't bother, love. I think they're a bit nervous in case if I'm not well, or something" (Mrs. Perlman).

"Sometimes they go to Rounday Park in the morning; if it's only for an hour, take me with, they don't" (Mrs. Pincus).

Help during Illness. To recover from an operation or illness most informants go to a convalescent home. After a couple of weeks, they may then go to a child's home to recuperate further. Mrs. Caplan stayed with her daughter-in-law, who took two weeks off from work to nurse her after major hip surgery. She then returned to her own flat, where her daughters took turns bringing her a hot meal every evening for a month. Mrs. Shapiro returned to her own flat after convalescing for two weeks following a serious operation. She was able to manage with the help of her daughter-in-law, who shopped, prepared meals, and straightened up. Later, she went to her son's home in Edinburgh to recuperate further. Mrs. Pincus went to her sister's home in Sheffield to recover from a stroke. She then returned to Leeds, where her daughter-in-law made her a cup of tea each morning and invited her almost every evening for dinner.[39] Because of this care, Mrs. Pincus decided not to apply for meals-on-wheels: "She wouldn't like me to, Libby. She thought it wasn't necessary. I thought of doing it, mind you, but then I changed my mind. . . . Only the very sick get them and they call me *shnorer* and all sorts. I managed. I managed. I went there three times a week and I got a good meal . . . I like to be independent."

As we have noted, independence is important to Leeds informants. Even when they're ill, they try to manage in their own homes.

Leeds and Cornell informants receive similar care from their children, but the people in Leeds are more comfortable accepting it. They are not afraid of being a burden. They recuperate in their own flats because they want to live again on their own, not because they are afraid of imposing. They accept the interest and concern of their children without reservation.[40] Willingly accepting what they cannot manage on their own, they draw on a wide range of support networks and receive help from neighbors and friends, siblings and children.

For short-term illnesses, family help is usually enough. Only occasionally does a social worker augment their care. My notes illustrate a typical situation:

"Mrs. Silverman had been very ill with a stomach flu for over a week, and I asked her how she managed. She became ill on Tuesday afternoon and drank only water. On Thursday her sister brought and steamed two days' worth of fish. On Friday, both her son and her sister brought soup for the Sabbath. She ate rice pudding most of the time, which she could warm up in the tin. Her son came every night during the time she was ill, only missing one Thursday. (When she is not ill, every evening her son or daughter-in-law calls her on the phone.) Mrs. King (the social worker) came, and Mrs. Landey, also a social worker, picked up a prescription to be filled last week. I asked how Mrs. King had known Mrs. Silverman was ill; she said the lady's brother-in-law had called to tell her. Mrs. King came twice, but only to make a cup of tea and see that she was O.K. Her son did the shopping, bringing a large amount of groceries and many tinned things on Sunday."

Parents also try to help their children when they are ill. Mrs. Perlman cared for her daughter-in-law when she was "poorly," and she did her cooking and ironing. Before her daughter's kidney operation, Mrs. Caplan went with her to the doctor. Leeds women continue to be "good mothers." "I would not let her down. A mother doesn't let a child down" (Mrs. Gottlieb).

Contact. Leeds informants and their adult children maintain close contact. Most sons call their parents every evening, or at least two or three times a week. "My son and daughter-in-law work, so I can't see them on weekdays, but we talk on the phone" (Mrs. Silverman). Unlike many Cornell sons, Leeds sons often stop by to visit: "Nearly every night he rings me, or he comes to see me on his way from work. He finishes early enough, he finishes at 5 o'clock. . . . Last week, he came nearly every night from Tuesday, Wednesday, Thursday, and last night he came for me, Friday, and he may come down tonight after they finish, they may do. After they get washed and changed, if they're going out for a meal, they come down dressed-up if they're going out" (Mrs. Pincus).

Leeds parents look forward to talking to children and occasionally call to chat if they are lonely or depressed: "I sit on me own and I cry and I pray for me phone to go and when our David calls me, I'm in heaven. . . . I do ring him sometimes. I just have a few words with him. I say, 'I'm very lonely and I'm about so many hours, so I thought I'd ring you, all right?'" (Mrs. Pincus). Children living in other English cities usually telephone once every week or two. Those on the Continent or in Canada or America write their parents and occasionally call.

Several women go to their children's homes for Friday dinners and Sunday afternoons. "Friday night I always go there for the Sabbath. It's a change being on me own. . . . Friday night's their night" (Mrs. Pincus). Mrs. Caplan says that since her husband passed away, "I have never in fifteen years been alone on a weekend." She goes to one daughter's for dinner on Friday night, to her second daughter's home on Saturday after *shul,* and then to her son's house for tea on Sunday. Other children visit their parents on Saturday afternoons and enjoy a cup of tea or a meal with them. Thus Leeds informants see their children, in general, more often than do Cornell parents.

Leeds parents look forward to these visits with their children. "Well, if they don't turn up one night or it runs into Sunday, I get very depressed, and I miss them a lot. I feel better when they come, you know" (Mrs. Pincus). The children seem sensitive to their parents' needs: "Wednesday night, I had *yortsayt* for my husband, *olevasholem,* so I didn't want to be on me own. So he said, 'You may as well come up and stay with us.' So I went up there Wednesday night" (Mrs. Pincus).

There is also mutual visiting with children living outside Leeds. Mrs. Shapiro takes a bus to Edinburgh to visit with her son and his family. She stays a month. Mrs. Perlman looked forward to visiting her daughter's home on the coast; she hoped that with companionship, good meals, and

someone to look after her, she would feel better. When adult children and
their families come to Leeds, they usually stay with the mother. Mrs.
Caplan's son, daughter-in-law, grandson, and dog often stay for five days
at a time in her three-room flat. Many informants keep a studio couch in
their living rooms for visiting children.

Holiday Visits. Passover in Leeds has the same significance for family
members that it has in Cleveland. Like their Cornell counterparts, none of
the Leeds group still prepared a *seyder* meal for the whole family. Mrs.
Caplan, for example, stopped soon after she moved to the Knightsdale
Estate because of the limited space in her flat.[41] During the spring I was
there, only three informants did not participate in the Passover *seyder* with
their families. Mrs. Silverman attends the communal *seyder* on the Estate,
because she finds it difficult to make the trip to her son's home. One year
her family joined her, and another time she was "thrilled and proud as
punch" to be selected to bless the Passover candles at the communal *seyder*.
Mrs. Gottlieb, who now goes to her niece's home, remembers sadly and
with nostalgia when her daughter still lived in Leeds: "I used to make the
meal for them all, and everybody used to say, 'Oh, how lovely to see the
way all your children come.'" Mrs. Stein, who is angry with her daughter-in-law, refused an invitation to join her son's family.

In-Laws. Some Leeds informants have comfortable relations with their
daughters-in-law. "My in-laws think as much of me as my own children
do, I'm blessed," said Mrs. Caplan. Many accept their daughters-in-law
because they are good wives to their sons.[42] "They're nice girls, they make
my sons happy, they're good wives and mothers" (Mrs. Caplan). "They're
not as close as a daughter would be. They'd come in the car, they'd come
in a bit, they'd sit down. She comes for me at the doctor, she sounds the
hooter and I've got to be ready. Do you know what I mean? Well, that's an
appointment, it's different. But when she brings me home, she just drops
me off, and she's off again. Now a daughter already would come in and sit
down for a few minutes and have a cup of tea with me. . . . I wouldn't tell
him. I wouldn't say anything about her to him. It's her husband, after all.
I never say a wrong word about her to him" (Mrs. Pincus).

Not everyone gets along well with in-laws, however. "You can't expect
a daughter-in-law to be a daughter," said Mrs. Perlman, who continued:
"She had a mother living down there in the maisonettes. It were all her
mother, and she would go to see to her. She's been a wonderful daughter
to her, and I'm very pleased. If she didn't have so much for the mother-in-

A communal Passover *seyder* held at the Knightsdale hall: women lighting the candles in the menorah.

Homemade gefilte fish for Passover in Leeds.

law, you can't make her. She always said she had a mother. But I can't get right close to her. . . . I'm the mother-in-law, and as you get older, you find it out."[43]

Despite such strains,[44] Leeds parents often receive assistance from their sons. "He does everything for me. . . . He does odd jobs, anything I want doing" (Mrs. Pincus). As noted above, sons call their mothers frequently and often come to visit. Mother-in-law and daughter-in-law also make an effort to cooperate. "I don't want to fall out with them, because I've got nobody else. And they are very good" (Mrs. Pincus). Leeds informants are not so dependent as some Cornell people on social welfare personnel if they do not get along with daughters-in-law.[45] Sons generally continue to be attentive, marketing when mothers are sick, visiting on their own, or doing odd jobs that need attention.

Advice. Leeds elderly have more comfortable relations with their off-spring than do Cornell parents.[46] Most try not to interfere in their children's lives and to give advice only when asked. Mrs. Caplan, for example, says that only after her children have explained their situations to her does she offer her opinion. They can take her advice or leave it: "I do not interfere; I want them to respect me." Mrs. Shapiro holds a similar philosophy: "I don't interfere with their lives, because they're young people. I'm getting on, you know, I'm not young. And I feel that people who are young should enjoy life and do what's good for them. Not like some mothers. They tell them to do this and do that. I say different. I feel they should, that's how I let me children, London or here. I never interfere with their lives, whatever they want, they do. They want to paper and to paint, they want to do. Some mothers, 'Oh, why do you do this, or do that!' I don't. Do what you like, love."

Other children resent unsolicited advice: "He wouldn't take it if I give it" (Mrs. Pincus). Leeds children try to influence parents' behavior by articulating their own feelings, as the following incident reveals:

"I told my grandson, they're very close, I says 'I don't understand your mother. After all, Patrick, why can't she phone me?'

" 'Gramma, I'm going to tell you a secret,' he says.

" 'Well?'

" 'Do you know why my mother doesn't phone you? She told me because every time she phones you, you play Hamlet with her. You shout at her and tell her off.'

" 'I only tell her for her own good, her own benefit.'

" 'Don't. Then she'll come more often.' "

Nevertheless, informants feel confident that they can discuss matters with their children, whom they consider to be friends: "Thank God, I've got good children, these days" (Mrs. Aronson). "I always tell my son and daughter-in-law, I don't tell my personal affairs to nobody, only my children. . . . They're my best friends. I can talk to them openly, they know all my business and everything" (Mrs. Shapiro). Mrs. Caplan tries to be independent but occasionally confides in her younger daughter: "She thinks like me, she reassures me." Or she may turn to her out-of-town son for advice: "He is a person without airs, with no side about him." Occasionally children also confide in parents: "My Barney is open. He tells me everything" (Mrs. Gottlieb). Informants and adult children often talk matters over and come to mutual agreement.

For Leeds parents, this involvement with children provides reassurance. They do not seem to feel left out and neglected, as many Cornell parents do. They see children as a source of love, support, and advice. "If my son was here, what, my son would be here every day. I know he would. . . . My son can take me on his knee and cuddle me, and he'll go past and give me a kiss on my head" (Mrs. Gottlieb). Parents also feel that they can help their children in return. This belief is illustrated by a comment of Mrs. Gottlieb, whose daughter's husband is seriously ill: "I'd still do for them if they needed me, if they needed my help. . . . We'd talk, she wouldn't have to do anything for me, but we'd talk and reminisce. . . . I would not let her down. A mother doesn't let a child down."

To Leeds parents the parental role is an ongoing involvement, a continuing concern throughout one's life. Mrs. Caplan's husband always told her, "Whatever we have, first comes the kids, you're next, and I'm last, if there's anything left over." She describes the years of sacrifice and hardship they endured to raise their four children. It is because of this lifelong commitment, she believes, that her children are now considerate of her: "I think we brought them up that way." Others share this opinion:

"I were lovely to them. Money is not everything. I had no money to help, but kindness. When you're good . . . they stayed two years with me when they got married. I used to get the dinners ready at night. . . . She says to somebody, she's got two mothers. Her mother does nothing like that. It were all me. That's why she keeps me as a mother" (Mrs. Perlman).

"I tell my son, 'Barney, I don't know how to thank you for what you've done for me.' He says, 'Mother, you don't have to thank me—I have you to thank for everything. You don't have to thank me. I have a lot to thank you for'" (Mrs. Gottlieb).

Thus Leeds and Cornell parents view kinship differently. For Leeds parents, kinship offers a sense of confidence, mutual involvement, and interdependence. The parental role never ends; women who continue to do things for their children are described as "good mothers." Children are also expected to help their parents and in-laws. By performing their duties, parent and child reflect upon and reaffirm the worth of the other. One male informant said to his daughter, "It is good to have kids like you." She replied, "Look at the stock we come from" (Mr. Segal).

Summary: Leeds Kinship Relationships

The children of Cornell and Leeds informants provide relatively similar services for their aged parents. They assist in illness, give financial help, telephone and visit regularly, and demonstrate concern. The crucial difference lies in the attitude of the informants themselves. Cornell parents seem uncertain and ambivalent. They want to be with their children, yet they are uncomfortable when they are. They feel that their children are too busy for them, too involved with business or their own families. Leeds informants, in contrast, seem genuinely to want to do things on their own, out of a sense of independence rather than a fear that they might be a burden. Leeds parents continue to give emotional support to their children; Cornell informants want to receive such support. What accounts for these differences?

One explanation is that Leeds informants benefited from being raised by their parents in England. They grew up in family units and lived near their own parents as they grew old. Informants learned from this experience, helping their aged parents as their parents had previously assisted them. A sense of confidence and assuredness in kin relationships seems to have grown out of these experiences, and these feelings have been transferred to the informants' children. "I didn't have to rely much on friends or strangers for help; first I had my mother behind me, and now my children" (Mrs. Caplan).

One exception is Mrs. Stein, whose atypical life history provides a useful test case. Her immigrant experience resembles that of Cornell informants: she came alone as a teenager to live with an aunt in Leeds. She does not have the same sense of trust, acceptance, and involvement with her children that other Leeds parents have. Rather, she expresses dissatisfaction and a longing for more signs of affection and demonstrations of love from her children. Like Cornell elderly, her son does not do enough for her: "He should come to spend an hour with the Mommy, a half-an-hour. He comes for five minutes. . . . I don't want nothing from them, I don't take nothing from them, I only want a little bit of respect and to appreciate what I do for them. Just respect as an old woman."[47]

A second factor explaining the difference in attitude between Cornell and Leeds parents may lie in their socioeconomic positions and life-styles. In America, many informants' children are well-to-do business people. They live in wealthy suburbs and belong to Reform or Conservative synagogues. Leeds children are not as affluent: They live in homes near their parents and have remained Orthodox Jews. They therefore share their parents' values and life-styles more fully than do Cornell informants' children.

A third contributory factor lies in the patterns of friendship and neighborhood relations in the two communities. This subject will be explored in the next three chapters.

3

The Urban Context: Old Neighborhoods and Social Networks

CHAPTER 2 DEALT WITH THE RELATIONS of parents and children. This chapter considers more distant kin—aunts, uncles, and cousins—and relations with neighbors and old friends. We will compare the Jewish immigrant experience in Cleveland and Leeds, discussing informants' kindred and neighborhood relationships within a context of changing domestic needs and patterns of residential mobility. How do the aged in Cornell and Leeds differ in their ability and willingness to draw on kin and neighborhood resources, and why?

CORNELL CHRONOLOGY

1910–1930: Immigration, Marriage, and Birth of Children
As we discussed in Chapter 1, many Cornell informants immigrated to the United States as teenagers, without parents or siblings, in the years just before World War I. When they arrived in Cleveland, they usually stayed with maternal kin, who helped support them.[1] These relatives lived in the old Jewish immigrant areas around Orange, Central, and Woodland avenues, areas into which Italians and blacks were beginning to move. Family members worked in the neighborhood—one as a *shoykhet*,[2] one as a blacksmith, and another as a dairy owner. Newly arrived young men found employment in nearby foundries or dairies. The unmarried girls got jobs in laundries, delicatessens, bakeries, or clothing factories. Mrs. Weiner wanted to save her earnings and so looked for a room on Hawthorne. She moved away from her uncle, who always "put a lien" on her wages to help support his eight children.

Informants married in their late teens or early twenties. They met their spouses informally, often through a casual introduction by a relative or mutual friend. Courtships were brief and weddings simple. The ceremony was usually held in a relative's home rather than at a synagogue.

The couple often continued living with relatives for a year or so. One couple went to Detroit and one to Akron to try their fortunes, but had to return to Cleveland and lived with relatives again (Mrs. Feingold and Mrs. Wexler).

Young couples chose their first apartments for economy and proximity to the homes of these close kinsmen.[3] Thus in the teens and early 1920s, most were still living in the Woodlawn and Central areas. Only a few had moved to the Mt. Pleasant-Kinsman district. Their first children were often born at this time.

Also during this brief but relatively stable period, a few informants made intimate lifelong friends. Some developed close relationships with neighbors or companions at work. Mrs. Weiner still sees the children of the family her husband lived with and in whose home they were married. Mrs. Samuels became friendly with a girl she worked with at the blouse factory, and Mrs. Brodsky visits a woman whose window faced hers in the old neighborhood and whose young children played with hers.[4]

Thus informants lived close to relatives and a few friends in declining older Jewish neighborhoods, where opportunities for economic advancement were limited. Many spouses worked in this neighborhood or sought employment in the rapidly expanding area around Kinsman Avenue. They worked as painters, contractors, trolley drivers, dry cleaners, and hucksters. Mrs. Brodsky recalls her husband hiring a horse and wagon for $3.00 a day, buying fruit on credit, and then peddling this produce in their Italian-Jewish neighborhood. Mrs. Samuels's husband moved his family to 93rd and Kinsman, where he worked as a milkman at the Meyer Dairy.

The two women who were born in this country and whose parents were well-to-do had different kinds of experiences. Mrs. Eisner, who was born at 14th Street and St. Clair Avenue, lived in that neighborhood from 1900 to 1910. The family occupied the rooms behind her father's furniture store. On weekends they would visit with *landslayt* on Woodlawn and 55th Street. In 1910 her father purchased a two-family home on Empire Way, a middle-class street off 105th Street. Her parents then commuted to business. Mrs. Eisner attended high school on 73rd and Cedar Avenue, and it was here that she met her lifelong friends. When she became engaged, there was much festivity, and her friends and relatives gave her many showers. Weddings were an important social event among the close-knit Jews who had earlier settled in Cleveland and had begun to make their fortunes: "There were not that many Jews in town, and among *our* Jews, it was a big thing when a girl got married, and the girls made showers" (Mrs. Eisner).

When she was married, her husband purchased a home around the corner, at Yale and 105th Street. Mr. and Mrs. Eisner continued to live there until they were divorced ten years later. She always maintained close contact with both her family and friends. What financial assets she has were left to her by an unmarried brother.

Mrs. Levi left Toronto after marrying her husband, who practiced medicine in Cleveland. He lived in the Slovenian area of 65th and St. Clair when the couple became engaged. After their wedding in Toronto, they moved to a private home on Pasadena, an upper-class street off 105th Street. Later they moved to 121st and Kinsman, where they remained for fifteen years. Here Dr. Levi was close to his medical office at 125th and Buckeye. Mrs. Levi did not mix with her neighbors, preferring to make friends through her temple sisterhood and Zionist organizations.

By the mid-1920s, almost all informants lived in the Kinsman-Mt. Pleasant area between 117th and 151st streets. This is a neighborhood of two-family houses and brick apartment buildings built for skilled tradesmen, working-class people, and small shopkeepers. Rents ranged from $34 to $46 a month. The Kinsman-Mt. Pleasant district was a boom area, built by a developer who used Italian and black labor. From the beginning, both Italians and Jews lived there. Although this neighborhood is contiguous to Shaker Heights, it did not have the status of the Jewish section around 105th Street. Informants' young children grew up in this area. An article by Violet Spevack in the *Cleveland Jewish News* (January 21, 1972, p. 15) describes with nostalgia how it was to grow up in this neighborhood:

> The long streets were always filled with kids playing baseball, . . . telephones had three party lines, . . . and large front porches held gobs of kids every night sitting on the swing and on the railings to joke around, exchange ideas, and neck—after the grown-ups disappeared.
>
> People talk about "Jewish identity" today. Heck, we had it then . . . in the homes and in the stores, . . . in the Council, Workmen's Circle, small *shuls*, in the playgrounds, and in the air that was wafted around. From those humble Jewish homes, from hard-working immigrant stock, have arisen a generation of highly successful business people, professional men, and community leaders.
>
> Rosh Hashana and Yom Kippur were great days for showing off brand new clothes (or those handed down from an older brother or sister) and parading from *shul* to *shul*, from 119th to 147th, . . . and passing all of the

kosher butcher shops, dry goods stores, delicatessens, fruit stores, . . . and all the other familiar places. . . .

One significant fact emerges from informants' discussions of relationships with neighbors and friends during their early married lives and child-rearing years. Cornell informants moved often, rarely staying in any location longer than five years. Their frequent changes of residence do not usually correspond with the expansion phase of the family cycle; instead they register changes in economic fortune.

The first years of marriage were financially difficult for immigrant men without a trade. Frequent modification in income led to frequent changes of address. Unfortunately, most informants only vaguely remember their various addresses, moving dates, or neighbors, but Mrs. Samuels clearly recalls the succession of apartments her family lived in. Her story is a detailed example of the transiency of Cornell informants during their child-rearing years.

In 1920 Mrs. Samuels and her husband, a milkman, lived in four "cheap," bug-infested, "cold" rooms on 57th and Kinsman Avenue. Afraid of being alone at night when her husband worked, Mrs. Samuels rented a room to a woman with a child. While this boarder worked during the day, Mrs. Samuels took care of her daughter. When Mrs. Samuels returned from the hospital with her first child, she was pleased that her boarder had cleaned the apartment and washed the curtains. Soon Mrs. Samuels's family decided to move. She wanted a ground-floor apartment because it was too difficult to take the baby carriage down three flights of stairs. They found four unheated rooms on Hawthorne. Here the family was close to the aunt of Mrs. Samuels's husband and near her own aunt's home. The family again took in a boarder, a woman who got married from their home. Mrs. Samuels remembers liking this Jewish area where she had "a very good neighbor upstairs, we were just like sisters."

While they were still living on Hawthorne Street, Mrs. Samuels's brother came from Chicago to teach her husband to be a painter. Mr. Samuels got a job in a paint factory, where he earned $22 a week. He gave up his job as a milkman to spend the summers painting. Soon the family moved to a heated suite on 97th Street off Cedar Avenue. The apartment building was soon sold, however, and the new owner increased the rent. The following year, the Samuelses located cheaper unheated rooms on Longfellow. When finances again improved, the family moved to 142nd and Kinsman, where their son started school.

In 1927, when he was thirty-six years old and his wife was thirty-four, Mr. Samuels lost his job at the paint factory and went to work for his brother in Canton, Ohio. Because they had invested all their savings in an unsuccessful building scheme, Mrs. Samuels had to put her furniture in storage and go live with an aunt. People gossiped and accused her of leaving her husband, but she was only trying to make ends meet. Mr. Samuels visited her on weekends and gave her what money he earned. She made a few dollars herself taking care of her sister-in-law's twin children.

In 1928 Mr. Samuels learned that one of his relatives was a "boss paintner." The family traveled to New Jersey to see him, remaining for nine months. When they returned to Cleveland, they lived with Mr. Samuels's aunt until they rented their own apartment with $100 they had borrowed against the value of their insurance policy. This was the top floor of a two-family home on 105th Street, near Hampden. Mr. Samuels decorated this apartment at his own expense, but when he was laid off work again, the owners became apprehensive about the rent and asked them to move. In 1929 the Samuelses found four rooms for $22 above a delicatessen on 105th Street, near Morison. During the Depression, the family bought a junk business in Collinwood and lived in the three rooms behind the office. When the Depression ended, they sold the business and moved back to Glenville.

This account of Mrs. Samuels's nine moves in nine years illustrates a number of experiences common to all Cornell elderly. First is the obvious fact of mobility. Each residential move except the first registers a change in the family's economic situation. Informants usually lived in Jewish neighborhoods and in buildings owned by Jewish landlords. Few ever owned their own homes. Only when they first came to America and during early years of marriage did they remain for long in one location. During this brief stable period they formed a few friendships. But because they moved so often, Cornell people were rarely able to form lasting relationships with neighbors.

Mrs. Samuels's account also illustrates the difficulties faced by men who came to America without a trade. The deteriorating Jewish-Italian neighborhoods where informants were forced to live offered few economic opportunities. Because much of the work was seasonal, they had to spread a few months' income over the entire year. Just at the time they were reaching the prime of their earning power, the Depression came. Many also made bad financial decisions.

Cornell people usually turned to aunts and cousins, rather than to friends or neighbors, for moral support and economic assistance during difficult times. Mrs. Brodsky's experience illustrates this point. Her husband, a huckster, rarely made enough money to support his family. When the utilities were turned off in their apartment, Mrs. Brodsky would return to work at the factory where she had been employed before her marriage. She made buttonholes for $6.00 a week while her husband stayed home with their three children. She bought kosher chicken wings, "insides," and little pieces of meat to put in a soup. "It did not cost too much. I never took pastrami or salami, I made a meal for them." Once during the Depression Mrs. Brodsky took her children to her cousin's home, confessing that she had no food. "I didn't want they [friends and neighbors] should know." At this time, kinsmen were still living near one another.[5]

Informants' economic plight grew worse during the Depression, but relations among kinsmen remained strong and supportive.[6] Most Cornell elderly were unwilling to ask for government assistance. Only Mr. Isenberg went on relief (but only for a short time), and another worked for the WPA (Mrs. Wexler's husband). Not until the early 1930s did most informants have their second children. Often there was as much as an eleven-year separation between the birth of the first and second babies.[7]

1930–1940: Children's Adolescence; and Some Broken Families

In the 1930s the sons of some informants were old enough for their *bar mitsves*. Few families could afford membership in a synagogue, however. Mrs. Eisner used her father's membership; Mrs. Brodsky paid a fee to have the ceremony in a *shul* and bought a bottle of *shnaps* to serve at the reception. Mrs. Samuels remembers that two friends, one of whom she had known before she was married, helped her to make her son's *bar mitzve* party. Too poor to have the ceremony in a *shul* or to buy the traditional wine and herring, she had her son's *bar mitzve* at the branch of the Jewish Community Center on 105th street, and her friends helped them celebrate at home. One woman baked a cake; a second bought meat for sandwiches. Mrs. Samuels reimbursed them with money claimed for an accident.

Few Cornell parents were members of synagogues, benevolent societies, or other voluntary associations.[8] "The family was more important than clubs," said Mrs. Levitt. Thus they did not use one of the common means of making friends and sustaining relationships. One exception is Mrs. Samuels, who sought sociability among the few Jews who

lived in Collinwood. "The couple of Jews in Collinwood were close together. . . . People wanted to join some place, to not be alone." The lady
who ran a Jewish grocery store on the corner took her to the Dvinsker
Jewish Aid Society meetings on 105th Street. The women went together
on the bus to weekly meetings, picnics, and other benefits.[9] Mrs. Samuels
continued her membership until 1970, when all the old members had
passed away.

In the years following the Depression, four Cornell informants faced
reversals in their personal lives. Mrs. Brodsky was widowed, Mrs. Wexler
and Mrs. Eisner were divorced, and Mr. Isenberg was separated from his
wife. The two divorced women went to work to support their children,
Mrs. Eisner selling men's furnishings at the May Company and Mrs.
Wexler sewing in a clothing factory. Family members, particularly sisters,
offered support and assistance at a time when divorce was uncommon in
the Jewish community. Often Mrs. Wexler took her children to Florida to
visit her sisters, who were her confidantes and friends: "In those days, a
divorce was looked upon as a very, very low thing. You know, people
didn't get divorced like they do today . . . everyone's divorced, nobody's
married, but years ago, divorce was looked on as something so unusual,
wrong, so I did not confide in my friends, I didn't want to, I was ashamed
. . . so it was really my sisters whom I confided in."

Mrs. Eisner and her children went to live in her parents' two-family
home. Her sister, who was also divorced and who lived upstairs, helped
give the children lunch and care for them. When her mother died, Mrs.
Eisner was not able to work, raise her children, and also cook for her
father, who strictly kept kosher. She decided to get her own apartment in
the 105th Street area, and her sister and father sold their house and also
moved. Mrs. Eisner continued to see them when they came to her home
for Sunday meals. Her brother and sister-in-law provided moral support,
the latter supplying the "niceties" by trying to teach her to drive and
giving a luncheon for her friends. A second sister-in-law gave her hand-
me-down clothes for her children. The neighborhood bridge group
dropped her from their card parties, but her old friends from high school
remained supportive.

Mrs. Brodsky, whose husband had been a huckster, was left a widow at
age forty. Neighbors helped to arrange for a funeral through the Chesed
Shel Emeth Cemetery Association. At their suggestion, she got a job
sewing at Lampl Sportswear, where she continued to work for twenty
years. Her aunt and cousin gave her clothing, which she altered with the

cousin's sewing machine to fit her children. Mrs. Brodsky was ashamed to let her neighbors know how difficult things were. One woman asked her, "How come you leave Sidney all alone?" She replied, "I have to go to work to feed my children. Do you want I should starve out my children?" When a fourth informant, Mr. Isenberg, was estranged from his wife, he went to live with his daughter and son-in-law.

During these years of economic and personal hardships, Cornell people relied on family members rather than friends and neighbors. They gave and loaned money or taught a new trade to a destitute relative. Aunts, cousins, and sisters acted as confidantes during the difficult times of divorce or poverty. Informants did not wish to discuss these matters with strangers, and they had little extra time to meet new friends.

1940–1960: Marriage of Children; Birth of Grandchildren

During the 1940s and 1950s, many informants moved to the Glenville and Superior Through region of East Cleveland. The two more wealthy informants, Mrs. Eisner and Mrs. Levi, were already living in the Cornell area. During these years, sons of informants and neighbors joined the armed services, but each mother seems to have endured her pain individually. When Mrs. Eisner's son did not return, again it was family members—a sister and a sister-in-law—who helped her through her tragedy.[10]

Daughters also got married during this time. A number of couples remained in the bride's home until after their first child was born. Female informants helped to care for both their daughters and the new grandchildren. The young couples usually paid for room and board, and the mothers did the cooking and laundry.

When the daughter and her husband did not live with the bride's parents, they moved near by. Informants saw their grandchildren often. They babysat and helped care for them when they were sick. Even when their children first moved to the suburbs, grandparents continued this pattern of assistance.[11] Mrs. Samuels took the bus two or three times a week so she could care for her grandchildren while her daughter-in-law went to visit a sick child in the hospital. Mrs. Wexler often made her grandchildren lunch and stayed to prepare and serve them dinner if her daughter was attending an evening class. On the Jewish holidays, the children and grandchildren came to the grandmothers' homes for the traditional meals.

For those few informants who worked, involvement with children and grandchildren was less intense. They had neither energy for nor interest in babysitting or cooking, although two working women took care of their first grandchildren when second or third babies were born (Mrs. Eisner and Mrs. Wexler).

Many informants were reunited with old neighbors near whom they had lived many years before. All had moved from the inner city to the Glenville and Superior Through areas. Thus old relationships were renewed and strengthened.

1960 to the Present: The Move to the Cornell Neighborhood; Grandchildren's Adolescence

In the late 1940s, blacks began to move into the Jewish area. By the late 1950s, few whites remained. Isolated, informants decided to move to the Cornell neighborhood. By this time, they were in their early sixties, children were in their thirties and forties, and grandchildren were becoming teenagers. Two women moved from New York to be with their children, thereby cutting themselves off from other family and friends and centering their lives on their children (Mrs. Nathan and Mrs. Levitt).

Certain patterns emerge from the chronology of informants' lives. One is the precariousness of their economic situation, for most were at the mercy of economic circumstances. For many parents, who gave part of their savings to help children buy homes or start businesses and whose Social Security checks are small, this pattern continues in old age.

Because their incomes were uncertain and their neighborhoods changed, Cornell people moved frequently. They developed few lasting relationships with neighbors. Only a few friendships date back to the days before informants were married or when their children were young. Thus they have little sense of identification with any particular neighborhood in Cleveland.

In times of economic and personal hardship, informants turned to family members as a source of support, assistance, friendship, and advice. "My sister Marian taught me a lot, she traveled the road ahead of me," said Mrs. Eisner. Another informant noted, "I was close with Mr. Samuels's family, so I didn't need neighbors or friends."

Thus Cornell parents, who did not develop the buttress of old friends and neighbors and who transferred their involvements with aunts, cousins, and sisters to their children and grandchildren, lack the wide network of associations that might enhance relationships with their children today. The consequences of this history of transience and resultant lack of stable peer relations are analyzed in the next chapter, while planning and policy suggestions to compensate for the results of thwarted prior opportunities in forming peer bonds will be advanced in the conclusion.

LEEDS CHRONOLOGY

1905–1955: Immigration, Childhood, Marriage, and Children

Informants' parents chose to live near kinsmen and *landslayt* when they first settled in Leeds. Even though their families were poor, their memories of childhood are happy: "At that time, everybody was friendly, everyone was jolly—it was lively. . . . We were all poor, they had nothing, nothing at all. Mind you, we weren't short of food. But we never had no nice homes, nice homes, if you know what I mean" (Mrs. Gottlieb).

Neighbors lived close together in small back-to-back houses. Most fathers were employed in the tailoring trades. Parents were religious, observed the Sabbath, and hired a *shabes goy* (a non-Jew) to come in to light the fires on the Sabbath. Common ties bound neighbors together, and there was mutual support and cooperation "when everyone was on the same plane, and none had a lot." Mrs. Caplan's mother, for example, had been a nurse in Russia; in Leeds she became the midwife for the neighborhood. Mrs. Caplan remembers her mother tearing sheets to make bandages. She is proud that the neighbors thought well of her mother, whom everyone called *bobe* (grandmother). Mrs. Gottlieb has similar memories: "If we heard anybody lost somebody, we'd all go in and we'd contribute. And mother used to bake. . . . They were so poor they couldn't even make a *bris*. So my sister made biscuits and my sister was *kvaterin*, godmother."[12]

Thus informants grew up knowing many people with similar backgrounds. After attending school together, all quit when they were thirteen to go to work. Most neighborhood girls worked in the same large clothing factories, and they would make their way together through the winding back streets. Many informants made lifelong friendships in these early days. One of Mrs. Caplan's close friends is the daughter of the *landslayt* to whose home her parents first came from Russia. She calls Mrs. Caplan her Yiddish name and refers to her parents as *"mume* and *feter,"* aunt and uncle. "We were very, very close *landslayt.*" Mrs. Caplan is also still friendly with the woman who moved next door to her mother when she was first married. Similarly, Mrs. Gottlieb remains friendly with a woman who was her girl friend for nine years before she was married. She also continues to see two sisters with whom she grew up: "They've been my friends all my life. We grew up together. I knew her before I got married. She got married five years later than me and then she lived with me in London. We lived together. She had only a bedroom and she ate with us. She bought her own food. We never had a word, never."

These longstanding friendships are based on the common experience of growing up in the same neighborhood, knowing one another's parents and siblings, continuing to live near one another after marriage, raising children together, and having husbands who worked in the same trades. "We have memories of things we have seen and done together," says Mrs. Caplan.

This social density continued in neighborhoods where informants lived after they were married. Several women moved near parents and aunts, maintaining close contact with them, too. Mrs. Caplan's mother lived on the next block: "I stayed in the neighborhood when I was married to be nearby parents." She remembers that her mother came every day to help her bathe her first baby. "When I got married, I lived with me mother because he lived in the army right after. When he got back, we moved to Roundhay Road for four years, but I didn't like it. I lived there four years and I come back to Meanwood Road, where I were used to, where I were near me mother. It was all mother, to tell you the truth" (Mrs. Perlman).

The husbands of Leeds informants were employed in the tailoring trades. They lived near the factories, and many walked home for their noon meal.[13] Spouses started work at 8 A.M., even on Saturdays and Sundays. "They had to work what the boss wanted." Only two husbands were self-employed. After one man had worked at Burton's for a while, he opened his own shop, where he made entire garments on the bespoke system and employed other tailors. Another husband owned a public house in London. During the war, he and his wife returned to Leeds, where he worked for a large manufacturer and later opened his own workshop.[14] A few spouses made a comfortable living, but many had a difficult time. "He'd get a job. He got a job and the shop burned down. We were unlucky, love, we were an unlucky couple," said Mrs. Perlman.

Half of the wives worked to supplement the family income or to help during wartime. Mrs. Stein, estranged from her husband, did cleaning, catering, and other odd jobs to support her children. Mrs. Pincus "worked markets"[15] on Saturdays after her husband became ill, and Mrs. Perlman took in sewing: "I had to take sewing in from any boss. . . . I worked harder after I were married than before." She describes going to the factories to fetch work to do at home: "I used to put it in the pram and sit him on it and wheel off. I don't know how I worked, I weren't supposed to be strong and all; I think it were more that I needed it that I did it. . . ."

Other women also worked during the war. Mrs. Silverman helped a neighbor sew weskits, and Mrs. Aronson worked for a relative in a popular Jewish fish-and-chips restaurant.

In addition to raising their families on small incomes, a few informants nursed sick husbands:

"Well, he had pleurisy at first. Then he got rheumatic fever. He didn't work for two years. We spent every penny we had. It's not like now, you know. . . . I had to work, the pensions weren't much then, sick benefits were very little. . . . Well, he was six years without legs. The first one come off when gangrene set in, the second one through thrombosis. . . . I was busy. Get up in the morning and light the fire, then get him out of bed when the fire was going, then pass him a bowl of water, had a little table here, and he sat in his wheelchair, then pass him his shaving tackle and water, give him clean clothes. Spotless clean. Every day a clean shirt, although he did nothing. . . . Iron and keep up, and bathe him in bed. Oh, I had enough to put up, no wonder I went gray" (Mrs. Pincus).

"He were a good one, but I had a hard life. I had to work hard; he were a sick man afterwards. . . . He were twenty-five years, off and on, ill . . . I nursed him all the time, I never gave him into a home, because he was clean and particular" (Mrs. Perlman).

Two women faced difficult marital problems. Mrs. Stein's husband gambled. After they had lived apart for many years, she divorced him. A second husband died of alcoholism in his fifties: "When he died, I wasn't sorry. I wasn't disturbed. I thought to myself, I have peace of mind now. . . . I didn't lose myself. I did everything that was right, that was correct, and I haven't looked back since" (Mrs. Gottlieb).[16]

The spouses of most Leeds informants died in the late 1950s and middle 1960s. Although they had difficult times, they tried not to let their troubles depress them: "I never let anything get the better of me. I've got a very good spirit. I had some very hard knocks with my husband. I never wanted sympathy or others to feel sorry for me" (Mrs. Gottlieb).[17]

Parents and siblings, who often lived on the same street or nearby, provided moral support and advice during these difficult periods. "I didn't have much. But I had the family all around me like that . . . ," said Mrs. Perlman. She reminisced that family members, both siblings and siblings-in-law, went to *shul* together and visited during the week: "They used to come to me on a Thursday when they went shopping in Chapeltown, they used to come and I used to make a lovely dinner for them. Blintzes, oh yes, I used to love it." Besides asking one another for advice and helping with domestic chores, siblings occasionally assisted each other financially. Mrs. Gottlieb, who spent the early years of her marriage in London, used to send a weekly food parcel to her brother. "Freda, love, if it weren't for you, we would starve," he told her. This pattern of support and advice to and from siblings continues in old age.

Informants also benefited from the company of neighbors and friends, with whom they formed close relationships over the years. Neighborhood life was stable and homogeneous in Leeds. Many informants lived in the same district, even the same house, for forty or forty-five years before moving to the Knightsdale Estate. People of similar background and economic position lived close together, and they knew one another well. "We lived neighbors over fifty years, and that's not a day you know, it's a long time," said Mrs. Aronson. "Leeds is a small town. And the Jews are very close knit and stick closely together. We all used to live in back-to-back houses and could hear everything going on. The children called all the adults 'aunt' and 'uncle' and the people were like related and everyone knew everyone. When you live as neighbors for a long time, you become related and they become like family. . . . I lived with neighbors and we became related. Their daughter married my brother, so you can't have anything nearer than that with a neighbor."

These Leeds districts were originally mostly Jewish. Over time they became "mixed" neighborhoods, however, and informants had non-Jewish neighbors too. "Where I lived before, it was a Jewish district, there were all Jews. In my street there were loads of houses, I don't know, about twelve blocks, and I think there were only about six English people altogether. Then all the Jews moved further up, they went out of the district. Everyone was moving further out to Chapeltown Road, the Savilles, and then they went a bit further . . . and then still further out" (Mrs. Aronson).

Many other Jews began to move out of these older areas. They left the back-to-back houses, communal toilet facilities, and cold running water for better neighborhoods, where non-Jewish people had been living. The

Chapeltown area changed from an entirely English district to one that comprised both Jews and Gentiles. "When a lot of Jewish people started coming in, the Christians moved out."

Mrs. Perlman, in comparing herself to a neighbor, explains that she moved into Chapeltown to give her children a better environment: "She lived fifty years in one place in a scullery house. Scullery, kitchen, and two bedrooms. They never had a bath, they never had hot and cold water. I couldn't have lived fifty years there. I wanted my children to get out of that. I lived in Meanwood Road with cold water . . . but when they grew up, I thought, no, . . . because they were bringing friends home and the friends were better off. So, well, I thought, it isn't nice, . . . I moved to the Maxboroughs. It were marvelous then, in the Savilles were all the richest people. But it weren't big rent. . . ."

Today, informants joke about the cold water and common toilet facilities. When they meet people from those days, they immediately launch into discussions of the old district, the neighbors, the common bakehouse, and the outdoor privy: "The toilet was for a walk, take an umbrella and a candle in the winter."

Leeds people were proud of their street and happy in the districts where they lived most of their lives. They usually got along well with both their Jewish and English neighbors, exchanging friendship, favors, and assistance. Informants have nostalgic memories of these old areas:

"I loved it there. . . . I had nice *goyim* neighbors, back-to-back and opposite, at the back and front, you come out and you see a person. I was very comfortable there—it was near to work and near to school, plenty of shops there. . . . Very nice neighbors, go on an errand for you when you're not well" (Mrs. Pincus).

"It were mixed in the Maxboroughs, Christians and Jewish. . . . I had one [Christian neighbor], a Middleton girl, and her husband was a Ukrainian, and they were marvelous. They even took me tea . . . and if I couldn't, she'd come in. I were in a few days after being in bed one time, and she came in . . . and made the fire and saw to me before she went to bed. . . . She were marvelous. She was young, she was only a young woman. . . . My husband used to sit in the garden at the back, and she wanted to go errands and she used to bring the pram and he used to look after the baby. So, of course, they repaid me that way. They were marvelous. . . . If there were anything I thought I couldn't manage, he'd be there, and that's with Christians and Jews, . . . so when I left the key, she broke down and cried" (Mrs. Perlman).

Thus informants generally found their Christian neighbors helpful, and several developed close friendships, which are still maintained. Many exchange Christmas cards. Mrs. Aronson writes to her neighbor's fifty-six-year-old son, who first moved into the neighborhood when he was three years old. She also goes to weddings and funerals of another non-Jewish woman's family; she has known her friend for fifty-two years. Her mother nursed her during her confinement: "She is a great friend of mine."[18] Mrs. Stein and her non-Jewish neighbor helped one another with food, money, child care, sympathy, and support.[19]

"We've been friends that we both had nothing. And when she used to come in to my place and she had nothing, or the shop was a long way off, 'I have no potatoes in the house, Anna.'

" 'Oh, go downstairs and get some, what you want.'

" 'Have you any sugar?'

" 'Go in the cabinet and get it. . . .' We never reckoned, we were good friends."

Mrs. Stein describes the various phases of this relationship and of their exchange of services:

"She looked after the three other ones when I was in the hospital. I had nowhere to leave them. . . . She used to help me. When I was poorly, or I couldn't do nothing, she used to come. When I had an operation, I was in hospital, she cooked for my kids and washed my kids and bathed my kids, and washed shirts, done everything. . . . When she was poorly, she was in the TB hospital for eight months. I've done it for her. . . . I cleaned and washed and I cooked. I had the key from the house. Every time he used to come from work, the kettle was on the fire and dinner was on the table. I used to go three times a week to see her in hospital. . . . All of them, funerals, weddings, I've always been with them and with the family.

"When Jonny died, she rang me straight away. Didn't take five minutes, I got the bus and I went to town and I took two carriers with me. . . . I went into the market and I filled them with stuff, with meat and chicken and butter and eggs and bread and cakes and sugar and butter—everything, I must have spent about three or four pounds. . . . I went in and said, 'Barbara, I'm sorry I didn't buy no flowers for Jonny, because I know you need that more important than the flowers for Jonny. . . .'

" 'My God!' she said, 'I've never known friends to be like that.' And she followed me, and she cried and I cried. Where can you find people like that? You can't find people like that now."[20]

Leeds informants and their old non-Jewish friends still share confidences. "If I'm upset a bit and I have no one to tell to, I ring up Norma and I talk to Norma. . . . She's a friend that I can speak to her. She knows my life and I know hers. She knows my *kinder*. If she has trouble with the children, she always rings me up and tells me. She confides in me and her daughter as well" (Mrs. Stein).

The friendships that Leeds informants made with their Jewish neighbors are also close and longstanding.[21] Many friends socialized as couples, often playing cards at each other's homes. Mrs. Caplan is friendly with the family who had been neighbors of her husband before they were married. The sisters were bridesmaids in her wedding, and the families visited every Sunday. The sisters took their elderly mother to stay at Mrs. Caplan's home when they wanted to go away for the day. When this old lady died, Mrs. Caplan went every night to the *shive* house for prayers and tried to comfort the family. They still talk on the telephone a few times each month, and Mrs. Caplan often confides in the younger sister. In describing this friend and their relationship, Mrs. Caplan says that they knew one another's mothers, and that she feels she can trust Evelyn's confidence and advice. "I tell her what's on my mind and worrying me. I can talk to Evelyn and tell her things, she is very motherly and understanding. . . . Evelyn has common sense."

Mrs. Pincus often visited two Jewish friends who lived a few streets away. "I had a friend in the Bexleys. . . . She lived next door to her cousin, and her cousin's brother was married to my sister, so I was friendly with her too." When she went on an errand, Mrs. Pincus often left her son with these friends, and they frequently accompanied her to the hospital when her son was ill. They visited often. "I used to go anytime, a few times a week, sometimes every day. I used to get the pram and wheel it down and stay for hours."

During hard times—both emotionally and financially—informants and their friends did favors for one another. Mrs. Caplan and a family who lived on a nearby street have remained friends for forty years. The man, a tailor, would make a coat for Mrs. Caplan's younger daughter when she had an extra piece of cloth. The family's relationship developed during the war, when the tailor enlisted in the army and his wife returned to work. Every day their four-year-old daughter would come to Mrs. Caplan's home for lunch and tea. In return, the mother always put something in the weekly parcel Mrs. Caplan sent to her son in the army. This neighbor also spent the Sabbath and High Holidays with the Caplans. The families still spend Passover together, and Mrs. Caplan, who is a widow, continues to go on holiday with them every year.[22]

These experiences contrast sharply with those of the Cornell group. Not only did the Leeds informants come to England with parents and siblings, but kin continued to live near each other and maintained close contact for many years. Informants lived in the same neighborhoods with family members and *landslayt* for thirty or forty years. While Cornell informants received assistance and encouragement from aunts, uncles, and cousins, these relationships seem to lack the intensity and duration of Leeds kin ties.

In Leeds, longstanding relationships were also developed with Jewish and non-Jewish neighbors, who lived close together for many years. A number of these relationships became intimate and enduring friend-ships—important sources of comfort and support, particularly during difficult times.

Jewish neighborhoods in Cleveland were less stable than those in Leeds. Cornell informants moved with each change in economic fortune. Although they lived side by side with other immigrant peoples, they chose to be friendly only with their Jewish neighbors. While informants were often close to neighbors for the few years they lived together, these rela-tionships did not usually survive the next move. Few Cornell people were therefore able to develop the longstanding, intimate relationships enjoyed by Leeds informants.

1955 to the Present: Move to the Knightsdale Estate; Birth of Grandchildren; Widowhood

When Leeds informants decided to leave their old neighborhoods and to move to the Knightsdale Estate, they did so reluctantly. In some cases, the decision was forced upon them by the Leeds Corporation, which had decided to tear down their houses. Sometimes the choice was dictated by changing personal and health needs. Many of their children had married and moved to their own homes. A few spouses had passed away. Widows no longer needed large houses, and it was difficult to repair and maintain them. Other women's husbands were sick or could no longer climb stairs. The Knightsdale Estate offered small, modern flats on one floor. Moving there also allowed people to be near children and siblings who had already moved to the Jewish area of Medina.

Coincident with changes in family needs were social changes in these old neighborhoods. Polish immigrants had moved into Chapeltown after the war, and West Indians and Pakistanis began to come in the 1950s. As in Cornell, informants no longer felt comfortable in their old neighborhoods:

"Hillcrest View was a *yidishe* neighborhood. The people were friendly and they had a nice *yidishe* clique. Then the children grew up and got married and the houses were big, and so people sold them to colored. The first one sold to a colored, and then talk about rats leaving a dying ship. . . . We were glad to get out. It is terrible, so I don't go there anymore" (Mrs. Silverman).

"I took ill then. I had my first heart attack, and when the *shvartsers* started coming, the darkies and the Poles, and the Indies and Pakistanis, my Miriam was only nine years old, and I went to my cousin and I said, 'Saul, I want to move out of that district. When Miriam will be older, I'll be terrified for her to come down the street, and what do I want a four-bedroom house, I haven't got the strength to keep it up' " (Mrs. Stein).

Mrs. Aronson vacillated in her descriptions of the old district, sometimes calling her home a "palace," sometimes saying "No decent person could live there." Informants generally remember their homes and their good neighbors fondly, however. "In fact, I didn't want to leave. I didn't feel like leaving Seaforth Avenue. It was that lovely house," said Mrs. Pincus.

Informants also tend to remember their homes in terms of the time when their husbands were alive and they were raising their families. When I asked Mrs. Caplan to compare her life on the all-Jewish Knightsdale Estate with life in a mixed neighborhood, she replied that she could not make such a comparison, that this was not the right question to ask. Her life was different in her old neighborhood of forty years, she said, because there she had her family and her husband with her. "My door was always open and the whole family would come and also our relatives. We had a lovely circle of friends. No, on the Estate," she said, "I am on me own."

The moves to the Knightsdale Estate and to the Cornell neighborhood occurred at about the same times. Informants' children were married, their grandchildren growing up. Parents were getting older, and many had lost their spouses. How they adjusted is the subject of the next two chapters.

4

Friendship, Neighborhood, and Kinship: Interrelated Networks in Cornell

CHAPTERS 4 AND 5 EXPLORE THE interrelation of kinship and friendship networks in Cornell and Leeds. After reviewing non-kin contacts from earlier periods, I discuss their influences on present-day attitudes toward and participation with both family and peers. How do these networks affect adjustments that parents must make in their lives? How does the cumulative effect of these adjustments influence the transition to the role of aged parent? And how do such adjustments help or hinder people as they attempt to present a desired self-image? These are the questions the two chapters will attempt to answer.

CORNELL

Before they moved to Cornell, my informants were busy with family, home, and work. Some women spent long days cooking, cleaning, and polishing, others went into business or worked in clothing factories. All were involved in the lives of their children, and many helped care for their grandchildren. They entertained their children often and invariably prepared and served the holiday meals. They offered their counsel and financial assistance, and both were appreciated.

In talking about their past, some women choose to remember when their husbands were alive and their families were with them. They describe the "good life, when they were a man's wife, when they rated." Then people "looked up to them and respected them because of their husband and children."

The move to Cornell was marked by various role and family changes. One man was estranged from his wife; many women were widowed. Two women left their kin in New York to be near their children. Children

95

bought homes of their own and moved away; a few left the Cleveland area altogether. Mrs. Samuels, whose daughter moved to Chicago, contrasts her present life with earlier memories: "My daughter is now far away from us. . . . Before, I would come to see them when I lived on Eddy Road. I used to take the bus, and she lived in Lyndhurst and I used to go there, years ago. But now those years are gone. . . . I was never lonesome."

As Cornell people grow older, their status continues to change, their roles becoming more ambiguous. The Cornell elderly are aware of these changes in status and prestige, but it is not always clear to them how these changes affect their role relations with their children or to what extent they themselves may have been instrumental in bringing them about. They interpret the changes in their family relationships in various ways. Most notice that their children no longer act toward them as they once did:[1]

"Now she doesn't seem to even want that [financial assistance] so much. I mean, it used to be 'Come on along, Ma,' because Ma would pick up either half or the [whole] check. But now that she's working, this time, she seems to want to be very much on her own. She doesn't want any hand-outs now" (Mrs. Eisner).

"They don't pay *that* much attention to me as they used to, but I don't mean lovingly . . ." (Mrs. Wexler).

In discussing their positions within the family, Cornell parents complain that they are frequently not informed of planned activities. When Mrs. Eisner's daughter-in-law was out of town for a Hadassah convention, she did not know what arrangements had been made to care for the children. They did not ask her to help, nor did they let her know their plans in advance.[2]

When parents volunteer suggestions or criticisms, they feel their comments are not well received. But they give them anyway. If they have to remain silent, informants feel resentful and belligerent. When Mrs. Nathan's nephew complained that her son and daughter-in-law were unfriendly, she replied, "I cannot mix in, I cannot get involved, I cannot say anything." Mrs. Samuels apologized to me for her daughter-in-law's oversight: "I have plenty to swallow, but I don't say anything." When I asked Mrs. Levi whom she would include at a family party, she replied, "I don't have the family affair. The family makes and they invite me, so whom should I invite?"[3]

Grandparental Role and Life-Cycle Changes

One way Cornell elderly perceive their changed status is in the transformation in their roles as grandparents. As they adjust to this change,
they come to terms with their altered status. They have great fondness for
their grandchildren: "I love the grandchildren, maybe even more than my
children. It's sort of a bonus like, the grandchildren are." They also
recognize, however, that they are needed, particularly when the grandchildren are young and require care. "The grandmother is wanted when
the children are small: she can be a sitter."

Although some women try to maintain a close involvement with their
grandchildren, their relationships lessen in intensity as the grandchildren
become teenagers. By the time grandchildren graduate from college, their
grandparents are embarrassed to give them their usual small birthday
gifts, and they usually stop. Some grandmothers still prepare traditional
foods for the grandchildren, but as they get older this task becomes more
difficult: "My grandson will come any time I invite him, but I don't invite
him that often anymore because it's hard work for me, even to have him
alone, because I feel like I want to make something special for him,
something special that he likes, and he doesn't like everything, so it's sort
of a nuisance. . . . So I don't even do that. . . . But I don't invite him so
much because I can't work so hard" (Mrs. Wexler).

Grandchildren visit or call their grandparents during school vacations
and drive them to family gatherings. When they come to visit, they may
vacuum or go grocery shopping. Mrs. Samuels was pleased when her
oldest granddaughter called from the hospital to tell her she had given
birth to a second child: "I am very glad they think of their Gramma."

Generally, however, Cornell parents are dissatisfied with their grandchildren—they do not visit them often enough or telephone to ask how
they are feeling and tell them what they are doing. "She does not take me
into her confidence," said Mrs. Levi. Informants excuse this situation in a
variety of ways, usually explaining that their grandchildren are busy. One
woman blames the years away at college: "Since they went away to school
and came back, each one of us is a little further away than they were
before they went. . . . It's a too long gap for a child, for even an eighteen-
year old, or seventeen-year old, it's a too long gap to be away from the
family for three years or four years. I know that's what sort of cools the
whole thing off, because they feel more independent, they were away
from home, and they got along, and why bother with the old people?"
(Mrs. Wexler).

Four generations of a family enjoy an affair together at the Jewish Center.

Informants feel that they can no longer give advice to older grandchildren. Mrs. Samuels, for example, decided not to propose a name for her new great-grandchild. She felt the distance between herself and her granddaughter was "too far" for her to make a suggestion. "When you become a grandmother . . . you are mothering to the grandchildren when they are little. But somehow when they grow in their teens, or older, they are more independent, they are more on their own, and the grandmother really can't tell them what to do . . . , they're too independent for that. They will listen to you when they are small, but when they grow into their teens, or older, they won't listen to the grandmother" (Mrs. Wexler).

Generally informants say that it is their children's responsibility to raise their grandchildren. "I wouldn't give my grandchild advice, because I don't feel responsible for them. I don't think it is my place to give 'um advice, because I might be very wrong. If they need advice, it's the parent's place, not mine. . . . I wouldn't take the responsibility" (Mrs. Wexler). The two more well-to-do informants, on the other hand, try to oversee the raising of their grandchildren and to correct what they interpret as failures. Mrs. Eisner occasionally pays for her diabetic grandson's medical appointments and checks to see that he regularly goes to the doctor. Mrs. Levi gives her grandchildren large gifts of money to compen-

sate for what she sees as their parents' frugality. Nonethelesss, even these
two women acknowledge the primacy of their children's role. They describe themselves as "interested, but afraid to interfere."

"I am proud of my grandchildren, you want to see them as flawless, but
having raised your own children, you see the pluses and minuses with
your own, but with your grandchildren, you see them only superficially.
You cannot take an initiative role, because their parents resent it. You
have to 'butt out.' They prefer that you not butt in with their children.
We all want to be important; here is their time to be important. My time is
past. Each wants his spot in the sun, to raise their own children. They
want to be the leading lady, and you have to step down. It's their turn. . . .
You can only play a superficial role, the role is one of being interested, but
afraid to interfere" (Mrs. Eisner).

"You're over the hill, they're on the hill, and the next are coming over
the hill. Your usefulness and services are expired. You have to cut the cord
from your children, to make a separation. You are interested in your
grandchildren, but theirs is a different world and you have to hear about
it. I visited Marty's apartment and I pretended that I could walk the steps,
even though I'd thought I would drop dead. It's all pretense, physically
you're just not there, but you don't want to be excluded, so you over-try.
You are unwilling to give up and show you're not able, you try to look like
you can and try to create an aura of being able. For example, my grandson
has three flights of outdoor steps, and when he wanted to have me again
for dinner, I said, 'Let's go out.' I don't blame them if they don't take me,
I'm a downer . . ." (Mrs. Eisner).

The change in the grandparent's role is publicly demonstrated at the
grandchild's wedding ceremony. At a formal ceremony, the grandmother
is usually the first family member to walk down the aisle. She may or may
not stand with the bride and groom at the altar, but it is her daughter, not
she, who plays a chief role in assisting the bride. In weddings held at
home, there is no traditional format, and the grandmother may not even
be included in the ceremony. "I was sort of behind like, with my girl
friends, and that's the way it was. . . . My *mekhuteneste* made some comment, 'How come you're not up there, sitting up there?' And I said, 'Well,
if they'd wanted me, they'd have asked me to come up.' So I didn't go up.
Either you ask me, or you don't. If you don't and it's all right, too. It's not
so world-destroying one way or the other. . . . I felt hurt, . . . but I
brushed it off" (Mrs. Eisner).

Later, Mrs. Eisner felt better when this same wealthy sister-in-law had a similar experience. When her daughter asked how she liked the ceremony, she snapped, "How could I see, I was sitting so far back!" The feelings of Cornell grandmothers can be summed up: "It's their party, I'm only a guest, I don't say nothing."

These marriage ceremonies do not help older Cornell people adjust to their changed roles within their families.[4] Any role they play is only indirectly acknowledged; there are no new duties, no new orientations. Unlike primitive societies, which at the time of marriage often emphasize the grandmother's role as the progenitrix of a line of daughters,[5] American society does not formally acknowledge a grandmotherly function in weddings. It provides no guidance for grandparents of newly married grandchildren.

Life-Cycle Changes in the Parental Role

Cornell informants respond to role changes with ambivalence. Parents say that they do not want to rely on their children, that they are jealous of their independence and guard their ability to continue to perform physical tasks. "A mother does not want to have her kids take care of her, she wants to be a strong person," says Mr. Fine. "This way you are the parent. Then you don't have to depend on them with anything, you know, they've got to depend on you." Nonetheless, these claims for independence sometimes sound defensive. Have they chosen independence, or has it been forced on them, they wonder.

Cornell informants also insist that they raised their children to be independent; children must lead their own lives. Yet uncertainty and ambivalence show through their remarks:

"I do not want my children to be so crazy for me as I was for my mother. I did not want them to be so close. I trained Sarah away from me; she should take care of her own life. My life was part of my mother's, and it's not healthy. I lived my life and had mine, yet I do not want them to overlook me, God forbid. What it is, is good enough. I'm sure she cares for me. She cares for me, the way we talk" (Mrs. Levitt).

"When you raise children you have to let go and then only if they wish it, will they come to you. You can't hang on, you can't beat a dead horse. You have to get them ready for life without you. . . , no one lives forever. Yet it's better than if they're dependent. . . . There are some bachelors I know who might have made fine husbands, yet their mothers held on to them. They want to be needed, and then they're the first to complain about all the work. It's a life of their own making" (Mrs. Eisner).

These people raised their children to be independent, but they also want voluntary demonstrations of love. Although they realize they no longer play a direct role in their children's lives, they have not successfully defined their new status. They are afraid of being abandoned by children who no longer need them. In social activities, for example, they choose the company of peers but only because their children are not available. They admit that if they have a choice, they prefer to spend time with their families. Mrs. Levitt frequently leaves her friends to visit with her daughter when she comes to the Jewish Center or the mall. Mrs. Eisner says that only when her family has no plans for Sunday does she "quick call a friend and make a date, so as not to be left sitting." "I go with the girls and they're my peers and we enjoy them, the girls whom I like, and we do what we want to do. We go to the show and we eat beforehand; but there's still that void, you know, it isn't mine and I *am* a parent and I *did* bear children and I suppose this is the way it is and the gap becomes greater, you know, the more you're away the greater the gap" (Mrs. Eisner).

Thus Cornell informants crave signs of affection, not only because they are lonely but because they have a profound need not to be forgotten as parents. Mrs. Eisner poignantly told me that her family had agreed to drive her to the eye doctor and wanted to take her out the following weekend: "I felt good, I felt wanted, . . . I'm not dropped, they're concerned about my health," she said. Mrs. Levitt expressed this same feeling: "To be wanted is the most important thing. If I were not wanted, I could not go on. I do not want them to overlook me."

Yet even as they discuss these feelings, Cornell parents try to protect themselves from disappointment. They explain repeatedly that they cannot expect their adult children to spend more time with them or to call them frequently. Their children are involved with business and in raising their own families, and some are not well physically:

"My daughter-in-law has three kids to take care of, and she was very sick. . . . My son has so much on his head. . . . My son was five years in the army, he's had plenty in his life. He's nervous as it is, now he's on a diet, he's hungry all the time. He don't feel good either" (Mrs. Samuels).

"My daughter-in-law has been very sick with a number of operations, and now she's going through the change of life . . ." (Mrs. Nathan).

"In the last few years, her problems are different and it just isn't there any more and there's no use beating a dead horse. It's different. . . . In the first place, she's tireder. She's getting middle-aged herself. And has great responsibility. Sophie's maternal and there's still a husband who needs serving, and the girl, and running the house, she keeps an immaculate house . . . and these things take a lot out of you. . . . And I appreciate she's tired and has other allegiances, prior, to her own daughter, and her son, and what's left, and there isn't much energy left. . . . I phoned her last night. I phone her, she doesn't really call me so much, I phone her because I'm not going to get a mad on, I'm not going to be on my muscle, for what? . . . and I could see she's tired" (Mrs. Eisner).

Mrs. Eisner admitted, however, that these explanations are merely excuses: "I could feel hurt or neglected by my son, but I imagine I excuse it by saying that he is a busy man, and there are demands on him. But it's always an excuse." Cornell informants hide their disappointment, but they also crave more attention and involvement in family affairs.

So they can be included in family activities, some refuse to admit they are ill or weak. Mrs. Eisner, who had an operation on her hip a few years ago, always enthusiastically answers "sure" when her children ask her to join them: "There will be no excuse not to include me because Mom couldn't." She carefully considers the consequences of refusing. Not going once is all right; but refusing two or three times may make her children think she can no longer go along at all, and they may stop asking her.

Other informants forgo commitments to keep kosher so they can be included in the traditional Passover *seyder*.[6] "I am kosher and Sarah is not kosher. She buys new pots and tries and shows me and buys kosher meat, but what, does it mean anything? It's not me as I want, but I have to dance as the music plays. I can't say no, they'll be hurt. She buys kosher meat, and she shows me, but I know it just isn't one dish" (Mrs. Levitt).

At the Jewish Passover celebration, people traditionally make public statements about family relationships and express their feelings about being with each other. The need to feel included is so strong that two women declined to participate in a communal *seyder* at the Carroll Arms, even though their children were not having *sdorim* at all. To them, the absence of family would have ruined the holiday.

"No, I won't go for the *seyder* in the building. . . . I feel that if I have to go to the *seyder* in the building, I'd rather stay in my own apartment, because I would feel too bad to be with them and not with all my kids. I would feel that I had come to a bad pass if I have to have a *seyder* in the building and not be around my own family" (Mrs. Wexler).

"I think I'd be lonelier than if I went out with the girls Saturday afternoon and called it quits. Because it's prolonged and it's not family and it's not those whom I'm really close with . . . a hurt rather than together. So I'll go out with the girls Saturday afternoon and come home. It won't be that difficult" (Mrs. Eisner).

Informants who have unsatisfactory relationships with their children, particularly their in-laws, attended the communal celebration. Mrs. Feingold explained that her daughter-in-law was ill and was not preparing for the holiday. Mrs. Nathan was more negative. She gave the rabbi twenty prayer books she had collected over the years because, she said, she was now too old to have large *sdorim* at her home. Having formally severed herself from her family for the holiday, she later remarked: "I'm different, they're different. I'm kosher, they're not particular. If I go there, it's like I'm in a jail—they are all doctors, lawyers, there are no stores, no place to go. It's a town for themselves. It's not my age, it's all young people there in Beachwood. I do not want to go."

In short, although these elderly parents acknowledge the change in their relations with their children, their descriptions of this new situation are often vague: "Things are not the same as they used to be." Among the role alterations are a general loss of authority and position within the family unit. Their advice is no longer sought, their financial assistance—which only a few can afford to offer—less readily accepted. They are not included in family discussions when decisions are made. (It must be noted, however, that these changes are not solely the result of children's distancing or loss of esteem. Aged parents view their relationships with their children differently too. They used to provide services and support; now they wish only to receive them. By limiting exchanges to one-way transactions, many have denied themselves a way to redefine and clarify their new position.)* Elderly parents seldom understand or accept these role changes, yet they have no clear vision of how things should be. If they do have a standard, it is idealized.

This mythical parent-child relationship is shown in the comments of one childless male informant: "It always lays on your mind that you have no children. . . . You feel lonely. . . . You can never make up for children: You could live in a house with walls made of diamonds, but still you feel lonely because there are no children. . . . All the old women sit and talk about their children and their grandchildren. That's all they talk about, they can make a hole in your head with their talk. I'm sick of listening to

---

*Readers may wish to turn to Chapter 7 for a discussion of the theoretical literature underlying the argument being advanced here.

it. If you have no children, you have nothing to tell back. After a while you'll go away, you get tired and jealous, both all together. You're alone; if you haven't got your own family, you're alone. . . . I see them all coming to take their parents. It is only one out of one hundred who don't have children. . . . No matter how bad they are, they are still the children, and it is better to have them than not to have any at all. . . . With no children, you have no ground under your feet—no one to lean on" (Mr. Fine).

Occasionally women comment on someone's "good children." Two such "good" daughters visit their mothers every day, often bringing home-cooked foods and doing the weekly shopping. They take their mothers to their own homes on weekends. But informants were never willing to articulate specifically what an ideal child would do for them, or to compare their own children to such an ideal.

Cornell parents adjust to their situations in a variety of ways. Some are willing to cope with their status as it is, even if it is not always what they would wish. These parents seem somewhat content and readily accept monthly dinner invitations as signs of their families' love and affection. "Some mothers curse their children, [but] I love my children, they're good to me," said Mrs. Brodsky. Others complain frequently about their adult children's behavior: "I'm all alone, I do not have nobody; I have three sons, but they're all for themselves, and I'm alone, but they'll all come to my funeral" (Mrs. Nathan). The first group can still make mutual adjustments with their children. For the second group, however, transactions seem to be blocked. As we attempt to analyze the reasons behind these various adjustments to an aged role, we must also examine the friendship relationships of Cornell informants. A network of friends provides an additional and influential context for defining one's status and hence one's relations with one's children.

Social Relations of Cornell Informants

Soon after my informants moved into the Cornell area, the social composition of the neighborhood started to change. In the early 1960s, when many arrived with friends from East Cleveland, groups of ten or twelve women would go to Euclid Beach Park for a day's outing. "The neighborhood was beautiful here ten years ago, there were no young people, just golden agers, . . . every apartment was filled by a golden ager." Then Cornell was still a Jewish area, with Jewish shops and a *shul* that kept people in the neighborhood. But during the middle and late 1960s, conditions changed. Many of the elderly left Cornell, and by the time of this study a decreased number remained in each apartment building. "It was a Jewish neighborhood before. It is not as much now. Some of the old Jews stayed, they were caught and couldn't get out. They didn't move as much as when they were young. A whole lot moved out, but the hippies moved in . . ." (Mrs. Wexler).

The elderly people who stayed in Cornell were unhappy about these changes. They felt it was no longer their neighborhood. One woman, complaining about the new people in her apartment building, said, "Everyone is for himself" (Mrs. Samuels). Others commented on the changes they had observed.

"In 1960, the area was nice then, the neighborhood was all white, there were no hippies, and one could walk out at night. . . . It is not too pleasant to live here now. No one is here now, just people with long hair and beards, whom we really have nothing against—they can be helpful and nice" (Mrs. Wexler).

"We go to the Pick-'n-Pay, which is now more dilapidated than in the past, people push you around, and items we used to buy are not there anymore, but I do get the Eagle Stamps. We don't go out in the evening, I don't know where to go. In the past, I used to go to Forest Hills Park, but now people cook there, and the grease from the pork chops poisons the air. I don't know where to go around here anymore" (Mrs. Feingold).

Undoubtedly, these changes are similar to those in other urban neighborhoods where Cornell informants lived when they were younger. Thus we can compare the kinds of social relationships informants developed then with the kinds they have formed in Cornell. Non-kin in these social relationships fall into three groups: neighborhood locals, associate friends, and old friends.

Neighborhood Locals. Neighborhood locals are neighbors who live in the same apartment house or next door. Because of physical disability or personality characteristics, some informants prefer to confine their relationships to these people alone. They often see one another daily. "I love people, I want people to come in. I like to be among Jewish people, even if I can't go to them. I love company. Somebody knocks on the door, I just love it," says Mrs. Samuels. People who rely solely on neighborhood locals are lonely and crave companionship. Their old life styles—"making yourself busy with the house, cooking, and cleaning"—are no longer possible because they are not strong enough.

For more active neighborhood local people, the Cornell area offers a

The customary exchange of gifts of food between neighbors during Purim.

variety of social meeting places. One central point is the supermarket. Mrs. Ables knows almost everyone she meets in the store: "I could be there all day if I didn't turn away sometimes when I see someone I know, or else I would be there all day talking."

Another gathering place for the neighborhood locals is Saul's Delicatessen, which, in spite of its reputation as a meeting place for people who have been in mental hospitals, draws some informants during the afternoons. "Many of the people in Saul's belong in or go to Fairhill for help," says Mrs. Wexler, who goes there anyway—"Time breaks, it shortens it for you. I have no one else." Another informant says: "I do not go into Saul's by the clock, but only one or two times a week only. They are not my friends; they are nice people, I have nothing against them, . . . I only know them from a distance. I do not go to their homes, and they do not come to mine; I just listen to them talk" (Mrs. Birnbaum). At Saul's, the Cornell group exchanges neighborhood gossip. They sit in the front of the restaurant, talking about everyone who enters and discussing each group member after he or she leaves. Some neighborhood locals see one another only at Saul's; they do not visit each other's homes.

Relationships among neighborhood locals rarely deepen over time. Informants say that it takes years to build trust and confidence. Explaining her lack of close friends, Mrs. Nathan commented, "I'm not long here. I only am eighteen years here, and I came with a sick husband." Because of the high mobility in Cornell, neighborhood composition shifts rapidly. The neighborhood locals have a limited number of socially compatible acquaintances remaining in the Cornell area. It is difficult to meet people with similar temperaments and interests. Neighbors may try to maintain contact with friends who leave the area, but these relationships soon peter out. Informants who used to work had little time to make new friends in Cornell.

Associate Friends. At the Jewish Center, Cornell residents can meet people who live outside of the neighborhood and can attend Jewish programs and activities.[8] Many meet acquaintances at the Jewish Center two or three times a week, they go to the mall on Saturdays for lunch or shopping, and they talk on the telephone. Because such voluntary associations have self-selective memberships, the Cornell elderly meet people of similar age, economic position, and interest. At club meetings and social affairs, associates sit at the same table, with the same people, with whom they have sat for fourteen years. The name of one group at the Jewish Center, for example, is the Mt. Pleasant Club, an echo of the old Jewish neighborhood where many informants used to live.

Temple sisterhoods and charitable organizations offer another social outlet for the few relatively well-to-do Cornell residents. Here they attend weekly discussion groups, luncheons, and project meetings with people they have known for many years. They also meet occasionally on Saturdays for lunch. But, just as it is with the neighborhood locals, there are limitations on the development of intimate relationships among associates.

Friendships between associates are usually not continued in the home, except for formal occasions, such as planned parties, when the family and other kin are not present. Those few associates who live near one another meet at the mailbox to talk in a "neutral place" or they chat on the telephone. They feel they already live close to neighbors and do not wish to become more friendly. They are afraid it will impinge on their privacy. "I don't visit, I don't extend myself to people in the building."[9] Associates rarely know one another's children. They can present only the image of themselves that they wish to convey. Associates cannot easily verify descriptions of family interaction unless they talk to others who know their associates in a different context.

Old Friends. Some informants have developed and maintained intimate friendships over many years. These allow them to feel confidence and acceptance. "With my friends, I like to be myself. A friend is someone you feel comfortable with, whom you don't have to try to impress," says Mrs. Eisner. Informants usually became friends with these people when they were new immigrants working together, when they were school- mates, or when they were raising young children. They may or may not have lived near one another later on. Friends are invited to one another's *simkhes,* and they know the members of each other's families. Although old friends may call only occasionally and visit only a few times a year, they are important to informants. Only one talks daily with her old, close friends. "I've never been wholly apart from them," says Mrs. Eisner.

These three types of social relationships are summarized in Figure 2. The table illustrates a number of significant points. First, the largest number of relationships fall into the associate friend category, the second largest into neighborhood locals, and the third into old friends. Second, informants tend to rely on a single type of relationship for assistance and emotional support. Third, the categories are not clearly bounded: Some neighborhood locals, for example, are also associate friends. Fourth, the "old friends" category may be unduly weighted for the Cornell group. A few informants, for example, named the children of their old neighbors and friends who have died; others named people with whom they had not kept in close contact, but who have recently moved to the Carroll Arms

Social Relations of Cornell Informants

Name of Informant	Type of Social Relationship				
	Neighborhood Locals		Associate Friends		Old Friends
Mrs. Wexler	4		0		0
Mrs. Nathan	3		0		(1)**
Mrs. Feingold	3		3		0
Mrs. Samuels	2		0		(2)
Mrs. Moskowitz	1	3*	0		0
Mrs. Levi	0	1	3		(1)
Mrs. Levitt	1	1	3		0
Mr. Isenberg	0		3	2	0
Mrs. Brodsky	0	3	0		1 + (1)
Mrs. Weiner	1		1		1 + (2)
Mrs. Eisner	1		1		4

*Relationships with unclear bounds are placed midway between categories (see explana- tion and discussion in point 3, above).

**Relationships that do not clearly qualify as old friends are enclosed in parentheses (see explanation and discussion in point 4, above).

and with whom they are just now renewing their friendships. (These "old friends" are designated by a number enclosed in parentheses.)

It is clear that elderly Cornell informants spend much of their time in the company of peers. Some visit each other at home and meet in the local supermarket. For them, neighborhood locals are the first to call upon for small favors and sociability. Others are members of organizations and see associates at weekly meetings and lunches. They enjoy associates and old friends for their companionship and sociability, rather than their ability to provide assistance. "As I get older, so do my friends," said one.

While peers provide sociability and status for the Cornell elderly, underlying their relationships is a strong current of competition, a need to project a desired self-image. Peers judge one another according to the attributes and attentiveness of adult children (which we will discuss below), general character, finances, appearance, accent, cleanliness, religiousness, conversational ability, and circle of friends. Being American-born and speaking good English are important: "They always think that I was born here. So I just let them think so. I don't want to go into a lot of explanation. Fine, I was born here" (Mrs. Wexler).

Informants are conscious of their status in these relationships, and they want to keep peer relations equal.[10] "I don't make up to anybody. When I sense I'm on the bottom rung of the ladder and others feel superior, I quit," said Mrs. Eisner. In all three types of social relationships, informants pay constant attention to position. If old friends, associates, or good neighbors attempt to "pull rank," the relationship is terminated. "She never made that she is bigger than I." Everyone tries to maintain or gain status, to make sure she is not overlooked. Informants "do not want to be taken for granted or used" (Mrs. Levitt). Describing an unsatisfactory relationship with her neighbor, one woman said: "She was looking to use people, she needed to because she was alone, but she would sap you if you permit it; you must watch this at this state of life; there was no give and take, only give and no take, so I quit" (Mrs. Eisner).

People arrive early at luncheons and at the Nutrition Program at the Jewish Center. They push and shove, anxious to be first. Mrs. Levitt asked her son to teach her how to use the washing machines in the Carroll Arms. She did not want to ask a neighbor, who might tell others. "If you let someone shop for you, the whole building knows they brought for you" (Mrs. Levitt). Some informants will not initiate telephone calls to neighbors and associates too often, for that person would then be "the big one." They gossip about people who get rent supplements and food

Lining up for lunch at the Nutrition Program at the Jewish Center.

A group of Cornell women who gather weekly to play cards.

stamps and pay less at the Jewish Center. They are jealous of their own positions and jealous of others'.

I observed one example of this desire to maintain equality in social dealings in a neighborhood poker game. I quote directly from my field notes:

"Finally I got to go to the card game which Mrs. Ables had been mentioning to me, and which she plays twice a week on Saturday and Monday.

"Mrs. Steinberg's home is a two-family, up and down, near the corner. Upon walking in and introducing me, the ladies immediately went into the dining room . . . and the game started—there was no initial talking in the living room. . . . All four women took out beaded change purses and proceeded to count their pennies and small change to themselves, and then publicly to one another, each taking a turn and making sure that the others saw that she started out 'honest.'. . . I asked how a new member could be admitted, and they said they would like someone new, but the person had to be elderly and definitely not a fighter, and that they did not want any fighting and that none of them were fighters. They told me they play the game 'to make the time pass.'. . . There was surprisingly little conversation between hands, and any talk that did occur was when the hands were being dealt, or the money taken in by the winner. . . . The ladies also laughed about the fact that they play for only 50¢, and that this is a game usually played for more money. In fact, both Miss M. and Mrs. Ables said when they tell other people about their game and are asked what money is involved, both reply $1.00, as they were 'embarrassed' to say only 50¢.

"The emphasis in the game did not seem to be on competition, except a little on Rita Kaminsky's part, when she reluctantly acknowledged that her hand had been beaten, or when Mrs. Ables reprimanded her for not raising when she had good cards. Rita protested in her own defense that she had noticed Mrs. Ables' cards, which made Mrs. Ables angry, and she flared up, saying she had caused her to lose and was tired of Rita using the same excuse, but Rita seemed unperturbed by the incident. There was no counting of pennies at the end to see who was high, and if a player lost all her pennies, she was allowed to play just as if she had money, neither borrowing from another player or the house, nor having to pay any back. For example, Miss M. lost all her money early in the game, but by the end, she had the biggest pile. Mrs. Ables, who held her own through most of the game, left with only about 8 to 12¢. When two people had a similar high hand, they split the pot. Everyone was very zealous in seeing that the other one put her initial penny in the pot at each hand, and everyone announced when she put her penny in. . . .

"About 4:00 P.M., Mrs. Ables asked for candy, and Mrs. Steinberg served 10 pieces of hard candy, and split one 12 oz. bottle of root beer among her guests. Mrs. Ables and Miss M. walked with me, but Rita left to go ahead to the store. . . . Mrs. Ables said Rita is worth lots of money, yet she will fight like crazy for a penny at the game, and she watches every penny. Indeed, Mrs. Ables was always telling her to put her penny in the pot and making digs in other ways, while Rita took an aggressive role in asking for the cards or in asking for the pot to be pushed over to her. Mrs. Ables said Rita is worth $60,000 and had had 6 husbands, with each of whom she made a deal to give her $10,000. Mrs. Ables said she did not want either her money or her children, as they are all cripples.

"I asked to return to the next game. . . . Mrs. Ables again stressed the noncompetitive emphasis of the game. She said the game is "like a family affair," and that they don't take in strangers who would play, win, leave with their money, and not come back. But that they play with the same people all the time, the money changing hands within the group. . . ."

The strong element of competition extends to status among peers. In all kinds of Cornell relationships, the attributes of children and the quality of intergenerational family relationships are important criteria in establishing status. Cornell parents use their children to compete for social status, conveying an idealized image of family relations to bolster their own uncertain position in the peer group. In the many activities where they interact only with age cohorts, they present themselves as loved and needed parents. Associates tell each other about the things their children do for them and the time they spend together. Even old friends try to project this image to one another and to themselves. On those few social occasions when children are present, their helpfulness to parents is used as an example of desirable behavior. Mrs. Levitt's son, for example, frequently takes her to the Jewish Center on Sunday mornings. Onlookers comment, "Your son is here to get you; you have a wonderful son." When her daughter comes to the Jewish Center for coffee, her friends remark, "Bessie, you are rich." Mrs. Levitt never reveals her unhappiness that her children rarely visit her at home. Instead she presents the image of a mother who gets along well with her children and whose company is desired: "He still takes me any place I want."[11]

Because of competition and uncertainty, Cornell parents are afraid to confess the strains in their relations with children. Never admitting disappointments, they emphasize only positive situations. Those few times when they do admit to old friends (or, less frequently, to associates or neighbors) that they are lonely and disappointed, they are never totally open. They say things "only up to a point. We do not admit that we expect more from our children, we cover these feelings." They discuss family problems "only superficially, it is not their business." "You never really tell all your feelings to anyone." "We know how far we can go."

Informants demand loyalty and an acceptance of this image in all their relationships. Even old friends are not permitted to expose each other's unhappiness, or the relationship will be terminated. "My friends ought to understand and stand behind me," said Mrs. Levitt, who ended a friendship of twenty years when the woman remarked that her son is better to her than her daughter and questioned whether her son would spend so much time with Mrs. Levitt if he were not single and in poor health. (These remarks reveal that the woman had no direct knowledge of Mrs. Levitt's family relationships. Mrs. Levitt is close-mouthed and resents any prying into her family affairs or allegations about her children, even from old associates.)

Ironically, it appears that on those rare occasions when friends do discuss being hurt—"We do come out with a pain; we're not completely closed off from one another"—the confidence also works to reinforce an abstract, ideal standard. It shows that "the grass is not greener on the other fence," says Mrs. Levitt. Mrs. Nathan revealed her disappointment that her children do not visit her more frequently when she tried to comfort a neighbor, who also missed her children. Even as she comforted her, however, Mrs. Nathan couldn't resist a comparison: "I don't make the fire bigger. I always try. I says, 'Don't think the kids ask me, or the kids do for me. You see how much they come, I'm here already so long and they don't come, and here they come to you Sunday to take you out. . . .' I make peace."

Because public observation of family relationships is limited and disappointments are concealed, the belief that other people have better relationships with their offspring is perpetuated. This works to make parents more uncertain about their own status. Comparing themselves with their peers, Cornell residents find their relationships with their own adult children lacking. "Sometimes I think that parents with a sweeter way have greater acceptance," confesses Mrs. Eisner.

Children's attributes and willingness to provide for parents are also used to raise status or to judge others.[12] Cornell informants see their children's accomplishments as extensions of themselves, and they frequently tell others about these successes. In talking about the gifts she gives to her grandson, one informant revealed this perspective: "That's part of you. I don't consider that even giving, now how do you like that? When I give my own, that's me. It's my own ego that I'm trying to boost in the world to have somebody say, 'Look at Lill's grandson, isn't he nice, isn't he fine?' That's part of my own ego. I don't even consider it a gift—it's me" (Mrs. Eisner).

When they talk about other people, informants and their friends discuss who their children are, what the husbands do for a living, and where they live. If a couple is well to do, it is always mentioned. Mrs. Nathan, who does not have comfortable relations with her own children and who is not physically well, talks frequently about how much money her son contributes to charity, what a beautiful home he owns in a wealthy suburb, and how he and his wife belong to a social club with doctors and lawyers: "My son pays an awful lot of money, an awful lot of money my son gives." At a luncheon, an old friend of an informant talked about each guest who entered. She elaborately described each family genealogy, occupation, and residence. Later, Mrs. Eisner commented, "She's on top of things." She explained her friend's need to know such details about other people as "compensation for her daughter who is not well."

Children's successes and provision of services also affect the formation and maintenance of social relationships and thereby influence family interaction. Informants use peer relationships to confirm their position with their own children. They establish relationships with age cohorts whose children have comparable social standing or treat their parents in a similar manner. "I know what she went through, so it's a little like I do." They cannot tolerate people who make them uncomfortable by reminding them that their own or their children's successes are less impressive than their friends'. Neighbors and associates thus reinforce one anothers' attitudes toward and adjustments to changed relationships with children. If a mother accepts the behavior of her children, so too do the mother's acquaintances. If she is discontented and unhappy, her neighbors and associates support her. Her expectations and behavior are thus confirmed by acquaintances with similar feelings. With few exceptions, Cornell parents do not observe others' actual family interactions, so they rarely alter their judgments or expectations to conform with reality.

Summary: Cornell Networks

I believe that one can relate the adjustments to an aged role (acceptance or rejection of changed family interaction) to the friendship relations informants have formed. Aged parents' ability to readjust their ideal expectations and to avoid role confusion, ambiguity, and feelings of rejection directly corresponds to their ability to sustain close friendships throughout their lives. Parents who are unwilling to accept their changed status, who hold painfully abstract, idealized conceptions of parent-child relations, and who frequently complain will generally lack old friends and confidants. They form relationships either with neighborhood locals or with associates.

Those few informants in Cornell who have the confidence of lifelong friends are better able to accept and adjust to their altered position. They can realistically evaluate their relationships with their own children and compare them with others'. Because they have known their old friends for many years, they also know each others' children. They have the advantage of looking behind the scenes, so they can make informed guesses about other people's family interactions and gain insight into their own. "Other people's situations are similar, but they don't admit it; you have got to learn from the other person's problems. My friend Evelyn S. tells half, and I guess half. I don't pry, it's not a pleasure, it's a painful situation" (Mrs. Eisner). These same parents use the insights they have gained to observe other people's behavior instead of believing everything they hear. "Mrs. Rothstein always talks about her brother, the doctor, or her brother, the lawyer, but on weekends she sits with her husband. And no brother, or doctor, or lawyer come to take her. They may tell me differently, but I have to go by what I see" (Mrs. Eisner).

Informants with old friends have learned more about their own positions as well. They have learned to make adjustments in their own behavior and in their expectations of children:

"I feel I go as far as I can. I can't make myself a burden, I can't make myself a pest, because then I'll have nothing. Some mothers think that they're very important, like Evelyn S. called me that her grandson was in, and he loved her and he kissed her and put his head in her lap, and I think, 'Bull crap. . . .' I hear some of them say their children call them, 'So Gramma, how are you? And I was worried. . . .' And they tell such bullshitting stories and I think where does that come from?

"You're accepted a lot less if you're always hurting—it h-u-r-t-s me—

then you really are dropped. Now I see with my girlfriend Evelyn, her son-in-law don't want to look at her . . . and I see a lot of the in-laws get a little tired of the mother-in-law being a leaner. And they brush 'em off anyway, so you may as well brush yourself off a little" (Mrs. Eisner).

Such parents have learned what is reasonable to expect from adult children, and they can adjust their own expectations to conform to reality, rather than to an ideal. By adjusting their expectations, they can adapt their behavior and accept their changed relations with their children. They are thus in a better position to negotiate. Cornell informants whose relationships have not allowed them to separate reality from myth continue to compare their children with others'. They make excuses for their children's inattentiveness, praising them to others—but complaining to themselves.

There seem to be three major kinds of adjustment to an aged role: (1) the traditional mother, whose primary reliance is on associate friends; (2) the adjusted mother, who maintains ties with old friends; and (3) the dissatisfied parent, whose relations are mainly with neighborhood locals. These correlate with the social relationships we have discussed. Interestingly, informants' home furnishings and family photographs also differ with adjustment and social network.

The Traditional Mother: Primary Reliance on Associate Friends (Five Informants—Mrs. Levitt, Mr. Isenberg, Mrs. Levi, Mrs. Feingold, Mrs. Moskowitz). These informants cling to the traditional maternal role. Adult children call two or three times a day, each jealously accusing the mother of favoring another child. Traditional mothers dominate their sons, who are often divorced or ill, but accept the behavior of their daughters on their daughters' terms. There is little role negotiation with children. Their sons are protective, driving them places or taking them home so they will not be lonely. Traditional mothers continue to play out old roles, bragging to friends about their good children. Thus they reinforce the myth of ideal parent-child relationships. Silently, however, they are lonely. "You see, I'm all alone, they never come to visit me at home." Their apartments are filled with carved, down-stuffed furniture from the early days of their marriages. There are wedding photographs and pictures of children, when they were young, displayed on the walls. There are a few photographs of grandchildren. Traditional mothers have no lifelong friends, and they quarrel often with neighbors and associates. (Mr. Isenberg is included in this category because he meets all the criteria except, obviously, motherhood.)

The Adjusted Mother: Primary Reliance on Old Friends (Three Informants—Mrs. Eisner, Mrs. Weiner, Mrs. Brodsky). These informants who are adjusted mothers have old friends with whom they maintain contact. They seem able to realistically appraise relations with adult children and to make necessary adjustments—for example, seeking the company of stimulating peers when children are busy. They are able to look behind other people's claims and to gain insight into their actual family relationships. Early in their children's marriages, they dispensed with some of the traditional aspects of the mother role, such as entertaining and cooking for children:

"I called it quits on the meals. After Saul got married, I called it quits with the cooking. . . . Too hard on me. Too hard maintaining a job, being clean . . . living a little. . . . It was just too much. . . .

"I had them over one night. . . . I had fruit cup—fresh fruit cup—sirloin patty with mushroom gravy, and mashed potatoes, and everything after work. And oh, was that a job! 'Ma, you'll excuse us, we're invited to Jo Doe's or Stanley's house, we've got to go.' And I thought, 'Gee whiz, look at all this dishes and preparing, and the dishes and I'm left with that, and really it's not my company that they're after' " (Mrs. Eisner).

While choosing to give up some of the directive dimensions of the maternal role—"I'm on the wane, no more of this matriarchy business"—these women have maintained a supportive role, often helping their daughters and sons-in-law financially. Now that their daughters seem less willing to accept gifts, they are also discontinuing this practice. "You can't buy affection or to be needed." While not always pleased with their altered positions, they seem willing to try to define and accept their new status. Negotiations with children are still possible. Adjusted mothers' apartments have only a few pieces of new furniture, and they were chosen for easy maintenance. They display no photographs of family members.

The Dissatisfied Parent: Primary Reliance on Neighborhood Locals (Three Informants—Mrs. Nathan, Mrs. Samuels, Mrs. Wexler). These informants are dissatisfied about lack of attention from their sons and daughters-in-law. Although complaining often and loudly, they are proud of their children's proximity and prosperity. One such informant's apartment is decorated with new furniture chosen by her daughter-in-law and paid for by her son—except for the dining room table, which she complained about so much that her son finally sent it back. She is angry that her daughter-in-law made her throw away so many things when she was

helping her move. She spends her time in the company of a few neighbors, all religious women like herself who are either secretive about family
relations or feel that they are unsatisfactory. She asks social welfare personnel to visit her because she is lonely, and she relies on them to take her
to the doctor.

Thus relations with peers seem to either support or hinder informants'
ability to define realistically their own status. When they confine their
relationships to neighborhood locals and associates, who often compete
with them and conceal their feelings and actual family situations, informants cling to an unrealistic, abstract model of parent-child interaction.
But when they enjoy reciprocal exchanges of services and support with
old friends, parents seem to be more realistic about family relationships
and can therefore evaluate and define their own kinship positions appro-
priately.

The quality of relationships with children also affects the formation and
maintenance of peer networks. Further, Cornell parents' earlier experiences in their own families of orientation were often characterized by
ambivalence and tension or by fantasies about what relations with their
elderly parents in Europe might have been. These experiences influence
present-day relationships with their own children—and they, in turn,
may inhibit informants' ability to develop intimate transactions with
friends. Thus friendship and kinship are interrelated.

At the funeral of a very elderly informant, the rabbi gave a eulogy on
which I made the following field notes:

"The rabbi spoke about man as like the blades of grass and the field
flowers, which can be mowed down by God's will. Then he read "A
Woman of Valour." He told that Fanny Moskowitz was eighty-seven
years old, that she had come to America when she was about twenty.
Thus she lived in America sixty-seven years or more. She had been married for forty years, and was a widow, fiercely independent, for over
twenty-three. But the message from her life—its meaning and remem-
brance—was not in the weight of the number of her years: it must be
sought in community.

"Fanny Moskowitz had tried living in the suburb for a while, but that
life was not for her. Hers was the old-world life of community and of
neighborhood. And these she found in Cornell and at the Jewish Center.
Here she could practice her way of life—of neighborliness, of doing things

for people, greeting people, being with people whom she knew, living with people. In fact, her last day was spent at the Jewish Center with some of the people with whom she lived on Cornell Avenue.

"While Fanny Moskowitz was part of an older way of life, she was very aware of the new way of life also. But she felt that the old way had strength and something to offer, and she wished to continue its strength— its concern for neighbors and its being with people and community. And so she chose to live that life. A life where even going shopping held promise of meeting people whom one knew and greeting them. This was indeed the meaning of her life—of a woman who loved to be with people and to lead an independent existence. Then the rabbi enumerated the members of her family—daughter, son-in-law, sister, nephew, grandchildren, and great-grandchildren—and urged that they express and accept their weakness and sorrow and take strength and comfort from their relationships with one another. . . ."

But the rabbi did not know, or at least failed to tell, the whole story. Mrs. Moskowitz's time with neighbors and friends was often spent in competition, jealousy, and uncertainty. She told me once that her relationships with her own family were not all she would have wished.

5

Friendship, Neighborhood, and Kinship: Interrelated Networks in Leeds

ALTHOUGH OF THE SAME GENERATION and often with similar backgrounds, the elderly in Leeds and those in Cornell differ in the nature of their social networks. As this chapter will show, interaction with children, friends, and neighbors affects the role adjustments of the Leeds aged and their Cornell counterparts differently.

LEEDS

Leeds informants moved to the Knightsdale Housing Estate between 1959 and 1966. By this time, their family lives had changed: Children were married and had moved away from home; the husbands of several women had passed away. The move to the Knightsdale Estate did not have the disruptive consequences on family and personal relations, however, that the move to Cornell had for Cleveland informants.[1] The Knightsdale Estate was built in a new, desirable Jewish section of Leeds. It offered the opportunity to live again near children and siblings, who were already in the area. The move thus helped to foster a continuation of the close family interaction informants had known in their previous neighborhoods.

Life on the Estate did not mark an abrupt change in the activities of Leeds informants. "When your children are grown and married, you spend more time with them than with your friends," said Mrs. Caplan. Some women remained physically strong and continued their usual tasks. They cooked and baked. The whole family came for Friday night dinner or Saturday tea. Many continued to have Passover *sdorim* in their homes.

120

Parental and Grandparental Roles and Life-Cycle Changes

Today, the same patterns continue. Unlike Cornell parents, these elderly are closely involved in family activities. Some parents go to visit children on weekends and stay to baby-sit. Others help prepare meals for working daughters-in-law.[2] Parents are included when families go to charitable functions or synagogue events, and children entertain them and their friends for tea. Informants are often on good terms with their children's friends. Mrs. Caplan calls her daughter's close friend her "adopted daughter." "The friends of my children are my friends," she says. When there is a *bar mitsve* or a wedding, parents and family members decide together which relatives and friends to invite. Often parents' lifelong friends are included because they are also close to the adult children. Mothers help address invitations and make biscuits to serve the guests. "My children keep me going," says Mrs. Caplan.

Like Cornell informants, Leeds parents were involved with their children's lives after they were married. Mrs. Perlman's son and his wife lived with her for two years after their wedding. Mrs. Stein housed her daughter and son-in-law for seven years while they were at Leeds University. Mrs. Caplan helped her two daughters and her daughter-in-law after the births of each of their children, once taking her daughter-in-law home and caring for her until the baby was born.

Leeds parents helped children when they were first married and their grandchildren were small, but they do not interpret these experiences as do Cornell people. For Leeds informants, helping is part of being "good mothers," and their involvement with children has continued. They have maintained some functions of their maternal role longer than have Cornell mothers.

The same is true of their relationships with their grandchildren. As noted earlier, Cornell parents feel that they were important only as baby-sitters for small grandchildren. Now that their grandchildren are older, they do not see them as often or influence them as much. Leeds parents, on the other hand, have maintained their earlier involvement with grandchildren. Mrs. Aronson's son, for example, asked his parents to take care of his two young children while he and his wife worked on Saturdays. The grandparents "enjoyed" this opportunity to be with the children. Today Mrs. Aronson continues this practice, even though her husband passed away nine years ago and she has moved from their family home to a flat on the Estate. Each Saturday her grandsons, who are now fourteen and seventeen, come to spend the day with her. On Thursdays she shops and on Fridays she prepares meals for them and their parents, who come late Saturday afternoons for tea. Although the work is "hard on me," Mrs. Aronson believes this practice will continue until her grandsons marry.

Others in Leeds are similarly involved with grandchildren. Mrs. Caplan goes to her daughter's home on the Sabbath. If the couple go out Saturday evening, she plays cards with the children. Mrs. Shapiro goes to Edinburgh twice a year to visit her son and his family. She often stays a month. While she is there, Mrs. Shapiro helps her daughter-in-law, who is a dental surgeon, gives the children lunch, and bakes their favorite pies to put in the freezer. Once she stayed an additional week so her daughter-in-law could visit old school friends in Paris. Mrs. Shapiro feels that she goes to Edinburgh not to help, but rather to see the family, who treat her well. They take her to restaurants, buy her new clothes, and escort her around the city. Mrs. Silverman gave her granddaughter lunch every day during the Passover holidays, and her grandson stayed with her on weekends when he was at Leeds University. Thus many in Leeds continue the traditional roles even when their grandchildren are in their early teens.

Generally Leeds grandchildren continue to visit their grandmothers, who receive "love and pleasure" from them. "I enjoy them, they are lovely," says Mrs. Caplan. Some grandchildren visit weekly, others when they are home on holiday or when their parents are out of town. Mrs. Pincus sees her small grandchildren every Sunday morning: "I really enjoy myself with them on Sunday. They make my day for me . . ., they make my week." Grandchildren may do small favors—fetch a prescription, fix a clock, plant flowers—but most are still too young to be of real assistance. Mrs. Gottlieb, whose grandsons are in their twenties, feels that if they lived in Leeds they would help her more: "They're all very handy, they'll do anything. If I was closer to them, they'd be very good to me, they'd help me." When grandchildren live close by, they often walk over for a visit. But when they move out of town, the contact with their grandmothers lessens. "I used to see her more often," says one.

When grandchildren come to visit during a holiday, they frequently stay for a meal. "They often pop round and have lunch," says one informant. Mrs. Gottlieb told of her grandson:

"When he comes, he phones me up, saying, 'Gramma, I'm home for the weekend. I'd like to see you.'

"I say, 'By all means come, love, come for dinner.'

"He says, 'Don't you think it would be too much for you, to come for dinner?'

" 'Too much for your Gramma? No!' Every time they come, they get a big meal here."

Not all informants cook for their grandchildren; some serve only tea and biscuits. "They don't come for meals, they don't expect it," says Mrs. Perlman.

Leeds elderly exchange gifts and cards with their grandchildren. They give grandchildren, young and old, money and gifts. In return, grandchildren send them cards and gifts as well. When Mrs. Perlman worried about her granddaughter's extravagance, her daughter replied, "Well, she loves you so much, it gives her pleasure."[3]

Grandparents are also involved in the ritual ceremonies of their grandchildren's *bar mitsves* and marriages. After her grandson's *bar mitsve*, Mrs. Caplan telephoned me to say she was both proud and happy and that she had wept a lot. There were many speeches following the ceremony, and all of them praised her. Her daughters spoke about their fine upbringing and good home life. When Mrs. Aronson's grandson finished his *bar mitsve* recitation, he immediately went to the gallery area, where the women sit, to kiss his mother and grandmother. The following day, Mrs. Aronson entertained her close neighbors with gateaux from the *bar mitsve* luncheon and shared her pleasure with them. "You should receive such *nakhes* [pleasure and pride, especially from the achievements of a child] from your children." Mrs. Caplan walked down the wedding aisle and stood near her daughter-in-law and granddaughter under the canopy. When the ceremony was over, she happily greeted all her friends and relatives as she walked back to the reception room.

Informants say that they are consulted on the guest list, but that the ultimate decision remains with the children. "The guest list is the choice of the parents, not the grandparents," says Mrs. Aronson. Old friends and neighbors, whom the children knew when they were growing up, are usually included, but newer friends from the Estate rarely come.

Although relationships with grandchildren are usually comfortable and accepting, they reflect the quality of interaction that Leeds informants have with their own adult children. If there is a strain, for example with a daughter-in-law, those tensions may also color grandparent-grandchild interaction. Mrs. Stein, for example, who rarely sees her Leeds daughter-in-law, is similarly irritated with her fourteen-year-old granddaughter, who does not often come to visit or offer to do errands. "She is a big girl, she's going on fourteen, couldn't she come up to see the grandmother? See if Gramma wants anything? She only comes if she wants money." Another woman, Mrs. Gottlieb, refused to attend her grandson's church wedding. Although her daughter had married a Gentile (whom Mrs. Gottlieb does not like), she had wanted her grandsons to be raised as Jews. She worked hard for their *bar mitsves:* "What I went through to make three *bar mitsves.* I arranged it with the synagogue. I got them over to the Orthodox. . . . I went on the committee of the synagogue and I used to bake and do everything for them. I worked like a horse only to get the children going. It didn't work. It cost me money and health, and I didn't achieve anything."

All her grandsons married non-Jewish women. "I thought if one child had married Jewish, it would be worth it. . . ." Mrs. Gottlieb saw the church wedding as a mockery of her efforts to give the boys a Jewish education, and she let her grandson know her feelings. Nonetheless, she entertained him and his new wife when they came to visit after their honeymoon, and she gave them money and things from her home. She remains disappointed with her daughter for marrying a Christian and for not raising her sons as Jews. "They're nice children, but they're not Jewish."

Like Cornell informants, Leeds parents are proud of their children's accomplishments, and they share their "pleasure and *nakhes*" with neighbors, acquaintances, and old friends. They also want people to know that they are loved and cared for. They tell friends and acquaintances about going to a son's home for tea and receiving a welcoming kiss from a daughter-in-law. Parents read aloud the letters they get from children living overseas and tell how much money is enclosed. They display wedding, *bar mitsve,* and graduation photographs of their children and show family clippings from the *Leeds Jewish Gazette.* They talk about what *simkhes* their children have attended. Children's accomplishments add status to themselves. When I was introduced to one woman, she volunteered to bring me a photograph of her son, so that I could see what a good family she comes from. Another woman, who is well known because she worked in a popular Jewish fish-and-chips restaurant, says her son complains that everywhere he goes people say to him, "I know who you are: you're Hatty Aronson's son." When another woman was depressed because she felt she had achieved little in her life, her son urged her to find pleasure in his

Sharing joys and sorrows with relatives and close friends.

accomplishments: "Look, Mommy, I'm driving a lovely car, and I've got a lovely wife, and you've got lovely grandchildren." The activities and accomplishments of children reflect on their parents, bringing them satisfaction and status.

But there is a code in Leeds against talking too much about one's children. People are criticized and disliked if they brag: "I don't tell all them, they think I'm swanking if I tell them. . . . I don't say nothing now" (Mrs. Shapiro).

Many informants are also reluctant to criticize their children publicly. They rarely discuss family problems, and then only with an intimate old friend. "They are my children, my children are my business, I don't tell them my children's business, nothing at all," said Mrs. Aronson. Mrs. Stein reiterated this norm: "It is wrong to talk about your children," and translated a Yiddish expression: "When you blow your nose, you wipe it on your own face." Mrs. Shapiro does not talk about her children even with her *mekhutonim*, wanting instead to be "one of them, taking it all in and never saying anything."

Nonetheless, Leeds parents also realize that "when you are full up to the top, you can talk . . ." and that "you've got to have somebody, everybody does." Most informants talk openly to an old friend or confident: "He was nice, I could tell him things, I could talk to him. . . . He was a good listener. He'd tell me about the family, tell me things about his family, tell me everything. . . . I told him things about my children I wouldn't tell anybody else" (Mrs. Gottlieb). Thus parents admit that they do confide their feelings to intimate friends: "Because I've known her all my life, and I've seen her two children when they were born and how they've grown up together. . . . We used to both go out with our children. . . . She confides in me and tells me about her children, her likes and dislikes, and she talks about them" (Mrs. Gottlieb).

Informants were also more open with me than were Cornell parents.[4] They do not make the same kinds of excuses for their kin. When Mrs. Gottlieb's neighbor returned from a trip to London, she was so distressed that her children had never telephoned to inquire if she were all right that she took a taxi from the station directly to Mrs. Gottlieb's flat. She did not tell her family that she had arrived for several hours.

After my first Passover *seyder* in Leeds, I visited Mrs. Gottlieb. She was telling an old friend about the holiday celebration at her niece's home, and what a wonderful family the girl has. Then she began to cry because her own family is not that way. Later she confessed how difficult holiday times are for her. Her son is in Los Angeles, and her daughter, who lives outside Leeds, is married to a non-Jew. "This shouldn't have happened to me. If my son were here, it would be different. His mother means everything to him," she said.

This incident shows that Leeds parents look to children for support and comfort, but that in times of despair, they talk openly about their feelings to trusted friends. Unlike Cornell parents, they do not defensively conceal their feelings by explaining that children are busy, ill, or living far away. Leeds parents still have room for continued negotiation and mutual adjustments within the family unit. One reason their adjustment to their aged role differs from Cornell people's is, I think, their sustained relations with old friends.

Social Relationships of Leeds Informants

Old Friends. Leeds parents lived in stable neighborhoods for thirty or more years. They made close friends, with whom they shared the experiences of raising families.[5] "Well, she's a friend. I can speak to her. She knows my life and I know hers, and when she has trouble with the children, she always rings me up and tells me, confides in me and her daughter as well. . . . And if I'm upset and I have no one to tell to, I ring up Mary. . . . I can talk to her. I know it wouldn't go any further. It doesn't go anywhere. . . . We know one another nearly forty years. She's been to all my children's weddings" (Mrs. Stein).

Having lived together in the same neighborhoods, their children are often friends as well. Leeds parents often confide in their old friends: "She knows all my life story. I know all her family very well, and she tells me about them." Thus the length of time people have known one another is an important dimension of their friendships. They may talk only a few times a year and see each other less often, but their conversations are about important matters. Parents tell their friends their troubles, and friends listen, sympathize, and try to help. By talking together openly and honestly, elderly parents develop a better understanding of adult children and what to expect realistically from them. The advantages of living closely with neighbors and observing the behavior of other people's children as they grew up continue into old age: "She clapped me around and she kissed me in the bus station. I cried, and she cried. She poured her heart out to me. She's in trouble, her daughter is in trouble, and the kids. She has nobody to talk to; it isn't the neighbors like we used to be" (Mrs. Stein).

Confidentiality and trust are also important dimensions of these friendships: "A good friend is a person whom you can trust, whom you can tell things to and it goes no further."[6] Mrs. Caplan compared her feelings for her friends with those for family members: "A feeling of stability, a feeling as though they're your own, they're my people. . . . We feel as though we belong. A friend is someone you will hear say, 'Come in,' and who will get the tea. With a friend you can say, 'I've come,' and they will ask, or just wait until you tell them why you're there."

Leeds informants and their old friends also help one another deal with other life crises, such as illness and widowhood: "She had a very ailing husband and my husband was ailing and we used to talk." Mrs. Silverman described visiting a friend after both their husbands had passed away. They prepared lunches for each other and comforted one another. Mrs. Caplan is grateful that her old friends insisted that she continue to go on vacation with them after her husband passed away. "You'll never be the odd one; this is what friends are for," they said. Mrs. Caplan said, "With them I'm happy." Every Saturday Mrs. Shapiro and an old friend shop together and have tea in town. "I've known her for forty years; when me husband died, we go out friends, like, on a Saturday."

Thus, in addition to children, informants can rely on old friends, who have helped them through difficult times. With the assurance of support from both kin and friends, Leeds elderly have been able to make a different adjustment to living with peers than have Cornell elderly.

Neighborhood Locals. When informants moved to the Knightsdale Estate, many were told, "It is like the Leylands, they'll be in and out of your home." The tenants often recognized each other from the old Jewish neighborhoods where they had grown up or worked together. "We all knew one another, more or less." Sisters or relatives through marriage also moved to the Estate. The Knightsdale Estate is thus composed of a homogeneous group of residents of similar background, religion, and socioeconomic status. But, although people were acquainted, many had never lived together; they had to establish new relationships. "Although we all know one another for a long time, we only saw each other occasionally, not often, and it is only now that we are all together, really for the first time, and this situation is new, unique" (Mrs. Caplan).

In forming new relationships with peers, Leeds elderly follow a code of independence, self-reliance, and service. They realize the need for relationships with neighbors. "As good as children are, neighbors are nearest to call on." In selecting fellow tenants as potential friends, they use criteria similar to those for old friends: trustworthiness and sincerity. "She does not talk about people and she does not repeat," says Mrs. Aronson. "She is a friend. She treats me as a friend, she confides in me, as well, and there is no exposure. She is very nice to me, a nice person. . . . She likes to come here, and we talk together, and she will not repeat anything that we say. That's a friend."

On the Knightsdale Estate, as in Cornell, neighborhood locals offer an important source of companionship. For women who nursed husbands and were not able to maintain old relationships, for those whose old friends have died, and for others who are no longer physically able to visit longstanding friends, the Estate offers potential companionship: "When I came to live here, I didn't know anybody. I was ever so lonely and miserable. I went to town every day. . . . And then I got friendly with this Dora and then they started coming in to me . . . and they all kept coming" (Mrs. Gottlieb).

Informants enjoy visits from neighbors, who drop in for a chat and a cup of tea. In the summer they sit outside together, playing cards and bingo. They appreciate each other's companionship: "You know, you go in and talk to a person, and it passes an hour." Even people they don't like can help pass the time: "I'm lonely, I have to wait for someone to come in," says Mrs. Perlman: "She comes in, you know I'm not one that would turn anyone away from me door, but really, I'm not pushy about her. I don't mind if she doesn't come, but sometimes, it's a bit of company."

Neighbors sit together on day trips, go to town, or travel together in the summer. Mrs. Caplan says that she no longer wishes to spend holidays with her children: "I do not want to baby-sit, and I can't walk that fast or far, and they go dancing in the evening. I prefer and want to be with friends my own age. We talk our own language."

Mrs. Caplan compared the difference between these new neighborhood local friends and her old friends. People talk with old friends about their family and children, she said, but they tell the "little daily hurts" to neighbors. These "little things are too petty and stupid to bother old friends with." Mrs. Caplan feels fortunate in having a good neighbor, who "sympathizes and understands how I feel. She is soft like me, she defends me, and she feels hurt for me." "You can talk to her," says Mrs. Aronson of her neighbor. "She's not a fool and she'll always tell me hers. She confides in me a lot and she'll ask me things. I'll quicker tell Goldie than anybody. Personal things I don't tell her, only what happened and I find her very nice."

Thus neighbors supplement the support of old friends and help one another adjust to new situations and overcome loneliness. "When you have your husband, you don't need as many people; you need more people when you're on your own." Neighborhood locals are valuable, for example, in helping cope with widowhood. After Mrs. Caplan's husband died, a close neighbor stayed with her every night for four months until she could manage on her own. She did not want to go to stay with her children, and her neighbor made it possible for her to remain in her own flat.[7] A second widow, Mrs. Silverman, kept to herself until a neighbor "caught" her and "pulled me into a circle of friends." These neighborhood locals encouraged her to join them for tea on Saturday and reassured her, saying, "You'll be all right." Mr. Harvey, who is still grieving for his wife, explains that he can "manage" when he goes in "for a couple of hours in the evening" to watch TV with a neighbor. Many informants describe meeting people on the Estate who have also lost spouses and are similarly lonely and seeking "other old friends."

Neighborhood locals also do favors for each other. A strict code of reciprocity governs these relationships. Leeds people are conscious of repayment and a necessary give-and-take. They discuss social relationships in economic terms: "She is paying me back for what I did for her; now she's retaliating" (Mrs. Silverman). Because one woman helped her neighbor by shopping and visiting with her ill husband, she could justify her neighbor's marketing for her when she was recovering from an operation. Mrs. Perlman is grateful to a male neighbor who gets her prescriptions and offers to carry groceries from the shops. She tries to repay him by sitting with his wife, who "suffers from her nerves," when he goes out with his brother: "Look how lovely I am with them. Now, I go in Saturday night. He has a brother come and he goes out an hour or so. Well, it's a break for him. And I think, how can I repay him when he's so good? So, I says, 'I'll come,' and so she won't be lonely and I sit. I do it, really, for his sake. I do it to repay, to repay. How can I repay it in any other way? It's very, very hard to repay, but I do."

Mrs. Gottlieb's generosity was repaid with concern and assistance:

"He's been very good to me. I'll never forget. I'm not talking about today, I'm talking about ten years ago. Mind you, I've been very, very good to him. Mr. A. was in trouble once with money, he must have gambled, and he came to me, and I helped him out and nobody knew about it. And he gave me back half, and it was a tidy bit, and then the other half I said to him, 'Forget it, forget it, it doesn't matter.'

"Well, he's never forgotten. . . . He offered a little while ago to give to me, I said, 'No, I don't want it. I told you no, and I don't want it, so forget it.' See, well he remembers. And I remember when he was younger . . . when the snow and the ice was on the ground and he used to come to my door and say, 'Don't go out, it's slippery, it's dangerous; tell me what you want.' And bring me everything. Well, to me, I can't tell you. . . .

"You see, so close we've always been. You know, he's been very good to me and I've been very good to him."

But Leeds informants also know which neighborhood locals do not return favors or demand too great a price in repayment. "I was very good to Nancy. I never baked without giving Nancy. . . . I always gave her and gave her. But Nancy wouldn't bring you anything. She can't carry anything, she won't put herself out. . . . She wouldn't, she likes herself. 'I'm sorry, I have a backache'" (Mrs. Gottlieb). Some ask too much in return: "She does things for you and then she wants a right lot of repaying, such as wanting you to be there with her all of the time. I don't call that a *mitzve* [a "good work"]. She also tells you, and others, how much she's done for you" (Mrs. Perlman).

Despite their desire for independence, informants realize that as they get older thay may have to rely more on neighborhood locals. They recognize the need to forge new relationships as social insurance: "You need to know someone and to have someone whom you might need to call on." Thus Knightsdale residents initiate kindnesses to create good will, even indebtedness. Mrs. Gottlieb, for example, began to invite for tea the younger brother-in-law of the neighbor to whom she had loaned money. This brother-in-law knew how good she had been to his family; they had told her, "You are one of the family now; if there's anything you want doing, you call." Mrs. Gottlieb gave him and his wife a jar of a special homemade Passover sweet and told them, "If I ever need a favor, I know I can come to you." Soon thereafter, she began to extend the relationship:

"When Mr. A. came in on Friday, I said, 'Herbie, are you going to the shop, to Malcomb's?'

"He said no, but he was going to Mark's, his brother-in-law.

"So I says, 'If Mark's going to the shop . . . ask him to get me a small bread.' And he brought it."

After the older neighbor died, the brother-in-law began to pick up his reciprocal exchanges with Mrs. Gottlieb. He brought her the *Leeds Jewish Gazette* on Friday mornings as the old man had done, and he came in for coffee after *shul* on Saturday mornings. Mrs. Gottlieb interprets this as evidence that she can call on him in the future. Other informants are similarly conscious of their possible future needs, and they court younger, stronger neighbors who might be able to help them.[8]

Mrs. Perlman not only encourages exchanges with younger neighborhood locals, but she has developed a close relationship with her home-help. She never refers to this woman as her "home-help," but rather as "my lady," and she always serves her a cup of tea. Mrs. Perlman's children gave her helper a large tin of biscuits for her family at Christmas. Mrs. Perlman's home-help drives her to get her pension check and a few groceries. She has volunteered to fetch the pension check on the weeks when she works for somebody else. Thus, by initiating favors and kindnesses, Mrs. Perlman has developed a supplementary resource.

Informants admit to being lonely, but they try to cope by keeping active and inviting people to visit. Many continue to bake and cook; they say this sort of activity "occupies my mind." They entertain at tea and card parties and serve home-baked pastry. Many are always prepared for unexpected guests. "I'm always ready to make people welcome. I'm always ready to

Leeds mothers are wonderful, generous cooks, who make delicious traditional foods.

cook a meal for anybody. I'm never lazy. I haven't got a lazy bone in me," says Mrs. Gottlieb.

"I got busy and I didn't go to the card evening. I stayed up late and I prepared a big dinner and they came at 1:00 and that table was set for a king. There was everything you could mention on the table. And he said, 'Auntie, we didn't expect anything like this. . . .'

"And I said, 'You know how I am and I like it.' I had chopped herring, soup, and *kneydlekh*, I had pickled meat, I had cold chicken, I had everything and the table was full. And they enjoyed themselves . . . and they were thrilled . . . and she phoned and she told my sister" (Mrs. Gottlieb).

Mrs. Aronson told me her various strategies for keeping busy and involved with people. "People are a comfort, so you do not have to stay alone." Every few weeks, she places a large order at her brother-in-law's delicatessen. Neighbors tell her what they want, and she takes these items to them in the communal hall. She feels she can go into the hall with a purpose. People call her over to chat, and she talks with everyone. "I use the projects to get out of the house and to be with people and to have contact with others, and people appreciate what I do. I have a good name on the Estate." She also knows a cobbler, who comes to her house to collect shoes to mend. Neighbors take their shoes to her and leave money to pay. Mrs. Aronson says she encourages this company. She likes to talk with the cobbler and with the people who bring and then collect their shoes: "I'm not alone all the time." She adds that her son is glad she has friends: "To be alone is to face four walls."[9]

In summary, Leeds informants look to neighborhood locals for companionship, comfort, support, and small errands and favors. Because they are certain of their status and have accepted an aged role, most Leeds elderly can build additional companionship among peers, who help them adjust to role changes and overcome loneliness. Although most informants do not discuss family affairs with neighborhood locals, some occasionally admit disappointments. Competition and jealousy do not inhibit these new relationships, the way they do in the Cornell neighborhood. Leeds parents do not use their children's accomplishments and services as criteria for status relations with new neighbors. Rather, they follow a code of self-reliance, independence, and service in building their own reputations among peers.

Associate Friends. In addition to keeping busy at home and visiting with friends and neighbors, informants occasionally go to the Day Center or the Leeds Friendship Club, both of which meet in the communal hall.[10] At these activities they mingle with people who are not their immediate neighbors.[11] "I go nearly every day. Look, I've been on Sunday to the Club, I've been on Monday twice, I've been today, I'm going tomorrow. I'm on duty to make tea. It keeps you busy," says Mrs. Shapiro.

Leeds informants prefer to take a service role as voluntary helpers rather than to be recipients of services. One woman is on three committees: "Being lonely, it is best to keep busy." Her son lives nearby, but he rarely finds her home when he comes to visit. She is busy serving tea or selling raffle tickets and candy at the bingo games. Others share her philosophy: "It had always been my plan when my children were married to do jobs for someone else, and so I assumed the job of cook and bottle washer at the Center" (Mrs. Caplan).

Although the Day Center meets on the Estate every day and sponsors several organized activities, many informants are reluctant to attend. To them the Center represents a failure to cope with loneliness and an inability to keep busy at home. "The Day Center is wonderful for people who have time on their hands and are very lonely; there are wonderful things for them to go to. But I could not sit at the Center and knit or crochet, I would prefer to help or to clean dishes. I'm not lonely enough, I don't need it. . ." (Mrs. Caplan).[12]

Similarly, informants are unwilling to eat at the Center's lunch pro-

A weekly meeting of the Leeds Jewish Friendship Club.

Buying eggs at the Leeds Jewish Friendship Club.

gram. "God forbid. I would rather go home and eat an egg by myself than stay here and have a meal" (Mrs. Shapiro). "I would be ashamed if I could look after myself to go to the Club for dinner," says Mrs. Stein. "People who are capable, they should have a pride of themselves. Where is the pride, the conscience, to go and sit down and have a meal and someone else to subsidize for them?"

As part of their code of service and involvement, informants volunteer in other charitable activities as well. Some belong to the WIZO chapter, which meets on the Estate. This service organization, the counterpart of the American Jewish Hadassah, raises money for Israel. Another woman and her neighbors wrap plastic silverware for the Kosher Kitchen. Some serve on the Tenants' Committee and the Ladies Welfare Society. They contribute to the Welfare Board and other Jewish charities. Voluntary work, serving others, and contributing to charities are important values among Leeds Jews. Through them, they demonstrate independence and maintain and raise their own status and esteem.

Knightsdale parents are also active in the small *shul* run by the Estate. Each week they attend Saturday morning services and serve as "hostesses," making coffee and setting out the cake and wine for the communal *kidesh* (the traditional blessing over the wine, followed by the communal sharing of wine, *shnaps*, and something sweet). This shared work is a source of companionship. "They're all nice and friendly up there, you know." For Mrs. Caplan, being active in the *shul* provides a link with her deceased husband as well: "It's homey here, I like it, I feel important, it's close by and I take pride in this *shul*—my husband helped to start it. I feel I belong here."[13] On the High Holidays, parents prefer to worship in this *shul* with peers rather than joining children at the larger synagogues. "It's a long way, it is too far to go." By accepting the love and support of their children, Leeds parents are able to forge an independent existence. They do not feel unwanted when they are not with family.

As they fight loneliness by keeping occupied, by serving others, and by making new acquaintances on the Estate, informants demonstrate survival strategies. One of these is self-reliance. "I don't sit in other people's houses, I've got plenty to do . . . I can assure you" (Mrs. Aronson). In their selection of friends they employ evaluative criteria that reinforce their sense of independence. "You see, this Mrs. T. says, 'Come in, love.' They want you to come in, but you can't create everybody. You can't create the whole Estate. It's too much and I can always find something to do. That's the difference" (Mrs. Gottlieb).

One criterion for evaluating potential associates is the neatness and attractiveness of their homes. Here the traditional Jewish values of the *baleboste*—the praiseworthy homemaker—are reinforced: "I like my place and I keep my place nice." People who are not well off financially save carefully to redecorate and keep up their homes.[14] "If you don't have money, I had to do it with what I saved up from my pension. It took me a whole seven years before my flat were redone. First I did the hall, then I saved for the kitchen, and then I saved again until I had enough to do the lounge" (Mrs. Perlman).

Although Knightsdale tenants rent their flats, they are willing to invest money to make them attractive. There is a sense of commitment and permanence that is lacking in Cornell informants—perhaps because they have moved from apartment to apartment all their lives.

Maintaining a home represents "keeping up" to Knightsdale informants. Mrs. Silverman, who left the Estate to go into the old-age home, misses her flat: "I hated to have to give up my lovely home, I was very comfortable there." Some parents have kept furnishings from their previous homes. Others display new possessions, polished silver, and sparkling crystal, which enhance their images as good housekeepers, modern women, and efficient managers of money. Nonetheless, even they obey the code against bragging or being ostentatious: "Nobody likes her. She talks too much, she brags a lot about her children, about herself, and about her flat. How wonderful, clean, and lovely, and how she washes her door down, and how she can't sit idle like some women" (P. Silver).

Personal appearance, public behavior, and speech are also criteria for selecting associates. "If a person wants his own independence and his own pride, they must look after themselves and look after their place" (Mrs. Stein). "Oh, I think appearance is a lot. If you see a clean woman, you always take more to her than anybody. Appearance is a lot" (Mrs. Pincus). Women should wear dresses and be "neat, clean, and tidy." But they should not overdress or try to be swank. "If someone dresses up, people will notice; and then when something happens, they will throw it up to them" (Mrs. Aronson).[15] People are also judged by the way they speak, the expressions they use, and their tone and volume. In public gatherings, people notice table manners and comment unfavorably on "hopping"—taking a lot of food or asking for extra tea.

At the communal hall on the Estate, informants are selective: "I'm stuffed, I'm particular whom I'm friendly with" (Mrs. Silverman). Some prefer to attend the small WIZO meeting rather than the 250-member

Members of the Tenants' Committee wash up after a Knightsdale affair.

A Knightsdale resident displays photographs, possessions, and gifts.

Leeds Friendship Club.[16] "I enjoy going there because it's quiet and nice, lovely people. At the Friendship Club, there are some horrible people, people who are *shnorers,* who only go for what they can get" (Mrs. Gottlieb). Informants try to avoid those "who try to take advantage, or to get something for nothing. They show you up."[17] "I used to sit at the 'posh table,' these women all do a lot of work, these are people who don't get anything for nothing, it would be degrading for them" (Mrs. Gottlieb). Thus informants prefer to associate with those who are also independent, who have status, and who do not accept charity.

The characteristics that the Leeds elderly esteem were exemplified by an eighty-year-old widower who died during my stay. After the memorial service that Estate members held in his honor, I asked informants to describe him:

"Mr. H. was spotless, he was clean, he kept his home beautiful, only since he's been poorly, he went for dinners. He used to cook himself, he used to do his own shopping and his cooking. . . . He was a nice man. He was a gentleman. . . . You could speak to him. You can have a conversation with him."

"He was such a nice man . . . quiet, inoffensive, jolly, never complained, kind. He went to *bentshen likht* [light Sabbath candles] for the old lady who lived next to him and who was going blind and could not see to light the candles."

"He was unaffected, kind, there were no two sides to him, he was a gentleman by birth. He made people feel wanted and he spoke to them."

"He was a gentleman, not rough, he would greet you if he saw you and ask how you are. He was not loudspoken, not rough, not insulting, and he did not talk about other people."

The following column, written by a fellow resident on the Knightsdale Estate (Mr. Segal), appeared in the *Leeds Jewish Gazette* after Mr. H.'s death.

A True Lamed Vavnik
One of the callers to whom I referred last week gave me the news of the passing of our dear friend, Mr. H. He was 82.

In the year of his birth, the well-known short story "Bontzye Shweig"— Bontzye the Silent—was written by Isaac L. Peretz.

Bontzye Shweig had "a quiet life, a quiet death and a quiet burial." He was "never heard to complain of either God or man. There was never a flash of hatred in his eyes."

As Peretz wrote, he must surely have sensed that Bontzye's prototype was being born in Mr. H.

On Simchat Torah, 5735, he could not take his place as Chatan Torah because he was in hospital. Ever after that time he had increasing spells of almost unbearable pain, recovering a little last Simchat Torah to take his place as Chatan Torah.

At the reception, he made the briefest of speeches, doing his utmost to hide the pains he was experiencing.

He was always the quiet man, a lovable man, making his presence felt by his reticence, by his undemonstrative actions, his almost stoic reserve.

I doubt if his name was well known in banking circles. Not many communal organisations knew him well, but he rarely missed shool in [Knightsdale] where he opened the Shabbat service as a lay reader.

He rarely missed his Thursday morning attendance at our Day Centre Discussion Group. Week after week he came in, quietly, an almost imperceptible smile of greeting as he went to his usual place.

It was a discussion group but like Bontzye he was always silent. I once asked him why he never took part in the discussions. His reply was, "I like to listen."

I recall one Thursday morning when he was not present when we opened our discussion. During my introductory remarks, I mentally counted the number of people present. There were 34, with myself 35. As I completed my count, he walked into the room. He was No. 36, a true Lamed Vavnik.

According to the Talmud, there are in the world no fewer than 36 righteous men in every generation upon whom the Shechina rests.

The Talmud also says that these 36 differ from other righteous persons in that they behold the Divine Presence with equal quality.

On this basis arose the legend of the Lamed Vav [Hebrew 36]—men of usually humble vocation whose special spiritual gifts are not generally recognised or appreciated but by whose merit the world exists. In times of crisis and danger, they reveal themselves and bring salvation to the people.

Lamed Vavniks are represented as hiding their sanctity and as not obtruding it for show. They usually follow humble vocations as artisans, unrecognised by the community and denying their identity when it is accidentally discovered.

As a man of Israel, he became one of us, worthy of being called up for Shelishi but not having the rights of a Cohen or the responsibilities of a Levi. Yet he acted as a Levi should. He served us.

He died quietly in his sleep. In the Ohel, before we went to his grave, no one gave him praise. The rabbi reminded us that we were in the month of Nisan and it was not permissible to give a Hesped, a funeral eulogy, during Nisan.

So, as quietly as he came to us, as quietly as he mixed with us, so quietly did we see him to his last worldly resting place. His voice, even his silent

voice, is stilled but every Shabbat morning, whoever opens the service, I
shall hear Mr. H. chanting Boruch, or, as he had it, Borich.

The Knightsdale Estate and the Friendship Club are composed of people of similar backgrounds. Members grew up in the same poor neighborhoods or worked together in the tailoring trades. Not only do they live
next to each other, but neighbors and associates sit together at social and
religious activities, meet while shopping or collecting pension checks, and
go on vacation together. Many ties bind them together. Housing patterns
and the location of the Day Center work geographically to reinforce social
homogeneity with physical intimacy. People can easily watch one
another's comings and goings. They frequently look out their windows
and comment on what others are doing.

There is a code of proper, expectable behavior among these Jewish
elderly, and peer pressure fosters conformity. Neighbors and associates
are careful of their reputations; gossip is greatly feared at Knightsdale.[18]
News passes quickly, as stories circulate first at the Day Center and
Friendship Club, and then are carried back to neighbors. "Yes, people do
gossip about one another," so informants are wary of those who come to
visit. "I don't want to know anybody's business and I don't want anybody
to know my business. If you can bring into my house, you can take out of
my house."

"They go in each other's houses and they talk about each other. That's
why I don't encourage them to come here, these people. Because they talk
about one another, and I don't want to be involved in any tettle-tattle. I
don't want it" (Mrs. Gottlieb).

"That's why I don't go. They sit talking about everybody. They never
left anybody alone. That's why I stopped going. Used to go every
Wednesday, sit and talk. . . . It was terrible. Front of their face, they were
marvelous. But as soon as they had their back turned, so many *yakhnes*"
(Mrs. Pincus).

One place gossip and peer pressure reinforce the code of independence
and self-reliance is the Jewish Welfare Board. People who receive help
from the Board are pitied, criticized, or ridiculed and are called *shnorer*.
On one occasion, Mrs. Pincus went on a subsidized day trip that her own
son had organized for the Board. She decided never to go again, saying,
"There's too much talking. 'How do I come? that I can afford.' I heard
someone say, 'She oughtn't to go. She's all right. She can pay for her
trips.' They thought that I was favored, David being on the committee."

Mrs. Perlman, who is not well and receives meals-on-wheels, is careful not to hang her laundry outside to dry. "Anyone will see, and say I can wash but I'm getting dinners. . . ." Thus fear of gossip encourages informants to remain independent as long as possible. Their pride and reputation are at stake.

Unlike social relations among Cornell associates, which are marked by efforts to convey idealized images of intergenerational relations to bolster their own uncertain positions, Leeds associates encourage one another to build their own prestige and status through independence, self-reliance, and service.

Summary: Leeds Networks

In analyzing the old-friend, neighborhood-local, and associate-friend relationships of Leeds informants (see Figure 3), a number of significant points emerge. First, most informants have relationships in each of the three categories. Eight have old friends with whom they share intimate relationships, nine enjoy the companionship of neighborhood locals on a daily basis, and six serve or visit with associates on committees. Thus for Leeds informants, the Knightsdale Estate offers a choice of compatible neighbors. The fact that tenants have lived together for several years also helps cement these relationships and allows trust and understanding. Cornell informants, on the other hand, principally rely on associate friends.

Leeds informants also benefit from the Day Center, the *shul*, and other organizations that hold meetings at the communal hall on the Estate. There they can socialize with other Estate members and with people from

Social Relations of Leeds Informants

Name of Informant	Type of Social Relationship			
	Neighborhood Locals		Associate Friends	Old Friends
Mrs. Perlman	4		0	0
Mrs. Silverman	2		0	1
Mrs. Stein	2		0	1
Mrs. Shapiro	1	2*	1	1
Mr. Segal	1		1	1	0
Mrs. Pincus	1		4	1
Mrs. Aronson	2		2	2
Mrs. Gottlieb	3		2	1	2
Mrs. Caplan	2	3	1	4

*All relationships that are not clearly bounded are placed midway between categories.

the community. They can get to know their peers in a variety of capacities. They also maintain close relationships with friends from the old neighborhoods, many of whom now live nearby in Medina.

Second, the three types of relationships involve complementary functions. Each helps elderly parents to accept an aged role and to readjust their expectations about relations with adult children.

Third, as is true in Cornell, the categories are not always clearly bounded: a number of Leeds informants attend meetings or serve on committees at the communal hall with the same neighbors they visit at home; others confide in associate friends.

Through a multiplicity of ties, neighborhood locals, associates, old friends, and family members know a great deal about one another. Through conversation and observation, they know how other people's children behave and learn what is reasonable to expect. Neighbors and associates see one another's children coming and going: "Yes, she has fine children, one is a doctor. They are nice to the mama. When I return from *shul* Saturday, all the children are *kidesh*-ing the mama." Often children have grown up together, and many live, work, or socialize with the adult children of other informants or neighbors. Adult children compare experiences, and each knows what the other does for his parents. Occasionally a mother will compare her child to another in an effort to bring him closer to her expectations. Or a close neighbor will defend an adult child against his mother's complaints. Clearly, Leeds elderly have benefited from experiences denied to Cornell parents.

Leeds informants generally assume one of two roles in adjusting to their aged status: that of adjusted mother or that of dissatisfied parent.

The Adjusted Mother, Subtype 1: Reliance on All Three Types of Social Relationships (Six Informants—Mrs. Caplan, Mrs. Gottlieb, Mrs. Aronson, Mrs. Pincus, Mr. Segal, Mrs. Shapiro). Adjusted mothers continue their traditional exchange of services with adult children: they baby-sit, entertain, and give birthday gifts. They visit each weekend with their children, who include their mothers in family gatherings, ask their advice, and share confidences. Although they are closely involved with children and grandchildren, adjusted mothers spend much of their time in the company of peers. They take initiating roles in charity and service activities. Rather than relying on the reflected accomplishments of their children, they create their own status. They can confide family problems or feelings of discouragement to old friends without fear of loss of status. These old friends are often companions from childhood or the early years of marriage; they know one another's parents, spouses, and children. There is continuity and security in these relationships, for old friends understand one's background and social position. Close friends also encourage negotiation with children, and they give informants confidence in building new relationships with neighbors. (Mr. Segal is included in this category because he meets all the criteria except, obviously, motherhood.)

The Adjusted Mother, Subtype 2: Primary Reliance on Neighborhood Locals (Two Informants—Mrs. Perlman, Mrs. Silverman). Because of illness, age, or years with an ailing spouse, these informants do not have the resource of old friends. Often, however, siblings act as confidants and sources of support and encouragement. For these parents, life on the Knightsdale Estate has offered potential new friendships, and they have built relationships of companionship and mutual assistance with their neighbors. A code of reciprocity governs and sustains these relationships. In general, interaction with children continues to be satisfactory. Aged, ill parents dependent on adult children for assistance in shopping and transportation repay these favors with continued emotional support. Leeds parents are grateful for the services of their children. Many adjusted parents of both subtypes have kept a few pieces of furniture from their former family homes, and they display, on dining room sideboards, wedding photographs of children and *bar mitsve* pictures of grandsons.

The Dissatisfied Parent (One Informant—Mrs. Stein). Mrs. Stein, the only Leeds parent in this category, did not enjoy the same experiences of family life as did other Leeds informants—she emigrated by herself to England when she was a young teenager, without siblings or parents. Her children have made successful careers and wealthy marriages. Today she either brags about their accomplishments or expresses dissatisfaction with her Leeds son and his wife in a manner reminiscent of Cornell informants. Mrs. Stein also compares her son to other people's children, whom she feels act better to their mothers: "He doesn't know what to do for her, he comes every day when there is a day from God. Now, what does she do for him, that I haven't done for my son? Nothing."

When she is not complaining about her children, she is bragging about them. Her neighbors and associates do not like this. "Oh, you'd think she was the only one who had a daughter. It gets other people's backs up." One woman continues: "People don't like her because she's a big bragger. Nobody's done anything as good as her Miriam and her other children. . . . How she used to rub it in how marvelous they were to her and this, that, and the other. 'You should have the same pleasure from your children as I have from mine,' and this is why people don't like her, she's not liked and she has a very big mouth as well."

Although Mrs. Stein has an intimate old friend with whom she shares family concerns and neighbors with whom she chats, she has not adjusted well to changes in relations with adult children. Clearly, sustained relations with old friends are only one factor assisting an elderly parent to accept an aged role. The quality of earlier relationships within the family of orientation and shared lifestyles of aged parents and adult children are also influential.

Postscript

We noted earlier that there is a code on the Knightsdale Estate against bragging or complaining about one's children. In one case, this code broke down. After illness and hospitalization, Mrs. Silverman decided to go into an old-age home. The neighbors and people with whom she had been friendly came only once to visit. She felt bad and made excuses for them: "I can't expect them to come every week. It's a long journey and they have to walk after taking the bus to [Medina] Corner. But, of course, my own family are attentive." Her conversation changed as she began to become a part of the old-age home environment. On the Estate, she emphasized how her friends helped her. In the home, she constantly refers to her family's nightly visits and her Sunday excursions with them. She needs not to feel abandoned: "It isn't that I'm not wanted that I'm in here." She offered the same reasons for choosing not to live at her son's home as Cornell informants give (the following is taken from my field notes): "She said she was very lonely even with her daughter-in-law coming home from work an hour early, and that she did not want the daughter-in-law to lose time. Mrs. Silverman did not want to be a nuisance to the children. It was awkward at home, as the toilet is upstairs and it is hard for her to do the stairs. She was also concerned with spoiling their life: If they want to go out in the evening, they would not want to leave her on her own. 'It's not convenient for me to live there—all of them work.'"

At the old-age home, people brag about their children. Their growing dependency on their children, the feeling of lowered status, and the fear of abandonment—the feelings that Cornell informants express in their neighborhood—are found in Leeds only in an old-age home.

6

Adjustment to an Old-Age Role

IN EXAMINING HOW TWO GROUPS OF elderly Jewish people have adjusted to an aged role, this study found two basic patterns. The Cornell elderly have not successfully redefined their new family status position. They hold an unrealistic and abstract model of parent-child relationships. Cornell parents conceal feelings of disappointment about the behavior of adult children, which they measure against this ideal standard, and they make excuses for their children's failures. They are also uncertain about their own status in the community. Informants compete for position with peers, presenting a desired image of a loved parent instead of confiding in neighbors or associates. A few depend on social welfare services or financial assistance.

Leeds informants' expectations about adult children are more realistic. They have managed to maintain, with only slight alterations, their parental and grandparental status. Through exchanges with friends, neighbors, and kin, they have defined their position in the community and their relations to children and friends. They confide intimate feelings to old friends and devise successful strategies to combat loneliness. Leeds people try to remain independent and rarely call on social service assistance.

My study of these two groups of elderly has shown, I think, that in role definition they are on their own. Western industrial societies do not define kinship roles explicitly. Class, ethnicity, occupation, age, sex, kinship—all are components of role definition. But their importance varies throughout the developmental cycle. Kinship responsibilities help to clarify young parents' obligations to others; and kinship ties assume importance again when those young parents have grown old. Neighbors often become friends, for example, because of similar shared concerns over children, who are the mediating link. As children grow older, parents' other roles begin to predominate, particularly at work. Only when people near retirement do they refocus on kinship ties. That is why an appropriate adjustment to old age heavily depends on how parents and children adapt to each other's life changes and communicate their needs and wishes.

145

A second problem follows from the first: Kinship obligations of elderly, retired parents are even less specific than those for younger people in Western societies. In neither Cornell nor Leeds could informants articulate a clearly defined set of rights and duties for interactions with adult children. Leeds informants were more explicit than their Cornell counterparts, however. British parents defined their responsibilities in terms of maintaining their traditional nurturing roles. Jewish life in northern England is more conservative than that in Cornell. Because peer pressures enforce conformity for both parents and children, Leeds informants have relatively clear kinship expectations. Cornell informants, in contrast, found discussions about kinship to be painful. They avoided talking about what their children should do for them, rarely mentioning disappointments and bragging instead about their children's services to them and their successes. They dealt with their own obligations only on an ideal level, often based on the past, when their children were newly married and their grandchildren babies. They could not articulate a clearly defined set of rights and duties for elderly, retired parents.

If society does not define one's role, it must be self-defined. But the process of self-definition cannot be abstract; one cannot successfully rely on ideal norms. For both British and American informants, public expressions and ideological statements about norms help in a limited way. English informants derive some guidance from reflecting on interactions with their own parents. But many Cornell elderly have no such experience; they must reflect on an idealized Eastern European code of reverence toward parents—a code they could not follow because they emigrated before their parents had grown old. Elderly Cornell people who must rely on formal cultural and religious models have great difficulty adjusting to their changing roles and positions.

How do people with no specific kinship obligations and with only unrealistic models interact with their children? How do they put new roles into effect? I hoped to find answers through a "contextual approach"—through observing, meeting, and talking to people in their own environments.

My study shows, I think, that socialization in old age depends heavily on the characteristics of others with whom the older person interacts. Friends, neighbors, acquaintances, and kin can help one another define their kinship roles. Friends are not substitutes for kin, nor do they take over kinship roles; but kinship and friendship together affect the adjustment to an aged role.

In fact, four factors seem generally to influence one's acceptance of an aged role. First, the process of successful adjustment to old age begins early in life. Living within a domestic unit during childhood and learning the negotiated dimensions of family living are crucial. A comparison of Leeds and Cornell people shows that if this process continues through adolescence—if one can have ongoing interaction with aging parents—one can learn about growing old in a kind of advanced socialization. In many cases, elderly parents provide appropriate models for successful adjustment in old age.

A second factor influencing adjustment to old age is a shared life style and economic position by parents and their own adult children. When generations have similar residences, incomes, and religious practices, as in Leeds, it is easier for parents and children to understand each other. Those few Cornell informants who share some economic equality with children are able to continue in their parental roles, to contribute to family decisions. They are not totally dependent, but can both initiate and reciprocate favors.

The third factor influencing adjustment to old age is access to lifelong friends. In both Leeds and Cornell, that depends in part on continuous residence in stable neighborhoods, where intimate friendships can be built up over time and where family members are known and confidences trusted.

Unfortunately, it is difficult to evaluate the relative importance of these factors. All are closely interwoven. It is obviously impossible to change Cornell informants' experiences. More extensive financial benefits, reform of Social Security, and access to health-care insurance would all increase their economic independence, but current economic and political conditions make such changes improbable. The friendship component can be influenced by public policy and planning, however. In Chapter 7, I shall comparatively examine the fourth factor affecting adjustment to an aged role—the quality of the residential environments where Leeds and Cornell elderly have settled in old age. Here I shall make concrete suggestions for housing estates and day center programs that would allow Cornell elderly, and other aged people, to continue to live in their present neighborhoods and possibly to build intimate friendships over time.

7

The Sociology and Anthropology
of the Elderly:
Studies and Proposals

THE AGED ARE A RELATIVELY RECENT subject of research in social-cultural anthropology. Before 1960, there was only one major published account of aging and that dealt with primitive societies.[1] While anthropologists relied on the knowledge and recollections of elderly informants for much of their data, they neglected the status of the elderly themselves. Even in life-cycle studies, which observe and describe stages, *rites de passage*, and age roles, the emphasis in anthropology was on infancy, childhood, or adolescence.

The same is true of kinship studies—social anthropologists have tended to concentrate on the young. Malinowski's classic monograph, *The Argonauts of the Western Pacific*, for example, discusses only one elderly person, the chief of Kiriwina, and then only in his role as negotiator in the Kula exchanges (Malinowski, 1922). Firth's study of Tikopia briefly mentions the ambivalence of filial relationships, but the weight of the data is on the formal roles of parents and children, the proper education of the young, and the general affection felt by grandchildren toward grandparents (Firth, 1936). Anthropologists' concentration on the young is partly due to the fact that few individuals in subsistence economies live to old age; those who do survive often retain comparatively good physical health and mental faculties and continue to pursue many of the activities of earlier adulthood (Clark, 1973). Moreover, anthropologists interested in kinship are usually concerned with its formal, organizational aspects, particularly in societies organized on the lineage principle. Such studies do pay attention to kinship statuses and genealogical relations, but mostly in terms of the power exercised by senior generations and their pivotal role in defining lineage identities. Seldom do they dwell on the actual kinship relations of specific elders within their own domestic groups. Even the

148

ownership and transmission of resources are considered significant only in terms of the elder's ability to maintain authority within the larger social group. This control is also reinforced by the elder's ritual position. Middleton's study of the Lugbara, for example, reveals how elders use supernatural sanctions and the belief in their sacred position to maintain authority (Middleton, 1965).

The cult of the dead further sustains the control of the elderly against their juniors' claims to independence and provides a set of sanctions to support group unity. Headship, which is competed for in ritual, is gained by the ability to invoke one's ancestors against others. In societies that practice ancestor worship and believe that the dead continue to influence the lives of their descendants, aged people are "natural" intermediaries with ancestors and the appropriate conductors of sacrifices. Elders are thus both present conductors and future receivers of sacrifices. Supernatural sanctions reinforce their position and society's belief in their ritual powers. Fortes, for example, discusses how filial piety is enforced by the jural and ritual authority of the father, the ancestor cult, and mystical power:

> In any system where the ancestors are the objects of worship (and even of cult), the elders are not only the nearest to the ancestors in genealogical terms (and in this respect are living ancestors with "one foot in the grave"), they are also the progenitors of the maximum number of descendants. . . . (Fortes, 1959).

Or, as Goody states:

> Elders are close to the ancestors; filial piety is blessed by the gods as well as by the philosophers; and supernatural sanctions are often intrinsic to a society's attitude toward, and treatment of, its aged members. (Goody, 1976, p.128)

Most anthropologists have believed that studies of lineage organization cover the elderly sufficiently so long as they analyze the conditions required for a retired elder to sustain his position.[2] In studies of nonlineage societies, whose aged do not have as clear a kinship status, anthropologists have generally neglected the particular position of the elderly.

Even in analyses of age-graded societies in East Africa, the status of retired elders is usually only briefly discussed. In his examination of an age-grade system, Dyson-Hudson reveals how the Karimojong enable men to relate to non-kin, even strangers, in patterned ways and to receive hospitality and protection among members of alien groups (Dyson-Hudson, 1966). Gulliver concentrates on the politically important junior elders, analyzing the age-grade system as one of the areas of jural decision making and social control (Gulliver, 1963).

In a comparative essay on age-sets among three Masai-type societies, Spencer reveals how intergenerational conflicts over highly valued and scarce resources, such as women and cattle, are prevented from endangering community harmony by the age organization, which provides means to avoid or manage them. Age grades are shown to divert strains and thus keep conflict under control (Spencer, 1976). Social anthropologists studying kinship have been concerned with how the structural characteristics of society affect intergenerational relationships—rules of inheritance, age grading, seniority rights, and the belief in the ritual power of the elderly as the apical ancestors of the living—not with the status of the aged per se.

Because most anthropological work on the elderly has been incidental to other research, the bulk of theoretical analysis has been left to sociologists. Their primary focus has been on the status and roles of retired people in contemporary industrial society, rather than on elder kinsmen in tribal societies.

In a recent theoretical work on adult socialization, Rosow argues that, "unlike earlier status changes in American life, people are not effectively socialized to old age" (Rosow, 1974, p.xii). With aging, the optimal conditions of socialization are reversed. Instead of new valued social positions with clear norms, role continuity, and status gains, old age represents a devalued social position, in which "restitutive and social control functions are minimal." Rosow finds that the norms for the aged are weak, ambiguous, and vague. Because Americans have no definite role expectations for the elderly, the aged suffer role losses and role discontinuity when they are widowed, retired, or ill. *Rites de passage* are few, and many resist socialization to a status that lacks responsibility, authority, and rewards. The basic institutions of American society devalue and exclude the elderly. They are viewed in invidious stereotypes and must struggle to preserve their self-esteem through youthful self-images.

While Rosow's argument might be accurate for society as a whole, other sociologists have questioned its application for personal interaction:

> While the loss of formal roles is undeniable in the lives of most older persons, and a shrinkage of life space occurs for the very old, it is nevertheless true that many informal roles remain, and that the typical older person is not without a role set nor without a set of "others." In most cases

> he participates in a number of family, leisure, and neighborhood roles. . . .
> Another factor is that the quality of roles, whether formal or informal,
> changes over time. Many roles in our society allow for considerable "role
> making." . . . This holds true particularly for roles anchored in primary
> groups. It is appropriate, therefore, to focus on . . . role negotiations; that
> is, change in the quality of a role relationship initiated by the partners
> themselves. (Neugarten and Hagestad, 1976, p.40)

Here, at the level of personal interaction, the roles of elderly people are
vague and therefore flexible, and the rights and duties of their position
must be negotiated with significant other people in their environment.
Socialization in old age depends heavily on those with whom the older
person must interact. The social context of interaction is what is important, not a formal set of rights and duties. Consequently, sociologists tend
to disregard fixed kinship statuses as a meaningful framework for role
definition of the aged.[3]

Anthropologists who have studied kinship in industrial societies have
also occasionally questioned the traditional stress on the formal system of
kinship as an organizing institutional framework. Bott, for example, contrasts the importance of kinship in primitive societies with its reduced
position in Western, urban society (Bott, 1964). In small-scale primitive
societies, kinship determines the rights to land and other productive resources and provides the basic framework of the social structure. There
are clearly formulated universal rules about the rights of and obligations to
kin, and societal members are able to state these norms explicitly. In
industrial societies, in contrast, kinship plays a minor part in the economic
and occupational structure. Few individuals depend upon their relatives
for access to a means of livelihood. As kin are bound by fewer economic
ties and obligations, they have less frequent and intense contact. Consequently, elementary families show greater individuation and variation in
kinship behavior and norms.

> In contrast with a small-scale primitive society, the articulation of the
> kinship system and the economic system in an industrial society is exceed-
> ingly variable and complex. Within broad limits, the operation of the eco-
> nomic system permits a wide variation of kinship norms and behavior. It
> creates variable conditions and permits a wide range of choice. Variability
> is a characteristic of the system. (Bott, 1964, p.118)

Instead of kinship providing the basic framework of the social structure,
"In Western urban setting, kinship provides a field for personal choice and
selectivity" (Bott, 1964, p.221). There is little consensus on familial

norms, and people find it difficult to state kinship norms explicitly. Schneider agrees with Bott's argument and suggests that kinship may be relevant only as a cultural idiom, a system of shared meanings and understandings (Schneider and Smith, 1973). To explain the basis of differences in family structure and kinship behavior, Schneider looks to nonkinship considerations such as class, occupation, ethnicity, age differentiation, and the sex-role system.

Needham extends a similar view of kinship into nonindustrial societies. In his introduction to *Rethinking Kinship and Marriage* (Needham, 1971), he rejects the traditional theories and methods of kinship study propounded by Radcliffe-Brown and Fortes. By confining kinship studies to formal and jural features, he argues, anthropologists have inhibited empirical examination and defined the focus of study too narrowly. Needham proposes instead that kinship studies concentrate on resolving particular problems and analyzing individual systems—that they analyze cultural detail in a local context. Such studies would be concerned not with social form but with the various meanings and functions of a social fact in different realms of meaning, including the symbolic and metaphoric. The study of affect, for example, tells us how people actually feel about formal social rules; it explains the emotional content of institutions. For Needham, kinship is not a discriminable class of phenomena or a distinct theory or method of investigation, but it is rather the analysis of a particular problem in different social contexts, traced as far as it will go. It simply is not possible, he argues, to determine what kinship is and what it is not before one studies it in a specific local context; one cannot "presume arbitrary boundaries to the significance of social categories" (Needham, 1971, p.cviii).

Some anthropologists, deemphasizing the jural aspects of kinship, have begun to focus instead on friendship networks. Bott, for example, has shown how friendship networks define the husband and wife roles of young married couples (Bott, 1964). Her analysis of domestic relationships in twenty urban families suggests "that the degree of segregation in the role relationships of husband and wife varies directly with the connectedness of the family's social network" (Bott, 1964, p.60). Families with a clearly defined sexual division of labor—male tasks vs. female tasks—have a close-knit network, and many of their friends, neighbors, and relatives know one another. In contrast, families with relatively joint-role relationships, whose spouses carry out many activities in common, have a loose-knit network: few relatives, neighbors, and friends know one another. Here the patterns in role relationships intertwine with the patterns in social relationships:

> When many people a person knows interact with one another, that is when the person's network is close-knit, and the members of his network tend to reach consensus on norms and they exert consistent informal pressure on one another to conform to the norms, to keep in touch with one another, and, if need be, to help one another. (Bott, 1964, p.60)

Such close-knit situations tend to prevail in working-class neighborhoods, where people are employed in the same or similar occupations and where residence is stable. Although the class structure, the economic and occupational system, and the ecology of cities all affect these networks, the role relationships and reciprocal expectations of husband and wife are influenced most by the friendship network. Since friendship networks vary widely in Western urban settings, so do kinship norms and behavior.

Exchange theory has much to contribute to the study of kinship roles in industrial society. Mauss's classic interpretation of gift exchange in primitive societies stresses the essence of obligation in gift giving, receiving, and repaying (Mauss, 1925). The giving of a gift creates a bond between two persons, and this bond establishes both rights and duties. The gift initiates and cements a social relationship—it is a statement about the relationship between giver and receiver. By presenting a gift, the giver establishes certain claims and expectations. By accepting the gift, the receiver acknowledges these duties; later, when he repays the gift, he establishes his own rights. The exchange of goods and services is thus a moral transaction—a contract—and as such implies obligation by both parties. Although most theoretical statements on exchange theory have focused on power relations rather than role definition, insights about the weight of obligation in reciprocations and bonding through exchange are necessary to a discussion of role transition—and thus to our study of the elderly.

Goffman pays more attention to the dramaturgical aspect than the bonding or obligatory dimension of exchange implied in role playing (Goffman, 1959). He reveals how the shared expectations and norms governing behavior are worked out in transactions. Each participant in the interaction projects his definition of the situation. His own conception of himself is an important part of this projection, and he tries to guide and control the conduct of others, especially their responsive treatment of him. By their responses, the other participants acknowledge or reject his claims, present self-definitions, and attempt to establish their own control. Through these interactions, individuals reciprocally influence one another's behavior: the part one individual plays is tailored to the parts played by the others. Goffman asserts that it is not sufficient for a participant merely to occupy a position: he must operationalize the role. He must enact the rights and duties attached to a given status, create the desired impression, and have others respond in reciprocal affirmation.

> A status, a position, a social place is not a material thing, to be possessed and then displayed; it is a pattern of appropriate conduct, coherent, embellished, and well articulated . . . it is something that must be enacted and portrayed, something that must be realized. (Goffman, 1959, p.75)

Thus interaction is a dialogue between performers.

For these transactions to succeed, the actors must also maintain a shared definition of the situation. There must be consensus—a shared basis of understanding—or communication will break down, and actions will have no common meaning or predictable responses. These points are particularly relevant to a discussion of the elderly. In Chapter 4, we considered how a group of Cleveland elderly, having had to rely too much on ideal models, were never able to define their own status position adequately. As a result, their relations with children and friends have suffered. A group of elderly in Leeds, England, on the other hand, have developed exchanges defining their status. These elderly informants feel certain of their position and relations; the Cleveland group members are more insecure and less able to cope.

PROPOSALS FOR ENCOURAGING SOCIALIZATION OF THE ELDERLY

Recent studies of the elderly concentrate on the social ties within age-segregated residences rather than on a total set of social exchanges between residents and their kin, old friends, and new acquaintances (Rosow, 1974; Ross, 1977; Hochschild, 1973). They deal with age as a principle of social organization, asking under what conditions and through what processes age provides a basis for community creation and encourages socialization to new roles and statuses. Kinship and friendship, according to these studies, are separate, nonconflicting, psychologically complementary relationships.

To encourage community creation and socialization, Rosow proposes large concentrations of socially similar older persons within a local residential setting. Such conditions would help the aged develop a new subculture by allowing them to create strong friendship groups with new group norms, positive reference groups, and qualified role models. Because the aged would be protected from the negative definitions of the larger society, their self-esteem would rise and they could be effectively socialized to new aged roles: "Even new elderly neighbors would become a stronger reference group to the aged than old friends who are not neighbors" (Rosow, p. 164). Thus, in his concentration on a community of peers Rosow does not consider the additional need to maintain and strengthen existing ties with kin and old friends.

Empirical evidence supporting Rosow's planning and policy suggestions for age-segregated housing comes from two anthropological studies. In her book *Old People, New Lives*, Ross examines the development of a community among a group of elderly workers living in an age-homogeneous residence in Paris (Ross, 1977). She finds that "More friendships, more social activity, more help in emergency, and higher morale are consistently observed in settings where old people are available as potential friends and neighbors" (Ross, 1977, p. 2). She distinguishes the conditions necessary for shared social relationships and a "we-feeling" to develop: common territory, social and cultural homogeneity, lack of perceived alternatives to living in the residence, and the presence of residents with leadership skills. Her study concentrates on peer relationships within the common residence and sees emergent social ties, development of community norms, and socialization to community values as evidence for an emerging subculture among aged residents.

Like Rosow, Ross separates relations with children from relations with peers. These are "two distinct spheres of social and emotional contact" (Ross, p. 187). She does not believe that kin and old friend networks are interrelated spheres, nor does she question how preexisting social relations affect residents' present adjustment:

> There is no indication that people participate in community life to compensate for lack of outside ties, or that frequent contact with children or friends from outside is contradictory to intense involvement in life inside the residence. Emotional ties to children seem to be part of a distinct aspect of residents' social lives. They are different from, and therefore not in competition with, emotional bonds with other residents. (Ross, p. 169)

Further validation for age-segregated housing comes from Hochschild's study of rural-born, working-class widows in Merrill Court, a San Francisco residence for the elderly (Hochschild, 1973). Hochschild believes that the elderly seek supplementary friendships to compensate for the relative weakening of kinship ties in American society. She suggests that reciprocal friendships and a subculture of the aged develop among peers as back-up relationships for individuals going through "problematic" states:

> From an individual's viewpoint, some periods of life, such as adolescence and old age, are better for forming sibling bonds than are other periods. Both just before starting a family and after raising one, before entering the economy and after leaving it, an individual is open to, and needs these back-up relationships. It is these stages that are "problematic" and it is these stages that, with longer education and earlier retirement, now last longer. It is in precisely these periods that social siblings are sought. (Hochschild, p.70)

Unlike Rosow and Ross, Hochschild notes that relationships with children and old friends do affect interaction among peers. Reciprocal peer relationships ". . . seem to emerge only when relations with children are in order" (Hochschild, p.88).

> The more one had friends outside the building, the more one had friends on other floors within the building. That is, the wider one's social radius outside the building, the wider it was inside the building as well. (Hochschild, p.51)

Among the residents of Merrill Court there are competition, rivalry, and a hierarchy of rank among residents, just as there are among Cornell informants. The highest position goes to those with large families or to parents who enjoy good relationships with their children.

> Those few whose family ties were feebly held together by Christmas cards and graduation notices did not "make up for it" by plunging themselves into Merrill Court affairs. They . . . remained aloof from the subculture as well. Moreover, those who had especially strong and rewarding family ties were . . . always on the phone or downstairs arranging for the bazaar or the Bowling Club banquet. In fact . . . those closest to their families were among the most active in Merrill Court society. (Hochschild, p.95)

Hochschild, however, chooses not to examine further the interconnections between family and friend networks, nor to show how relations with kin are used to build status with peers. Her analysis is written from a psychological perspective. She interprets kinship relations between elderly mothers and adult daughters in terms of the psychological mechanisms and emotional dependencies of identification and altruistic surrender and sees relations among peers in terms of a reciprocity of equals. Within her psychological framework, kinship and friendship are again interpreted as noncompetitive, complementary relationships.

Unlike Ross, Rosow, and Hochschild, I believe that preexisting social relationships with old friends and kin are crucial for establishing workable self-definitions and for adjusting to new roles, and that such relationships are important aspects of community formation. Previous policy and planning proposals do not pay adequate attention to developing and maintaining necessary kin and old friend exchanges. Neither Rosow, Ross, nor Hochschild explains different adaptations to old age; neither does any of them examine housing location, social welfare programs, government policy, or other circumstances that might lead to maladjustments or to other adjustments in different population groups. As we have learned from Leeds and Cleveland, different patterns of aging cannot be attributed to a single set of variables, such as sex or ethnic background. They involve many variables, and therefore what is advisable for one group is not necessarily a desirable planning proposal for another.

POLICY AND PLANNING SUGGESTIONS FOR ESTATES FOR THE ELDERLY

Current anthropological and sociological studies on aging support a policy of age-segregated housing for the elderly. Such residences are designed to encourage new social relationships which in turn develop social participation, morale, and self-esteem. Thus they counteract loneliness and isolation. The Knightsdale Estate has these virtues; but exactly which factors contribute to its success?

As we have said, informants moved to the Knightsdale Estate when they were in their late fifties and early sixties. The Estate was constructed in a developing Jewish section of Leeds, and tenants saw it as a desirable place to retire, where they could be near children and family. Built for Jews of "necessitous means," the Estate is composed of a homogeneous group of people of similar socioeconomic position and religious background. Initially there were a few families with children on the Estate, but now most of the residents are elderly and widowed. The first tenants were purposely selected for their leadership skills, and the Jewish Welfare Board encouraged them to form a Tenants' Association.

The Tenants' Association set up social, religious, and welfare committees. Residents established a *shul* and voluntarily called on sick neighbors,

The Knightsdale *shul:* The cloth was hand-embroidered by one Estate member in memory of the deceased spouse of another Estate member.

Following the traditional Orthodox custom, the men and women sit separately at the Knightsdale *shul.*

and the social committee hosted day trips and bingo and card evenings. Through these activities, tenants became acquainted with their new neighbors, and many residents developed a sense of involvement and commitment to the Estate. Today, fifteen years later, informants still serve on these committees and remain actively involved in Estate activities. Many say that they are too old to join something new but that they remain because they are used to the work and enjoy the participation. Assignments to make tea and serve biscuits at parties keep informants involved in social activities and promote a sense of status.

One strengthening activity on the Estate is the Knightsdale *shul*. Services are held there on all Jewish holidays, every Friday night, and every Sabbath morning. Two younger men from the Leeds community lead the more difficult portions of the prayers, but the organizational work is done by the *shul* committee. The Knightsdale *shul* is organized differently from other Leeds congregations, which reward wealthy, generous male members by calling them to the front to read from the Scriptures. The Knightsdale *shul* promotes a sense of equality and involvement among congregants. The leaders try to honor every man present, calling them up to read by their Jewish names. A particular attempt is made to make new worshipers feel welcome.

In addition, the Knightsdale *shul* holds a *kidesh* every Saturday morning after the service. The worshipers share a glass of wine and wish one another a "good Sabbath." The women on the *shul* committee prepare the tables and make the coffee. The tenants pledge the wine each Jewish New Year. Prayer books are donated in honor of a deceased husband or parent, and the biscuits are supplied by the individual who hosts the *kidesh* that week, usually to honor a deceased relative. A strong sense of involvement and commitment is thereby encouraged for both men and women.

Like the card games, Friendship Club, WIZO meetings, and Day Center activities, which are all held in the communal hall, *shul* services encourage the formation of new relationships and allow tenants to view one another in a variety of capacities. Even the physical layout of the Estate encourages residents to get to know each other better. Housing styles are varied on the Knightsdale Estate. In each section, people are grouped closely with neighbors, who walk to the communal hall for religious services and programs. Residents can see and talk to neighbors through their kitchen or living room windows, or they can easily go out to talk with someone passing by. By watching what is going on outside, residents can feel socially involved and understand each other's social routines. They can see how often people's children come to visit and how long they stay. Since many know these children personally, they often visit with them and their parents.

A system of social welfare is an integral part of the management of the Knightsdale Estate. Two social workers interview all applicants. They serve as referral agents, helping tenants apply for supplementary benefits or meals-on-wheels. Also available to handle emergencies, these social workers give the aged a feeling of security. Residents know that if they need help to remain independent and in their homes, somehow they will get what they need. Many tenants, for example, have a home-help who comes once a fortnight to help clean their flats. When necessary, she accompanies informants as they shop or fetch a pension check. The elderly can also rely on government transport to take them to a hospital appointment or physical therapy. Doctors make housecalls. With socialized medicine, people have no large bills for doctors' fees, medication, or eyeglasses. Some of the flats have a night watchman, whom the elderly can call by pressing a bell near the bed. A walking warden also visits physically frail tenants and those with few close kin. She is there to do errands and to fetch pension checks, groceries, or medicine if their home-help has not come or if they require extra assistance.

All these factors—socioeconomic and ethnic homogeneity, community and religious services, the community-forming functions of the *shul*, the physical plan, proximity to children and old friends, the feeling of security—work to encourage social relationships, participation, and high morale, and to combat isolation and loneliness.

Cornell is a different situation entirely. When informants first moved there, they lived with old friends and neighbors from previous neighborhoods. Cornell had a high percentage of Jewish people with similar backgrounds and socioeconomic positions. People socialized in the apartment houses and shops, and they knew one another's families and children. Younger neighbors helped with marketing and other errands. Neighbors and friends discussed common feelings about children, offered moral support and assistance in illness or tragedy, provided companionship, and exchanged services. It is this kind of companionship and exchange of services that sustain many elderly, making it possible for them to live independently of children and institutions. Similar types of reciprocal relationships must be encouraged and supported in any planning proposals.

In the early 1970s, conditions deteriorated for the elderly in Cornell.

Rents were raised, maintenance services were not provided, and the *shul* was sold. Many elderly Jews moved away. As had happened many times before in their lives, informants lost their companions. Contact among friends gradually became less frequent. But with the construction in 1975 of a federally subsidized high-rise for people of retirement age, the Jewish character of Cornell was renewed. Seventy-five percent of the occupants of this new structure are Jewish. Many moved to be near Jewish age-mates and to have a clean, new, affordable apartment.

Neighbors are establishing relationships, but many residents are still unable to define their roles because previous exchanges with kin and friends have not prepared them to do so. A "we-feeling" and sense of community have not emerged among the homogeneous residents of the Carroll Arms, and many remain uncertain, isolated, and unwilling to join organized activities. It is necessary to examine carefully those physical and sociological factors which appear to thwart the emergence of community in Cornell and thereby inhibit possible further role adjustment. Only then can we suggest positive planning alternatives.

In contrast to the Knightsdale Estate, the Cornell high-rise was built as an urban renewal project aimed at destroying a blighted area, rather than integrating the elderly into a developing community. Accessible shopping and transportation make the area a good choice for a residence for the elderly. However, the builders made no effort to devise a comprehensive physical and social service plan nor to provide or encourage the medical and religious facilities and services needed by a large aged population.

The physical environment, with its absence of medical facilities, makes day-to-day living more difficult for those who live in Cornell than those who live in Leeds. As discussed in Chapter 2, one of the most difficult tasks is getting to the doctor. Many physicians have moved to the prestigious medical buildings in the eastern suburbs. These centers are easily accessible only to those who drive. Cornell residents must take three different buses and a minimum of three hours just to get to a doctor's office. Some informants ask their children to drive them to an initial appointment, but for the follow-up visit they take a taxicab or put off going. Other residents also need assistance with shopping and cleaning and again feel guilty about troubling children. Thus Cornell informants lack the assuredness that Leeds elderly gain through a national health plan and the program of home-help.

In other important ways the Carroll Arms is not linked with the surrounding neighborhood. Unlike the Leeds communal hall, which serves as a meeting place for the Leeds Friendship Club and the Day Center—both of which bring other elderly to the Estate—the Cornell assembly room is reserved only for Carroll Arms events. When the building was first opened, the Jewish agencies asked to sponsor programs and a drop-in center for neighborhood elderly, but their requests were denied.

The Jewish Center remains the meeting place for many Cornell elderly and is where they spend their days. Because of its programming, the Center competes with the Arms. On Sunday afternoon, when both institutions sponsor special events, the rivalry is apparent. There is little cooperation between the Carroll Arms management and social service agencies to support needy tenants, or to help them remain in their apartments for as long as possible. Tenants who develop service needs as they age are instead expected to relocate to settings that provide the appropriate help. Thus the Carroll Arms lacks the integration of residence, programming, and social services that makes the Knightsdale Estate a community and creates an atmosphere where residents get to know one another in a variety of capacities.

Further, the Cornell high-rise was not built as part of a strongly integrated neighborhood but was constructed as an urban renewal project. The management discourages identification with the neighborhood, has avoided collaboration with neighborhood, religious, social service, and civic organizations, and has thwarted tenants' efforts to form committees and to participate in decision making and the management of the residence. Rather than developing a sense of community within the Carroll Arms, tenants continue their involvement in organizations outside the building and neighborhood. They volunteer their time and skills elsewhere. External sources of prestige are more important than status within the immediate neighborhood. A new status heirarchy and alternative reward system based on voluntary work within the Arms has not evolved, as it has in Leeds. Thus, Arms residents are denied another avenue for developing a sense of identity and self-worth.

Proposals for Change

On the basis of the comparative data of Leeds and Cornell, I have suggested that four factors assist the elderly in adjusting to an aged role. These contributors are: (1) the quality of early family relations; (2) a shared life-style of aged parents and adult children; (3) the presence of lifelong, intimate friends; and (4) the quality of the residential environment where the elderly settle in old age. Although it is not possible to assess the relative weight of these interrelated factors, it seems clear that the number of close friendships people are able to sustain throughout their lives does affect their adjustment to new roles in old age. Can social policy and physical planning affect this factor? By integrating residential housing, population composition, tenant-initiated social programming, and supportive services, can society encourage the formation of intimate friendships and the development of a sense of community? I believe so. The Leeds housing estate represents one example of a positive situation that evolved over time, while the Cornell case now calls for compensatory alternatives to better meet the needs of the present residents. From our knowledge of these two cases and of the natural support system that evolved in the pre-1970 Cornell neighborhood, we can suggest a number of proposals for fostering greater social interaction and involvement:

1. The Jewish community and other sectarian groups with large elderly constituencies should become strong advocates of continued federal funding for the construction of more housing for the elderly.[4] These structures should be built where the aged find it desirable to live—close to shopping, kosher butchers or ethnic food stores, restaurants, religious institutions, public transportation, and medical facilities. As one woman said, "It's wonderful to be in a neighborhood where there are doors to go in. You see a person. There are people and it's interesting." Such housing should give the aged an opportunity to remain in familiar areas as their needs change and help them develop longstanding friendships with neighbors. Scattered-site and high-rise structures should be constructed, and existing housing stock renovated to town-houses and shared-living residences, perhaps with provision of meals and other necessities. *What is important is that the elderly have a range of housing options.*

2. Since many elderly prefer to remain in their own apartments or homes, concerned groups should work to secure a program of supplements to help with rising housing costs and to assist with maintenance and repair costs. There should also be special grants and low-interest loans to enable the elderly to rehabilitate their homes and to increase housing efficiency for retirement living, even for people with disabilities. Many elderly people feel familiar, comfortable, and secure because they have contemporaries in their apartment buildings or on their blocks.

3. To keep the elderly from being isolated in new buildings or high-rise structures, there should be more creative use of surrounding housing, and social involvement should be encouraged. The programs and services of the central building should also be made available to *all* neighborhood

residents. In the Cornell neighborhood, for example, large apartments with two or more bedrooms are often occupied by single persons. Perhaps they originally moved in with parents or siblings who have since died, but now with more room available they may be eager to share their suites. Religious groups could become rental agents, sponsoring "mixers" and encouraging people of similar interests to meet and match their housing needs, or they might hire student volunteers to paint and repair apartments in elevator buildings and then coordinate the renting of such suites to elderly (or mixed-age) tenants. Social Security checks could be pooled to pay for the rent, and social workers could handle problems of interpersonal relations. Such group or cooperative arrangements would encourage surrogate family ties and an exchange of services and, by increasing selective health care and housekeeping services, could possibly enable a group of frail elderly to remain together longer before requiring institutional care. Another possibility is to subdivide these large apartments into a number of smaller units.

For example, in Glasgow, Scotland, the Jewish Welfare Board purchased suites in apartment buildings in Jewish areas. These were refurbished and rented to elderly persons at subsidized rents, thus enabling tenants to remain in a familiar Jewish neighborhood close to friends, neighbors, and accessible services. The Glasgow flats are not all in one building: They are located throughout the area to encourage the occupants to mix with other neighbors. The Glasgow plan permits the use of existing structures, which are refurbished to house the elderly, and also encourages older residents to mix with younger neighbors, who are potentially available to provide services, to shop, and to pay an occasional friendly visit.

4. Such measures aimed at maintaining the stability of a neighborhood would, one hopes, encourage developers to rehabilitate other buildings or to construct new units to fit a range of economic and age levels. They might, for example, refurbish two-family homes or remodel apartment buildings into condominiums suitable for people without children, or for couples whose families are grown. Having made a financial investment in these properties, new owners would be committed to and involved in maintaining property values in the neighborhood. In the past years, a number of apartment buildings in the Cornell area have been made into condominiums. However, because of the lack of a unified program on the part of the Jewish community, elderly tenants have been forced out. The aged are isolated in the Carroll Arms. Had the Jewish community pur-

chased one or two suites in each condominium or encouraged legislation permitting elderly tenants to remain for one year, tenants might have been able to locate alternative housing in the area, thereby reducing displacement and relocation traumas.

5. Active involvement by concerned groups, such as the Jewish Federation, in maintaining neighborhoods suitable for the elderly should also include the development of a comprehensive program of social welfare services and preventive health care aimed at keeping people independent for as long as possible. An assessment team composed of a social worker trained in gerontology and a nurse with public health experience should be available to evaluate the social and health status of the elderly from a holistic base, determine their needs, and work out a service plan where necessary. This team should be experienced in working with older persons and be knowledgeable in community resources so that it could be an advocate for and access appropriate services. By having a case load in the area, the team would get to know the residents and their friends, neighbors, and kin and be able to detect unmet needs and develop suitable programs. As trust and confidence in the team grew, so would the older persons' sense of security. Residents would know that people were available to discuss economic, health, or personal problems and to help them gain access to community resources.

Home-health aides and homemakers should also be available to furnish necessary assistance during periods of serious illness or following discharge from hospital care. Similar ongoing services may also be needed as frailty and level of impairment increase, so that those elderly who desire aid and for whom it is reasonable, can remain in their own homes. An activity director might also be part of the assessment team to discuss which residents need further encouragement to become involved in activities. Transportation should be available to take residents to medical appointments (or a health-care team could visit the neighborhood weekly) and to visit old friends in other areas of the city. During the winter months, outreach workers or volunteers could assist with food shopping, although ideally younger neighbors would help with shopping and transportation.

With the shrinkage of government social service delivery funds, these programs may be difficult to realize. But trained volunteers in church and sectarian groups may choose to offer these services under the direction of a professional, as in Leeds.

6. Active involvement in the interests of neighborhood elderly also

provides a significant opportunity for local churches or synagogues to assume an innovative role, such as that played by the Knightsdale *shul* in Leeds. Rich in religious resources and close to aging populations, the Leeds synagogue is a convenient meeting place for the aged and a center where a sense of religious involvement and community are fostered and nourished. When the local Cornell *shul* was sold, many residents felt abandoned. "The center had fallen out of our lives," said one. Had the Federation and the synagogue combined funds, they could have bought the *shul* for a relatively small sum.

With the limited resources available to religious groups today, it is unrealistic to expect one synagogue or church to sponsor such a program or to expect a neighborhood of elderly people on Social Security to support a congregation. With assistance from the Jewish Federation, however, the *shul* could be maintained and staffed by a retired rabbi, a lay person overseen by the Federation chaplaincy service, or even by the learned members of the community themselves, as is the case in Leeds. At little cost, neighborhood residents could conduct weekly services and initiate and coordinate social activities. By integrating religious programs, social action, and social activities, the *shul* or church could encourage the elderly to overcome their isolation and to develop friendships, surrogate family ties, and a sense of service and community involvement. Active participation in a religious group that is present and involved can change a neighborhood into a community.

Today, various Jewish agencies are attempting to fill the religious and social vacuum in the Cornell area by providing social outreach programs, cultural programs, and High Holiday religious services. For example, for the past few years the Jewish Community Federation of Cleveland, through its Heights Area Project, has sponsored Rosh Hashana and Yom Kippur services for the Cornell elderly who cannot ride on holidays. Last year, the Federation hosted a communal *seyder* in which seventy-four local residents participated. If the synagogue were still in Cornell, these activities would have been held there instead of at the branch library or in the recreation room of the new high-rise building. If a *shul* were in the area, perhaps residents would take more initiative in making their own arrangements for High Holiday services and for the Passover *seyder*. A heightened sense of involvement and self-esteem would result, with less dependence on social welfare persons. (With the next generation of well-educated, physically healthy, American-born elderly, religious institutions may no longer provide the symbolic focus of the community.

A group of men reading from the Scriptures during High Holiday services, sponsored by the Cleveland Jewish Community Federation, at the
Carroll Arms.

Educational/arts institutions and achievements in these areas should be
examined as possibly furnishing parallel functions, with clusters of the
elderly living on or near college campuses. Ideally, such situations should
encourage exchanges among equals.)

Two Programs at Work

There are two programs, both recently initiated by the Department of
Aging, City of Cleveland, which support and use planning principles
similar to those I am advocating. These projects merit brief description to
illustrate how my suggestions have practical and replicable application in
varied settings.

Project GOh (The Golden Age Outreach for Health) is a self-help,
neighbor-to-neighbor network providing basic social services and preventive health care to older residents in the Fairfax community of Cleveland.
This neighborhood is a 76-block urban inner-city area of 18,000 residents;
98 percent are black and 45 percent of the families live below poverty
level. Many Fairfax residents are over sixty years of age and have owned
and carefully maintained their own homes for 35 to 45 years.

The GOh program seeks to maximize family and neighborhood involvement in the social and health care of the Fairfax elderly. Elderly and middle-aged community residents from organized street clubs are trained to provide simple social and health assessment and care to all older neighbors. Every ten days, each elderly person is visited in his or her home by the street health worker, who administers basic health evaluation tests. If there is a change in condition, a nurse sees that person the same day; and if necessary, a doctor also makes a house call. In addition, a volunteer network of family, friends, neighbors, street club, and local church members also helps the street health worker network to deliver concrete services. Necessary assistance is given with shopping, check-cashing, lawn-mowing, transportation, etc. GOh thus builds on existing informal support systems rather than developing new ones.

GOh's professional core staff includes two geriatric outreach workers, a public health nurse, a part-time social worker, a part-time physician, and a director. The project aims at overcoming the loneliness, fear, forgetfulness, and depression that are often rampant in poor, elderly neighborhoods. A cost-effective program, it also seeks to combat minor health problems and thus to lead to less frequent and more appropriate admissions to hospitals and nursing homes. Project GOh is being examined as a national model for community self-help, combining a health-care and social service package. It nicely complements and underscores the planning proposals that emerge from my cross-national field research.

A second project, also under the auspices of Project GOh, aims at maintaining the stability of older neighborhoods in a way that again parallels and extends my proposals as outlined in suggestion 4. Project Swap proposes a "housing swap" between elderly homeowners and younger families in the Fairfax area. The goal is to increase the supply and range of options for desirable living arrangements for both the elderly and young families, while eliminating the need to leave the area.

Street health workers report that many older people want to be relieved of the demands of the large houses in which they raised their families. Loss of health and income increasingly erode the ability of the aged to maintain and live comfortably in their houses. Yet if they seek to dispose of their property, they have no satisfactory alternative living arrangements that would allow them to remain in their own neighborhood. Many apartments are overcrowded by young families who eventually move out of the neighborhood due to lack of adequate available housing. This transiency undermines the quality of the housing stock, lessens stability of such institutions as the schools, and hurts the commercial viability of small neighborhood businesses. If young families had access to the larger houses in the neighborhood, at an affordable rent, neighborhood stability would be enhanced.

Project Swap proposes to relieve the shortage by converting appropriate units within familiar residential neighborhoods. It will purchase and convert a variety of dwellings in the neighborhood into a range of alternative housing arrangements for families whose children are grown. Residents will be free to dispose of their larger homes for use by families with small children and thereby convert ownership into a more liquid asset. The project would provide access to maintenance services, link the elderly residents to the neighborhood's unique GOh program, assign transportation service to the seniors' residences, and counsel younger families to be supportive of the previous owners. The proposed project will render large residences economically feasible for families; apartment and group living financially advantageous to the elderly currently owning the houses; a range of housing options available for middle-aged and older people without children; and the "swap" convenient to all by eliminating the need to leave their neighborhood.

The Theory Behind the Proposals

In the proposals I have advanced, my concern is with all elderly groups. I am not advocating age-segregated neighborhoods, but the maintenance of older communities where the elderly are familiar with the environment and the people. Stable neighborhoods with some new dwelling units and a more creative use of existing housing stock, suitable for both elderly people and younger couples, would allow people to develop long-term, intimate friendships. Such relations would help the elderly define their position and negotiate realistic role relationships with their children. It is essential that the aged live near not only their contemporaries but people in their fifties and sixties—people who still drive cars and are able and free to shop for a sick neighbor or to come in for a visit.

Thus all my proposals for the elderly should also be aimed at keeping and/or bringing people in their fifties and sixties into the neighborhood and involving them in community and religious activities. The presence of the young elderly, who could remain in the area as their own housing needs change, would give stability to the neighborhood, provide them with the opportunity to forge social relationships and neighborhood contacts so crucial in their own later years, and furnish an available resource to aged neighbors in time of need.

I have a second set of proposals as well. They involve (1) the physical layout, to encourage opportunities for interaction; and (2) the sociological design, to permit leaders to emerge, to allow internal status differentiation to occur, and to encourage participation in community-wide events by residents. Here I believe that concerned community groups should also take the initiative to build housing for the elderly in prestigious suburbs, close to children, more well-to-do friends, and medical facilities. In Leeds, such housing supports intergenerational ties by enabling parents and children to live near one another and informants to visit old friends. Again, parents who choose to live near their children should be urged to move to these areas when they are in their fifties and early sixties and can become actively involved in community events. The physical layouts of these residences should aim at giving tenants maximum access to, and visibility of, one another. Perhaps a balcony could surround the whole building, enabling people to visit easily and observe the local scene. There should also be garden chairs so people could sit together in the summer. Activities in these buildings and in the community centers, churches, and synagogues should occasionally include children and grandchildren, so residents could get to know other people's families. At present, almost all social programming is age-graded; it discourages, rather than develops, close parent-child relationships in a new social context. It does not permit people to gather "backstage" information.

A social service team made up of a social worker, an activities director, homemakers, and home-health aides should also be assigned to the immediate area. Transportation facilities must be available. Tenants should be encouraged to set up their own tenants' association, and there should be many organized activities where they get to know one another in a variety of capacities. Careful attention must be given to the choice of a building manager. An effort must be made to find an individual who encourages initiative and self-respect through group participation in decision making. Unfortunately, many tenants feel that the present manager of the Carroll Arms in Cornell thwarts efforts at tenant self-initiative by creating an atmosphere of fear, ridicule, and intimidation, which is shown by my field notes on one of his public speeches:

"Mr. Weinberg (the manager) said it was rumored that he did not like people sitting together in the lobby. He asked the people present how many thought Carroll Arms was an 'old home' (no one raised her hand), and how many wanted to live in an old home (again, no response). He then asked the people to picture the lobby of an old home with everyone sitting in a straight line talking to one another, or to themselves. He said he did not want the Carroll Arms to look this way. Mr. Weinberg announced that he had ordered $6,500 worth of new furniture—that it was there to make a good impression, and to sit on only when people were waiting to be picked up, and not all day long. 'If I had wanted people to sit in the lobby, I did not need this new furniture. I could have ordered benches, or, better yet, rockers for everyone.'"

In such statements, the manager emphasized the negative image of the elderly as sedentary and unproductive. The frightening comparison of the Carroll Arms to a home for the aged reinforced the elderly's fear that they are not wanted. After this talk, Mrs. Eisner said she believed that Mr. Weinberg did not like old people and was afraid of getting old himself. He liked to intimidate people, she said, and many accept it, because he has "clout." The manager has thwarted efforts to initiate a tenants' union, and the tenants have no intermediary body that can negotiate complaints or problems. There are few channels to build status, self-esteem, and an interdependent community. "People are really frightened of what will happen to them. People are scared of the idea that what they do or say will jeopardize their position as tenants in the Carroll Arms."

Thus, in the Carroll Arms in Cornell, an already insecure and uncertain group of elderly people are kept in a frightened and dependent position by what they perceive as a paternalistic management system. Because this residence for the poor and the aged encourages neither self-respect nor self-reliance, it makes adjustment to their increasing years more difficult.

Community has been defined as a possession of a common territory, "we-feeling," and a social organization unique to a body of individuals (Ross, 1977). In Leeds, such a community developed, while in Cornell it failed to evolve. In Leeds, the different skills and capabilities of the residents were encouraged, and role differentiation, interdependence, and a strong sense of self-identity have emerged among the tenants. Leeds informants, who had already begun a successful adjustment to old age, moved to the Knightsdale Estate, and the Estate and the development of a successful community further encouraged this process. In Cleveland, informants had had difficulty adjusting to their increasing years, and residence at the Carroll Arms hindered a possible better adjustment.

Appendix A
Aide-Mémoire *and Case History Schema*

BASIC DATA

Name
Address, including apartment number
Marital status and number of living children
Age

OBSERVATIONS

The following are used only as (1) a general guide when interviewing to direct discussion and conversation and (2) a means of checking the completeness of the data when I write up an interview.

A. Date and amount of time spent with each informant for either a formal interview, social visit, or shared activity.

B. Attitude of informant—cooperation and interaction, or visit considered an intrusion.

C. Physical description of the informant and other members of the household—clothing, appearance, ailments, disposition.

D. Description of the home—photographs displayed, heirlooms, memorabilia, TV set, repair of furniture, condition of home. (If meeting not held at informant's home, why not? Where was interview held?)

NEIGHBORHOOD INFORMATION

(Note how people introduce themselves to me and to one another—what they choose to emphasize.)

1. How long have you lived in this neighborhood?

2. Where did you live before? How long? Type of residence? Why did you move?

3. Where did you live before that? How long? Why did you move?

4. Where did you spend the major portion of your adult life?

5. Why did you choose to move specifically to the Cornell (Knightsdale) area? (For friends, relatives, Jewish neighborhood, apartment available, inexpensive rent, convenience, transportation, shopping?)

6. Has the neighborhood changed since you moved in? How? Describe your feelings.

7. Do you notice any strain or tension between the groups who live in Cornell, or do they get along? Hippies? Blacks? Elderly? Young people with families? Unmarried couples?

8. (If negative feelings.) Why do you remain here? (For bus transportation, convenience of stores, illness, lack of money to move, no energy, cheap rent, no one to help you move, attachment to neighborhood, responsibility for a neighbor, good friends?)

9. What is it like to live in a neighborhood that is really not the one you would choose, or that has a negative image? (Do you think Cornell still has a bad reputation?) How do you cope? Or do you have positive feelings? Do you tell people where you're from?

10. (If informant lives in an apartment.) Did you ever consider moving to the Carroll Arms, or to another project outside this neighborhood? (What complaints—rooms too small, kitchen too small, do not like the electric stove, can't use the elevator, too old, furniture isn't nice, rather move to a better neighborhood, household composition?)

(Knightsdale alternate.) (1) Would you like to live in a Council flat? (2) Where do you shop—greengrocer or dairy? (3) Do you have a *personal* relationship with the shopkeeper? Can you buy on credit, for example?

11. (If informant lives in the Carroll Arms.) Why did you move in here? Why did you choose to stay in the same neighborhood? Who helped you fill out the application? Who helped you move in? Who bought your furniture, hung the drapes? Who taught you to use the stove, elevator, washers?

12. Since you moved into the neighborhood, or the Carroll Arms, have you lost contact or decreased intimacy with any friends or neighbors from before? Tell me about them.

13. Have you made any new friends here, or met people whom you used to know a long time ago? Tell me about them.

14. Number of people who live in your household? Relationship? Age? Occupation? How long have you lived together?

15. Amount of rent—has it increased? Will you be able to stay? Get opinions on general repair of apartment, building exterior, halls, heat, laundry room, safety, noise, traffic, dogs, motorcycles, neighborhood upkeep.

16. If you share an apartment with someone, is it out of choice or necessity? For companionship, comfort, safety, financial necessity? Are there conflicts, annoyances, antagonisms, things you learn to live with and accept? What are the advantages?

17. If you live with someone, do you cook for both? Cook separately? Divide and share expenses? Shop separately? Keep separate kitchens but eat a meal together?

18. Possible changes in neighborhood and feelings and reactions: What do you think about the possibility that the library will be closed? That the Pick-n-Pay store may move? That more apartment buildings may be torn down to build parking lots? That there is no *shul?* No movie? (Push for political consciousness and possible social action—do you attend meetings, write letters, call mayor, talk to friends? If informant does not take action, try to find out why not.) (Adapt for Leeds.)

19. If you had your choice, where would you like to live? (Nearer children, more well-to-do neighborhood, one with a better reputation, a "more Jewish" area, one with Jewish stores or a *shul*, nearer friends?)

20. When you go out, do you see people you recognize? Is this one reason why you might feel comfortable in this neighborhood? Is this a friendly neighborhood? Would you say it has a sense of "community"—that people know and care about one another, have lived together a long time, share things, see and talk to one another, gossip about one another?

21. What streets are included in the Cornell area? What would you say the boundaries are? Do you know people on all these streets?

22. Do you go to Saul's regularly? The Beverage Shop? Dan's? Whom do you look for? Whom do you meet there? Do you have a regular crowd? Do you go there often? Do you go there with someone? (Adapt for Leeds.)

23. Do you feel more free here than in other neighborhoods, like Shaker Heights, where you have to dress up and have your hair done to go out?

24. What TV programs do you watch? Any daytime programs? Why do you enjoy them? What newspapers and magazines do you read? Do you subscribe to them, or get them from a friend, or read them at the library?

NEIGHBORS

(Always try to compare the Carroll Arms with former building situations. Adapt for Leeds.)

25. Do you have friends and neighbors in this building? In the area?

26. What is the difference between a neighbor and a friend? (Probe.)

27. Who are your neighbors? Where do they live? Age? Sex? Number and residence of their children? Do you know all of the people in your building? Age? Occupation? Religion? Marital status, etc.

28. How did you meet your neighbors? How often do you see each other? Where? Why, of all the people who live around you, did you choose to be friendly with these people over the others? What do you like or not like about them? Do you depend on them and need them in any way? Do they depend upon and need you? Do you turn to each other in times of crisis?

29. Do you ever feel afraid or unsafe?

30. Do you have any neighbors who do not live in your building (or on your floor, or hall)? Do you have any neighbors in buildings down the block, across the street, or on other streets close by? (Try to get a sense of the physical and geographic limitations and boundaries of the concept of a neighbor.)

31. Is there anyone who drops in daily, or makes sure you are OK? Anyone whom you watch out for? Is there anyone whom you watch TV with? Shop for or with? Keep apartment keys for? Share newspapers with? Eat a meal with? Sit and talk together? Bring in something if you bake or make soup—or who brings it in to you? Anyone whom you can borrow an egg or flour from? Whom you help in illness, or who helped you? Whom you can borrow money from? Who will dial the telephone for you or read the mail? Who will pick up a kosher chicken? Whom you go to *shul* with? Whom you go to visit when you're feeling blue, or go for a walk with? Anyone who calls when he or she sees your lights on after you've been away? (Be sure to get the *reciprocal* dimensions of these exchanges.)

32. *Should* a neighbor do for you, or *should* you do for a neighbor? Get what a "good neighbor" should do—norms, expectations:

transportation	shop, get pension
housework—help cook	advise
emergency help (not financial)	help when husband ill, or recently died
money	go to doctor with
talk to when blue	cut hair or nails, etc.
check daily to see if OK	

Do your neighbors do any of these things? Or you for them? (Keep probing for the reciprocal nature of exchanges between neighbors.) Do you visit with neighbors? Do you get a chance to meet new neighbors?

33. Did you ever have a neighbor who became a friend—someone who was a neighbor first and then became a friend?

34. As you get older, do you rely on neighbors more, and children or friends less?

35. Do you ever ask a neighbor to do something or to get you something, so as not to bother a child?

36. Have you any former neighbor with whom you are no longer friendly? What was the cause of the breakup? (Push for boundaries and a statement of what a neighbor should be and what the transgression was.) Is there anyone who seems not to want to be close to you, who avoids you?

37. Is there anyone in the neighborhood who is not really a friend, but whom you have looked out for and helped?

38. Are there things you sometimes tell a neighbor that you don't tell friends or family?

39. Do your neighbors ever influence your behavior or change the way you think about a problem?

40. Has anyone in your family, or your friends, influenced your relationship with a neighbor? Has anyone encouraged or discouraged a relationship?

41. Is there anyone who made a pest of himself, or made too great emotional demands? Anyone who never shared, kept everything to himself, complained too much?

FRIENDSHIP (Adapt for Leeds.)

42. Years ago, when you first moved into the Cornell area, did you have more friends here than you do now? What happened to them? If they moved away, have you kept in touch with one another?

43. Are some of your present friends people you knew or recognized from having lived together in the old neighborhood?

44. What is a friend? (What, in contrast, is an acquaintance?)

45. Ask about each friend individually: Who are your friends, their names?

Age	Residence
Religion	Health
Marital status	Drive a car—or do their children
Number of children	take them and their friends places?

Where did you meet? How long have you known each other? What do you admire or like about this person? Criteria of selection? How often do you get together? Where? Would you like to see more of them? Do you talk on the phone? How often? Who calls whom? Have the relationships changed through the years?

Criteria used in judgment: Why are these people your friends? What do you like or not like about them? Do you depend on and need them in any way, or do they depend on you? Do they ever do anything to help you, or do you help them?

46. Do you have any new friends? Where did you meet? What do you like about them?

47. Have any arguments or fights with friends either strained or broken your relationships? Is there anyone with whom you used to be friends, but no longer are?

48. Friendship—ideal vs. actual (norms, expectations).

What *should* a friend do? What do your friends actually do for you, and what do you do for them? (Consider each friend individually.)

transportation	watch out for
housework—help cook	help when husband ill
go downtown together	go to doctor with—to hospital
emergency help (not financial)	cut hair, nails, etc.
money	check in daily to see you're all right
call when blue	invite you to family *simkhe*
shop	talk over problems with kids
advice	talk over problem with—hard times, a hurt, someone not nice

(Keep probing the reciprocal nature of friendship—the give and take—what do you do for friends in return for what they do for you? Do you ever get annoyed or feel "used"?)

49. Do you have a sense of obligation and responsibility to your friends? What enforces this feeling?

50. Do you rely on friends more as you get older? Do you see them instead of children or relatives? Are they more important—why?

51. Are friends ever substitutes for family? (To go out to a restaurant with, to spend Saturdays or holidays with—Thanksgiving? Passover? To call on for help and support in time of emergency or illness?)

52. Do you sometimes hesitate to call on family and so rely on friends and neighbors? If so, when and for what kinds of things—shopping, small errands?

53. Do you talk about common family problems with friends? Do you help and support one another? Do your friends ever influence your behavior or change the way you think about a problem?

54. Do any of your friends know one another? (Network? Star configuration?)

55. Is there anyone whom you help, or you helped in the past, who is not really your friend but who relies on you?

56. (If informant is single, divorced, or widowed.) Are you seeing anyone? Did you in the past? Anyone who wanted to marry you? Was this person a friend? Do you go out with friends to theater, cinema, for tea?

57. Did you have more friends when you lived in the old neighborhood? Have you kept up with any of them?

58. Do you think if your friends moved away tomorrow that they would still be your friends?

59. Has anyone in your family, or a neighbor, influenced your relationship with a friend? Or has a friend influenced your relationship with another friend?

KINSHIP AND LIFE HISTORY

60. Take a *complete* genealogy of *all* relations—both consanguineal and affinal.
Name
Sibling order plus ages, or dates of birth and death

Occupation
Residence
Information on contact—reasons for contact or noncontact, frequency of and type
    of contact (letters, phone, visit, when, where, who pays, etc.), attitudes, depth
    of relationships, etc.
Religion
Spouse and spouse's family and relatives (relations with spouse, contact, feelings
    toward, etc.).
Who among these individuals is considered "family"?

PERSONAL BACKGROUND

61. Where were you born? Farm? Village? *Shtetl*? Town? City? Country or
province where raised? Year born?
62. Education—years of school completed. What languages do you speak, read,
write?
63. When did you come to America? (Britain?) With whom? Who was here to
meet you? Who gave you a place to stay? From whose home were you married?
64. Parents and grandparents—age at death, where living, occupation?
65. Relations with your parents and grandparents, also aunts and uncles. How
did they influence your life? Has their influence affected how you deal with your
own children? Did you used to meet at your mother's house? How did you feel
about your parents, grandparents, aunts, and uncles when they grew old—
admiration, respect, that they lived too long, that they imposed on your life?
66. Did either of your parents live with you, or a sibling, after you were
married? Tell me about it. (If unmarried, did you live with your parents, or they
with you, until they died?)

SIBLINGS

(Review names of brothers and sisters, their ages, residences, spouses, children,
and grandchildren.)
68. How *should* one act toward a brother or a sister? What responsibilities or
obligations are owed them when they are over 60? And what do they owe you?

care during illness	transportation
money	housework
advice	emotional or moral support
gifts	"staying close"
emergency help	visits

(Be sure to get the reciprocal dimension of each exchange. Also, for each of these
ideals, ask if the ideal matches the relationship with the sibling; if not, why not?
Also check on each of these responsibilities for nieces and nephews.)
69. Do your sisters or brothers ever annoy or anger you? Are there any problems with wills, estates, or treasured heirlooms? Different "side of town"?
70. Do you feel a sense of obligation toward your brothers and sisters? Is seeing
them a duty and a responsibility? (If so, what makes you feel that way? What
makes you see them?) Or is it a source of joy and satisfaction?

71. As you grow older, do you notice a change in your relationship with your sisters and brothers? Is your relationship with your sisters and brothers becoming more important as you grow older? Is this relationship increasing in comparison to your relationship with your children? How, if at all, is it changing?

72. Describe your relations with family members. Are they, for example, a source of strain, tension, and friction? Or of security and moral support? (If strain, do friends compensate for this problem? How, then, do friends differ from relatives?)

73. How do friends differ from relatives?

74. Are any of your relatives also friends? If so, who?

MARITAL HISTORY

(Review marriage information—who married, when, where, how did you meet, how long married, when did spouse die, was there a divorce or more than one marriage?)

75. How long have you been widowed?

76. Funeral—who came to visit you? Who helped with arrangements?

77. Economic position—what was your spouse's occupation? Were you poor, or well-off?

78. Did you ever work? Doing what?

79. Did you ever consider remarriage? Why or why not?

CHILDREN

(Review data on children—age, sex, residence, how long it takes to get to their homes, religion of child's spouse and relationships with, religious congregation children belong to. Also review data on grandchildren—age, sex, residence, religion, occupation, amount of contact, and spouse of grandchild and spouse's family and religion. Great-grandchildren—names, ages, residence, contact. What are the names you call all these people? What names do they call you?)

80. Ideology and actual practice—*should* a child provide for a parent, or a parent for a child? (On each item, also ask if the ideal corresponds with the real or actual, and how.) Get reciprocal exchanges; get qualitative data—norms and expectations.

housing
help in illness
money? food? clothes? gifts?
advice
shopping? cooking? housecleaning?
decorating
emergency help

go to the doctor with
transportation
visit at home—yours or theirs
closeness
emotional support
someone to call when you're blue, etc.

81. Did you, or your spouse, give a child money, or a loan, for a home, business, etc? *Should* a parent do these things?

82. Can you drop in on your kids, or do you call them first? Do they just drop in on you, or call? How do you feel about this?

83. Has there been any change in your role as mother as your children have grown and have had their own children, and as you have become a grandmother or

great-grandmother? (Get informant to discuss changes in role over life span, e.g., when family used to come for Friday night, *seyder*, etc., and when she stopped cooking for the family. Changes in role as children seek her advice and counsel less, or consult her about fewer matters.) Difference in role as mother, grandmother, and great-grandmother. Different attitudes and relationships. Activities for children, daughters during confinement, baby sitting. (Observe dimensions of intergenerational relations carefully; try to meet children and grandchildren of informants.)

84. Do you feel closer to your daughter(s) than to your son(s)?

85. If your children *really* wanted you, would you go and live with them? If you were very sick and needed care? Short-term care? Long-term care? What other solution might you prefer—in-home nurses? Old-age home? Convalescent home? Hospital?

86. Why do people who are over sixty seem not to prepare or make plans for the future, such as for illness? Do you think about such things? How, for example, do you feel about old age homes: Montefiore Home? Menorah Park? (Adapt for Leeds.)

87. Do you ever talk over your feelings of disappointment with your kids, or try to get them to meet your expectations in other ways? Do they ever talk over what they want or expect from you?

88. Who makes decisions in your family, gets and keeps people together? Entertains family groups? Sees that cemetery plots are cared for? Makes decisions? Whose opinions are important? (Try to get a sense of the elderly woman as a matriarch.)

89. Whom do you talk to to find out what's going on in the family—the children, grandchildren, great-grandchildren?

90. Have any of your friends or neighbors ever influenced your relations with your family? How or how not? Has a family member influenced your behavior with another family member?

COUSINS

(Review data on cousins, and if there are cousins with whom close contact is maintained, ask questions about a reciprocal exchange of services.)

housing   go to doctor with
help in illness   transportation
money? food? clothes?   visits
advice   moral support
shop? cook? houseclean?   to call when blue
emergency help

EXTRA-COMMUNITY RESOURCES

Health

91. Get a history of illnesses and hospitalizations.

92. Whom did you first call for help when you were ill, or fell? Whom would you call now?

93. Who visited you in the hospital or sent cards or called?

94. Where did you convalesce each time? Would you go to any of these places again?

95. If you were taken ill for two weeks, whom would you call on to take care of you? What have you done in the past?

96. If you became too ill to care for yourself, what would you do? (Move in with children, siblings, nieces, or nephews? Try to get in-home help? Go to a home?) Does your doctor live far away? Does he ever visit you?

97. Discuss relationships with doctors—physicians whom they see regularly and whom they rely on for moral support, advice, or friendship.

Income (Adapt for Leeds)

98. Pensions? Social Security (supplemental income; assistance from Board)? Money in the bank? In a joint account? Aid for the aged? Supplemental Social Security? Cash from other sources—rent from a boarder, securities, credit cards? Inheritance?

99. Whom will you leave your things to when you pass away? Do you have a will? Will you leave more to some than to others? Why? (Press to find out if allocations will be equal or not, and reasons behind decision.)

100. Did you ever consider applying for food stamps? If not, why not? How do you feel about food stamps and Social Security?

101. How do you feel about meals-on-wheels?

102. Do you have difficulty meeting expenses—food, rent, clothing? Do you have any serious health problems that are not being taken care of because of financial problems? Do you see a specialist?

103. Do you receive help from children or relatives (small gifts, clothing, cash, etc.)?

Relationship with Social Service Agencies

104. *Cleveland*	*Leeds*
	Day Center
Welfare visitor	Lunch program
Shopper	Heating bills
Meals-on-wheels	Board trips
Homemaker or home-help	Ladies Aid parcels, Passover package
Social worker	Old clothes, furniture, household
	goods, blankets

Are these services satisfactory? Could you benefit from other family services?

105. Help from the Jewish Society for the Blind? Vouchers for taxis? Clinic for drugs, doctors, equipment?

106. Where did you find out about these services? How did you come to apply? Did anyone help or encourage you? Do your children know? Did you tell them? What were their reactions? Do your friends know? How do you feel about receiving these services?

107. Do you belong to or attend any clubs, sisterhoods, hobby groups? Other clubs and organizations—Hadassah, Chabad, senior citizens groups, JC Friendship Club, (Ladies Guild, WIZO, Friendly Society, Pioneer Women, etc.)? Why

do you go to meetings? What do you particularly like or enjoy about these groups? Whom do you meet and see there? Do any members of your family or relatives belong? Have you made any new friends there? How often do you go? Is there any status or prestige value in belonging? How much are dues? Membership fees? Charges for special affairs? Can you always afford to go? Are these groups expensive to belong to?

108. Do you try to attend local lectures, events, meetings? Whom do you usually go with? What groups or topics particularly interest you?

109. Are you a member of the JC (Friendship Club)? If not, why not? Did you ever belong in the past? (Dues too high, time, transportation, not comfortable with the type of people who go there, not your type of people. Do you think single, unmarried people are less welcome?) What do you enjoy about the JC? Why do you continue to go? Friends you see and meet there? Anyone else in your family also a member? Membership fees and charge for special events and activities?

110. Do you ever go to the Nutrition Program (Lunch Program) at the JC (Day Center)? (Food, sociability, a way to pass the time?) Whom do you go there with, whom do you sit with? Fee? How often do you go?

111. Do you attend Conversations with Lill (Mr. Segal's discussion) at the JC (Day Center)? Why do you enjoy it? What activities, if any, do you attend at the Day Center?

112. Did you attend the Jewish Family Service lunches at the Cornell Library? Did you enjoy them? Do you feel you need a neighborhood drop-in center where people can stop in for coffee and meet friends and neighbors? (Adapt for Leeds.)

113. Do you belong to a synagogue or *shul*? Which one? Dues? How often do you attend? Whom do you go with? How do you get there? Does your family also belong? Did you belong in the past? To which congregation? Did you used to go to the old Cornell *shul*, or to Rabbi Stein in the neighborhood? Where do you go now for High Holy Day services? Whom do you go there with, or walk with? Whom do you meet there? Who makes the arrangements for seats? Do you attend services with your children or other family members? Does the fact that your children live far away, or do not belong to an Orthodox *shul*, make it difficult or impossible for you to spend holidays with them? Would you rather attend with friends in your own area, with people more like yourself? Do you belong to a burial society?

114. What do you do for Passover? Where do you go for *seyder?*

115. Sabbath observances? Keep kosher? Light candles? Go to services? Not light fire, carry money, or ride? Not cook or use electricity? Whom do you visit with on the Sabbath? How do you spend the day? Whom do you eat the Sabbath meal with? In the past? Go to *shul?*

116. Do you vote? Interested in politics, news events, Israel, current events?

117. What would you say were the major time divisions marking the major events of your life? How would you divide your life into significant times, turning points, major time periods?

118. Where were some of the happiest and best times of your life?

119. What were some of the hardest or unhappiest times?

120. What kind of life have you had generally? How did you think your life was going to turn out—did it work out the way you thought it would—why or why not?

QUESTIONS TO DISCUSS BROADLY WITH PEOPLE WHO NEVER MARRIED

121. Did you work to support yourself? Type of work? Did you enjoy it? When did you retire? Was your work important to you?

122. As the oldest (youngest) child, did you feel a responsibility for caring for your parents, supporting them, giving them a home? When did your father, mother pass away? Siblings die? Discuss these events.

123. If you were to become ill suddenly, whom would you call on for help? To help you if you were sick for two weeks? If you needed more extended care? If you needed money? Help with shopping or housework? If you felt blue and depressed? To prepare food for you? To take you to the doctor? Can you call on a brother or sister? A niece or nephew? Why or why not? How do you feel about asking a sibling or niece or nephew for help? *Should* a brother or sister, or a nephew or niece help you, or *should* you help them if they need you? How does the ideal fit the reality? Also ask about: housing, advice, transportation, visiting, moral support, call when blue, etc.

124. Do you look out for your nieces or nephews in any way? Are you closer to some nieces and nephews than others? Why—more close with the parent, same sex? Are there some nieces or nephews whom you visit often, give gifts to, call, write, feel close to?

125. Can you count on your brothers or sisters for help, or your nephews or nieces? Would you ever consider going to live with them? If they *really* wanted you?

126. Do you ever discuss these feelings or problems with anyone?

127. Do you ever think of family members—such as nieces or nephews—as being like your own children, or a substitute for them? What about great-nieces being like grandchildren?

128. How do you feel about not being married? Are men who never married treated differently from unmarried women? If you had it to live over, would you make the same decision? Are there advantages or disadvantages to not being married? Some women today are consciously deciding not to marry and to devote themselves to their life's work. What do you think of their decisions?

QUESTIONS FOR PEOPLE WITHOUT CHILDREN

129. If you were to become ill suddenly, whom would you call on for help? For help if you were sick for two weeks? If you needed more extended care? If you needed money? Help with shopping, cooking, or housework? If you felt blue and depressed, lonely or needed advice? If you needed someone to take you to the doctor, or for other transportation? Could you call on a brother, sister, nephew, niece, cousin? Why or why not? A friend or neighbor? How do you feel about asking family members, relatives, friends or neighbors for help? Social service agencies?

130. *Should* a brother or sister, nephew or niece, cousin, help you? In your case, does the ideal fit reality?—sickness, cooking, shopping, housework, taking to doctor, moral support, etc.?

131. Do you look out for your nieces and nephews in any way—gifts, letters, phone, visit? Are you closer to some nieces and nephews than others? Why?

Cousins? Why? Could you call upon or rely on any of these people if you had to? What about their children?

132. Do you ever feel as though your nieces and nephews are like your own children? What about your great-nieces and nephews—are they like grandchildren? Do you send gifts, cards?

133. Did you want to have children, or decide not to? Did you consider adoption?

134. Does not having children affect your relationships with family in any way? Relationships with friends?

135. Do you think other people's children are really a source of help? Are children a source of help and support in time of emergency—if so, what resources do you have to compensate?

136. Do you ever discuss these feelings with anyone?

137. Who makes decisions in your family, gets people together and entertains? Whom do you talk to to find out what's going on in your family?

LIFE CRISIS INFORMATION

(Record data on life crises which occur to informant or members of family, or to friends. Always take advantage of opportunities for participant observation.)

FUNERALS

Who notified you?
What relatives were expected to tell other kin?
Who put the announcement in the newspaper?
Who made arrangements; paid for funeral expenses?
Who attended the funeral and signed the guest book?
Who sat with the family at the funeral home?
Was there anyone whom you thought should have attended, but didn't?
Were you surprised at the number in attendance?
Who were the pallbearers; how was this decided?
Who went to the cemetery?
Who officiated; did you like the choice of rabbi; who decided?
At whose home did the family gather after the cemetery?
Who came back to the house?
Who prepared the food?
Who ate first—immediate family?
Who sat *shive*, said the prayers?
Who came to visit, sent cards, made donations?
Did you approve of the way things were handled, were you consulted, and on what?
Who picked out the coffin; who will decide on a date for the stone-setting?
Note all ritual and ceremony.
(Some questions to ask when deceased was not a close member of the family.)
What funerals of friends or neighbors did you attend recently? How did you find out about the death? Why did you attend? Whom did you go with? Did you send donation, card, or visit the family?

WEDDINGS

Who was invited to the wedding—family members, relatives, friends, neighbors?

Who made up the guest list—were you asked to give your list, were you restricted to numbers, were there others whom you would have liked to invite, how did you decide whom to invite—was this a source of anger or ill feelings with family or friends?

Were you pleased with the religious nature of the ceremony?

What preparations were you involved in?

How do you feel about the groom (bride) and his/her family?

Did any of your friends or neighbors send presents?

Were there any kin whom you thought should have been invited, but weren't?

Tell me about seeing all these relatives: did you get together before or after the wedding for parties and visits? Who came?

Did you march down the aisle?

Did you give a gift?

Did you enjoy yourself and feel a part of things or pushed to the side?

(Did you attend any weddings of the children of friends or neighbors recently? Tell me about them.)

BRIS (RITUAL CIRCUMCISION)

Who was invited to the *bris?*

Were you allowed to invite anyone?

Was there any question if there would be a *bris*, and did you have anything to say about it?

How was the baby named and for whom, and did you influence the decision?

Who called to tell you the baby was born, when the *bris* would be, what the name of the baby would be?

Did you give the baby a present? How often do you see the baby, other grandchildren and great-grandchildren?

(Did you attend the *bris* of a friend's or neighbor's grandchild?)

JEWISH HIGH HOLY DAYS AND PASSOVER

Whom did you get cards from or send cards to, receive calls from, or call to wish a happy holiday?

Did anyone bake and bring something over or invite you in; did you take anything over to neighbors or friends?

Where did you go for services?

Whose home did you go to to eat?

Whom did you go to services with?

Who made arrangements for you?

Would you rather be with family or friends?

Whom do you light *yortsayt* candles for, or Sabbath candles for?

BIRTHDAYS

Do you send cards and gifts to your children?
Who calls, writes, visits, sends cards or a gift?
What did you do on your birthday this year, and did you enjoy yourself?
How do you deal with disappointments?

MOTHER'S DAY OR FATHER'S DAY

What did you do this year?
Who sends you cards or gifts?
Who decides what you will do?
Do you ever feel left out or lonely?

Comments: Make assessments and comments in notes about the reliability and completeness of the information given. If possible, participant observation should be done wherever possible to fill in data and details the informant chooses, or forgets, to include. Thus, every opportunity is taken to participate both in social and religious functions of informants with their neighbors, family, and friends and to be with them at activities sponsored by social service agencies.

Appendix B
Charts Detailing Life History Data
and Exchange of
Services and Support for Individual Informants

Mrs. Wexler

Age	Health	Marital Status	Household Status
73	Poor health, has had a stroke	Divorced	Lives alone

Children	Local	Non-Local	Occupation	Ages
Deborah	X		Teacher	53
Ann		Los Angeles	Teacher	44

Grandchildren	Ages
3	13 to 24

Siblings	Local	Non-Local	Ages
Evelyn		Florida	76
Rose		Florida	72
Manuel		Los Angeles	67

Length of Residence in Present Neighborhood	Preceding Neighborhood
12 years, currently at the Carroll Arms	Cleveland Heights (6 years on Richmond Road)

Mrs. Wexler

Service or Resource	Self	Children	Grand-children	Sib-lings	Neighbor-Friend	Associational-Friend	Confidant-Friend	Social Service
Assistance								
Transportation	X	X						
Shop for Food or Medicine	X	X						
Go to Doctor with	X	X			X			
Housework or Cooking	X							
Pay Bills	X							
Laundry	X							
Money		X		X				Rent supplement
Call in Emergency		X		X	X			Food stamps
Help in Illness		X		X	X			
Emotional Services								
Share Joys & Sorrows				X				
Advice & Talk over		X						
Talk to Daily		X			X			
Visit at Home		X	X					
Spend Saturdays with								
Spend Holidays with								
Jewish		X	X					
Secular	X	X	X					
Go on Vacation with								
Call when Blue		X						
Invite to a Family Affair								
Meet at Clubs & Organizations					X local deli			

Mrs. Nathan

Age	Health	Marital Status	Household Status
79	Poor health—bad eyesight from circulatory problems	Widow	Lives alone (moved to Cornell with husband)

Children	Local	Non-Local	Occupation	Ages
Saul	X		Runs his own company	50
Mark		New York	Men's clothing	54
David		Milwaukee	Salesman	57

Grandchildren	Ages
7	Youngest is 14

Siblings	Local	Non-Local	Ages
Brother		Israel	

Length of Residence in Present Neighborhood	Preceding Neighborhood
20 years—currently at the Carroll Arms	New York City

Service or Resource	Self	Children	Grand-children	Sib-lings	Neighbor-Friend	Associational-Friend	Confidant-Friend	Social Service
Assistance								
Transportation	X				X			Social worker
Shop for Food or Medicine	X				X			Shopper Meals-on-Wheels
Go to Doctor with	X							Social worker
Housework or Cooking	X							Meals-on-Wheels
Pay Bills	X							
Laundry	X							
Money		X paid rent						
Call in Emergency		X			X			
Help in Illness		X			X			
Emotional Services								
Share Joys & Sorrows					X		(X)*	
Advice & Talk over		X						
Talk to Daily					X			
Visit at Home		X	X	X	X			
Spend Saturdays with					X			
Spend Holidays with					X			
Jewish	X							Passover *seyder*
Secular		X						High Holidays
Go on Vacation with					X			
Call when Blue								
Invite to a Family Affair								
Meet at Clubs & Organizations								

*Relationships that do not clearly qualify as old friends are enclosed in parentheses.

Mrs. Feingold

Age	Health	Marital Status	Household Status
75	Poor health, in pain most of time	Married	Lives with spouse

Children	Local	Non-Local	Occupation	Ages
Donald		Palm Beach	Salesman	48
Harold	X	Moved to San Diego	Salesman	45

Grandchildren	Ages
5	16 to 24

Siblings	Local	Non-Local	Ages
Pearl (half-sister)	X		
Faye (half-sister)		Houston	90

Length of Residence in Present Neighborhood	Preceding Neighborhood
16 years—currently at the Carroll Arms	East Cleveland, lived 7 years on Elderwood

Service or Resource	Self	Children	Grand-children	Sib-lings	Neighbor-Friend	Associational-Friend	Confidant-Friend	Social Service
Assistance								
Transportation	X cab					X		JC Bus
Shop for Food or Medicine	X	X used to	X		X			Shopper
Go to Doctor with	X			X	X	X		
Housework or Cooking	X							
Pay Bills	X							
Laundry	X							
Money		X Fla. son						
Call in Emergency		X			X			
Help in Illness		X			X	X		
Emotional Services								
Share Joys & Sorrows					X			
Advice & Talk over		X			X			
Talk to Daily					X			
Visit at Home		X			X			
Spend Saturdays with						X		
Spend Holidays with								
Jewish		X						Passover *seyder*
Secular								
Go on Vacation with								
Call when Blue								
Invite to a Family Affair								
Meet at Clubs & Organizations						X		

Mrs. Samuels

Age	Health	Marital Status	Household Status
80	Blind, has arthritis	Widowed in April, 1975	Lives alone

Children	Local	Non-Local	Occupation	Ages
David	X		Has own contracting business	55
Janet		Chicago	Works at Penney's	

Grandchildren	Ages
9	12 to 28
1 great-grandchild	

Siblings	Local	Non-Local	Ages
2 siblings		Kiev, Russia	
1 half-sister		Los Angeles	

Length of Residence in Present Neighborhood	Preceding Neighborhood
12½ years	East Cleveland (Eddy Road)

Service or Resource	Self	Children	Grand-children	Sib-lings	Neighbor-Friend	Associational-Friend	Confidant-Friend	Social Service
Assistance								Society for the Blind
Transportation		X					(X)	
Shop for Food or Medicine		X			X		(X)	
Go to Doctor with	X	X						
Housework or Cooking								
Pay Bills		X			X			
Laundry	X							
Money		X buy food						
Call in Emergency		X						
Help in Illness		X			X		(X)	
Emotional Services								
Share Joys & Sorrows					X		(X)	
Advice & Talk over					X			
Talk to Daily		X			X		(X)	
Visit at Home		X	X		X		(X)	
Spend Saturdays with	X							
Spend Holidays with								
Jewish		X						
Secular		X						
Go on Vacation with								
Call when Blue		X			X		(X)	
Invite to a Family Affair								
Meet at Clubs & Organizations								

Mrs. Moskowitz

Age 90	*Health* Heart condition	*Marital Status* Widow	*Household Status* Lives as a boarder	

Children	*Local*	*Non-Local*	*Occupation*	*Ages*
Shirley (Bert, died as a young adult)	X		Works in husband's medical office	65 +

Grandchildren	*Ages*
2	35, 45

Siblings	*Local*	*Non-Local*	*Ages*
Ada	X		65–70

Length of Residence in Present Neighborhood	*Preceding Neighborhood*
12 years	Lived with daughter

Service or Resource	Self	Children	Grand-children	Sib-lings	Neighbor-Friend	Associational-Friend	Confidant-Friend	Social Service
Assistance								
Transportation	X							JC Bus
Shop for Food or Medicine	X							
Go to Doctor with		X	X					
Housework or Cooking	X							
Pay Bills		X						
Laundry	X							
Money		X						
Call in Emergency		X			X			
Help in Illness		X	X	X	X			
Emotional Services								
Share Joys & Sorrows						X*		
Advice & Talk over								
Talk to Daily		X		X	X	X		
Visit at Home		X	X	X		X		
Spend Saturdays with						X		
Spend Holidays with								
Jewish		X	X	X				
Secular		X	X	X				
Go on Vacation with								
Call when Blue								
Invite to a Family Affair								
Meet at Clubs & Organizations					X	X		

*Relationships with unclear bounds are placed midway between categories.

Mrs. Levi

Age	*Health*		*Marital Status*		*Household Status*
80	Good		Widow for 12 years		Lives alone

Children	*Local*	*Non-Local*	*Occupation*	*Ages*
Henrietta	X		Active in Hadassah chapter	57
Evelyn	X		Social worker	45

Grandchildren	*Ages*
6	15 to 24

Siblings	*Local*	*Non-Local*	*Ages*
Martin, Faye, Ida, Rose, Elaine		Toronto	75, 70, 65, 62, 60

Preceding Neighborhood
Kinsman (18 years), moved to Cornell with husband and daughters

Length of Residence in Present Neighborhood
35 years

Mrs. Levi

Service or Resource	Self	Children	Grand-children	Sib-lings	Neighbor-Friend	Associational-Friend	Confidant-Friend	Social Service
Assistance								
Transportation	X	X				X		
Shop for Food or Medicine	X	X						
Go to Doctor with		X	X					
Housework or Cooking	X							
Pay Bills	X							
Laundry	X daughter drives							
Money								
Call in Emergency		X			X			
Help in Illness		X						
Emotional Services								
Share Joys & Sorrows				X			X	
Advice & Talk over		X		X				
Talk to Daily		X				X		
Visit at Home		X	X	X	X			
Spend Saturdays with		X				X		
Spend Holidays with								
Jewish		X						
Secular		X						
Go on Vacation with		X		X			X	
Call when Blue		X					X	
Invite to a Family Affair				X			X	
Meet at Clubs & Organizations						X		

Mrs. Levitt

Age	Health			Marital Status	Household Status
84	Good health, has recovered from major surgery			Widow for 24 years	Lives alone

Children	Local	Non-Local	Occupation	Ages
Norman	X		Salesman	55
Sarah	X		Homemaker	44

Grandchildren		Ages
3		12 to 19

Siblings	Local	Non-Local	Ages
Deceased		New York	

Length of Residence in Present Neighborhood	Preceding Neighborhood
14 years, currently at the Carroll Arms	East Cleveland (6 years on Eddy Road; before that lived in Brooklyn)

Mrs. Levitt

Service or Resource	Self	Children	Grand-children	Sib-lings	Neighbor-Friend	Associational-Friend	Confidant-Friend	Social Service
Assistance								
Transportation		X					X children drive	JC Bus
Shop for Food or Medicine	X	X						
Go to Doctor with		X						
Housework or Cooking	X		X vacuum					
Pay Bills	X							
Laundry	X	X						
Money		X son helps						Rent supplement
Call in Emergency		X						
Help in Illness		X son helps						
Emotional Services								
Share Joys & Sorrows								
Advice & Talk over		X son				X		
Talk to Daily		X			X			
Visit at Home		X	X		X	X		
Spend Saturdays with						X		
Spend Holidays with								
Jewish		X daughter						
Secular		X						
Go on Vacation with						X		
Call when Blue						X		
Invite to a Family Affair						X		
Meet at Clubs & Organizations						X		

Mr. Isenberg

Age	Health	Marital Status	Household Status
89	Good	Separated	Lives as a boarder

Children	Local	Non-Local	Occupation	Ages
Norm	X		Disabled	56
Bea	X		Homemaker	54

Grandchildren			Ages
6			14 to 30

Siblings	Local	Non-Local	Ages
Deceased	X		

Length of Residence in Present Neighborhood	Preceding Neighborhood
8 years	Kinsman

Mr. Isenberg

Service or Resource	Self	Children	Grand-children	Sib-lings	Neighbor-Friend	Associational-Friend	Confidant-Friend	Social Service
Assistance								
Transportation	X							
Shop for Food or Medicine								JC Lunch
Go to Doctor with		X						
Housework or Cooking		X daughter cooks						
Pay Bills		X						
Laundry		X						
Money								
Call in Emergency		X						
Help in Illness		X						
Emotional Services								
Share Joys & Sorrows							X	
Advice & Talk over		X					X	
Talk to Daily						X	X	
Visit at Home						X	X	
Spend Saturdays with								
Spend Holidays with								
Jewish		X						
Secular		X	X					
Go on Vacation with								
Call when Blue								
Invite to a Family Affair								
Meet at Clubs & Organizations						X	X	

Mrs. Brodsky

Age	Health
72	Good health, but has eye trouble

	Marital Status
	Widow for 40 years

	Household Status
	Lives alone; had been a boarder

Children	Local	Non-Local	Occupation	Ages
Sarah	X		Secretary-bookkeeper	55
Shirley	X		Bookkeeper	53
Sidney	X		Salesman	50

Grandchildren		Ages
7		14 to 27

Siblings	Local	Non-Local	Ages
All deceased		Europe	

Length of Residence in Present Neighborhood	Preceding Neighborhood
15 years, currently at the Carroll Arms	Kinsman

Mrs. Brodsky

Service or Resource	Self	Children	Grand-children	Sib-lings	Neighbor-Friend	Associational-Friend	Confidant-Friend	Social Service
Assistance								
Transportation	X							
Shop for Food or Medicine	X					X		
Go to Doctor with	X	X	X			X		
Housework or Cooking	X							
Pay Bills	X							
Laundry	X							
Money								Rent supplement
Call in Emergency		X						Food stamps
Help in Illness		X				X		
Emotional Services								
Share Joys & Sorrows						X	X	
Advice & Talk over						X		
Talk to Daily						X		
Visit at Home		X				X	X	
Spend Saturdays with						X		
Spend Holidays with								
Jewish		X						Passover *seyder*
Secular		X						
Go on Vacation with						X		
Call when Blue						X	X	
Invite to a Family Affair								
Meet at Clubs & Organizations						X	X	

Mrs. Weiner

Age	Health		Marital Status	Household Status
74	Good		Widow for 14 years	Son lives with her

Children	Local	Non-Local	Occupation	Ages
Harold		Portland	School teacher	43
Dora	X		Homemaker	48

Grandchildren				Ages
2				18, 22

Siblings	Local	Non-Local		Ages
Brother	X	Los Angeles		
Half sister		Miami		

Length of Residence in Present Neighborhood	Preceding Neighborhood
13 years	Kinsman

Mrs. Weiner

Service or Resource	Self	Children	Grand-children	Sib-lings	Neighbor-Friend	Associational-Friend	Confidant-Friend	Social Service
Assistance								
Transportation		X						
Shop for Food or Medicine	X	X						
Go to Doctor with		X						
Housework or Cooking	X							
Pay Bills		X						
Laundry	X	X						
Money		X						
Call in Emergency								
Help in Illness								
Emotional Services								
Share Joys & Sorrows				X				
Advice & Talk over								
Talk to Daily		X			X			
Visit at Home		X	X	X				
Spend Saturdays with		X						
Spend Holidays with								
Jewish		X	X				X	Passover *seyder*
Secular		X	X					
Go on Vacation with								
Call when Blue							X	
Invite to a Family Affair						X	X	
Meet at Clubs & Organizations						X		

Mrs. Eisner

Age	*Health*			*Marital Status*		*Household Status*
75	Good health, has had a hip operation			Divorced		Lives alone

Children	*Local*	*Non-Local*		*Occupation*		*Ages*
Sophie	X			Secretary		47
Saul	X			Attorney		44
(Leonard, died in World War II)						

Grandchildren		*Ages*
5		9 to 27

Siblings	*Local*	*Non-Local*	*Ages*
Marian	X (nursing home)		86
Isaac		Miami	84

Length of Residence in Present Neighborhood	*Preceding Neighborhood*
17 years, currently at the Carroll Arms	Cleveland Heights (10 years in Cedar-Fairmount area)

Mrs. Eissner

Service or Resource	Self	Children	Grand-children	Sib-lings	Neighbor-Friend	Associational-Friend	Confidant-Friend	Social Service
Assistance								
Transportation	X	X			X			X reimburses the cost of gas
Shop for Food or Medicine	X							
Go to Doctor with	X	X					X	
Housework or Cooking	X							
Pay Bills	X							
Laundry	X							
Money	X							
Call in Emergency		X					X	
Help in Illness		X					X	
Emotional Services								
Share Joys & Sorrows							X	
Advice & Talk over		X					X	
Talk to Daily		X		X			X	
Visit at Home			X					
Spend Saturdays with						X	X	
Spend Holidays with								
Jewish		X						High Holidays
Secular		X		X				
Go on Vacation with		X						
Call when Blue								
Invite to a Family Affair							X	
Meet at Clubs & Organizations						X	X	

Mrs. Perlman

Age	Health	Marital Status	Household Status
81	Has arthritis, tires easily	Widow	Lives alone

Children	Local	Non-Local	Occupation	Ages
Fanny		Scarborough	Widow	57
David	X		Tailor	55
John	X		Cosmetician	44

Grandchildren
Milly (Leeds), Susan (London), Adam (Leeds)   *Ages* 16, 19, and 26

Siblings	Local	Non-Local	Ages
Rita	X		79
Hilda	X		77
Ben	X		70

Length of Residence in Present Neighborhood
9 years

Preceding Neighborhood
Chapeltown (34 years)

Mrs. Perlman

Service or Resource	Self	Children	Grand-children	Sib-lings	Neighbor-Friend	Associational-Friend	Confidant-Friend	Social Service
Assistance								
Transportation		X						Home-help
Shop for Food or Medicine		X in-laws			X			go with home-help
Go to Doctor with		X						
Housework or Cooking	X							Home-help Meals-on-Wheels
Pay Bills		X			X			
Laundry	X	X						
Money								
Call in Emergency		X			X			
Help in Illness		X			X			
Emotional Services								
Share Joys & Sorrows					X			
Advice & Talk over		X						
Talk to Daily					X			
Visit at Home		X		X	X			
Spend Saturdays with					X			
Spend Holidays with								
Jewish		X						
Secular		X						
Go on Vacation with		X daughter						
Call when Blue								
Invite to a Family Affair								
Meet at Clubs & Organizations								

Mrs. Silverman

Age	Health			Marital Status		Household Status
81	Has rheumatism			Widow for 9 years		Lives alone

Children	Local	Non-Local	Occupation	Ages
Son	X		Government work	51

Grandchildren		Ages
2 grandchildren		17 and 31
2 great-grandchildren		

Siblings	Local	Non-Local	Ages
Molly	X		70
Minnie		London	61

Length of Residence in Present Neighborhood
14 years (husband was living when they moved in); Mrs. S. has recently moved to old-age home.

Preceding Neighborhood
Chapeltown (13 years)

Service or Resource	Self	Children	Grand-children	Sib-lings	Neighbor-Friend	Associational-Friend	Confidant-Friend	Social Service
Assistance								
Transportation		X	X					
Shop for Food or Medicine					X			
Go to Doctor with		X	X					
Housework or Cooking	X							Home-help
Pay Bills					X			
Laundry	X	X						
Money								X Allowance from Board
Call in Emergency		X		X				
Help in Illness		X		X	X			X
Emotional Services								
Share Joys & Sorrows							X	
Advice & Talk over		X						
Talk to Daily					X			
Visit at Home		X	X	X	X			
Spend Saturdays with		X			X			
Spend Holidays with			X breakfast					
Jewish								Passover *seyder*
Secular		X						
Go on Vacation with					X			
Call when Blue					X			
Invite to a Family Affair								
Meet at Clubs & Organizations					X			

Mrs. Stein

Age	Health		Marital Status	Household Status
66	Poor health, heart condition diabetes		Divorced	Lives alone

Children	Local	Non-Local	Occupation	Ages
Hess		America	Lawyer	43
Mark	X		Educator	39
Sandy		France	Secretary, wife of professor	36
Miriam		America	Homemaker, wife of doctor	25

Grandchildren	Ages
8	2 to 16

Siblings	Local	Non-Local	Ages
Deceased			

Length of Residence in Present Neighborhood
Teenager was living with her when they moved to the Estate

Preceding Neighborhood
Chapeltown (16 years)

Mrs. Stein

Service or Resource	Self	Children	Grand-children	Sib-lings	Neighbor-Friend	Associational-Friend	Confidant-Friend	Social Service
Assistance								
Transportation	X	X						
Shop for Food or Medicine	X	X takes to mrkt						
Go to Doctor with	X							
Housework or Cooking	X							Home-help
Pay Bills	X							
Laundry	X	X drives her						
Money								
Call in Emergency		X						
Help in Illness		X						
Emotional Services								
Share Joys & Sorrows							X	
Advice & Talk over							X	
Talk to Daily		X						
Visit at Home		X			X			
Spend Saturdays with					X			
Spend Holidays with								
Jewish								
Secular								
Go on Vacation with	X daughter							
Call when Blue							X	
Invite to a Family Affair							X	
Meet at Clubs & Organizations								

Mrs. Shapiro

Age	Health	Marital Status	Household Status
81	Good health, successful recovery from major surgery	Widow for 17 years	Lives alone

Children	Local	Non-Local	Occupation	Ages
Son	X		Owns tailoring shop	47
Son		Edinburgh	Professor	53

Grandchildren	Ages
2 grandsons in Edinburgh	14, 16
2 grandsons in Leeds	16, 18

Siblings	Local	Non-Local	Ages
2 deceased		Brazil, Israel	

Length of Residence in Present Neighborhood	Preceding Neighborhood
17 years	Kosher Kitchens House (16 years)

Mrs. Shapiro

Service or Resource	Self	Children	Grand-children	Sib-lings	Neighbor-Friend	Associational-Friend	Confidant-Friend	Social Service
Assistance								
Transportation	X							
Shop for Food or Medicine	X							
Go to Doctor with		X						
Housework or Cooking	X							
Pay Bills	X							
Laundry	X							
Money								
Call in Emergency		X			X			
Help in Illness		X						
Emotional Services								
Share Joys & Sorrows		X			X	X	X	
Advice & Talk over		X			X			
Talk to Daily					X			
Visit at Home		X	X		X			
Spend Saturdays with							X	
Spend Holidays with								
Jewish		X Edinburgh						
Secular		X						
Go on Vacation with					X		X	
Call when Blue					X			
Invite to a Family Affair					X		X	
Meet at Clubs & Organizations					X	X		

Mr. Segal

Age	Health	Marital Status	Household Status
80	Good health, still employed	Widower	Lives alone

Children	Local	Non-Local	Occupation	Ages
Betty	X		Civil service	40+
Mark		Nottingham	Solicitor	—
Eva		America	—	39

Grandchildren	Ages
8	Youngest is 19

Siblings	Local	Non-Local	Ages
Deceased			

Length of Residence in Present Neighborhood	Preceding Neighborhood
Wife was living when they moved to the Estate	

Mr. Segal

Service or Resource	Self	Children	Grand-children	Sib-lings	Neighbor-Friend	Associational-Friend	Confidant-Friend	Social Service
Assistance								
Transportation	X							
Shop for Food or Medicine	X							
Go to Doctor with					X			
Housework or Cooking	X							
Pay Bills	X							
Laundry		X						
Money								
Call in Emergency		X						
Help in Illness		X						
Emotional Services								
Share Joys & Sorrows						X		
Advice & Talk over								
Talk to Daily								
Visit at Home		X				X		
Spend Saturdays with		X						
Spend Holidays with								
Jewish		X						
Secular								
Go on Vacation with	X							
Call when Blue								
Invite to a Family Affair								
Meet at Clubs & Organizations						X	X	

Mrs. Pincus

Age	*Health*	*Marital Status*	*Household Status*
72	Has had a stroke	Widow for 11 years	Lives alone

Children	*Local*	*Non-Local*	*Occupation*	*Ages*
David	X		Works for father-in-law	31

Grandchildren	*Ages*
2	4, 6

Siblings	*Local*	*Non-Local*	*Ages*
Dora, Rose, Sarah		Sheffield	75, 68, 64,
Faye, Hattie		Sheffield	64, 57

Length of Residence in Present Neighborhood	*Preceding Neighborhood*
14 years (moved into Estate with husband and son)	Harehills Lane (20 years)

Service or Resource	Self	Children	Grand-children	Sib-lings	Neighbor-Friend	Associational-Friend	Confidant-Friend	Social Service
Assistance								
Transportation		X						
Shop for Food or Medicine		X			X			
Go to Doctor with	X	X						
Housework or Cooking	X							
Pay Bills		X						
Laundry	X	X						
Money								
Call in Emergency		X						
Help in Illness		X		X	X	X		
Emotional Services								
Share Joys & Sorrows		X		X	X			
Advice & Talk over		X		X				
Talk to Daily		X			X			
Visit at Home		X	X	X	X	X		
Spend Saturdays with					X			
Spend Holidays with								
Jewish		X Fri. night		X Passover X High Holidays				
Secular		X						
Go on Vacation with				X				
Call when Blue		X			X			
Invite to a Family Affair						X	X	
Meet at Clubs & Organizations						X		

Mrs. Aronson

Age	*Health*			*Marital Status*	*Household Status*	
76	Good health			Widow for 10 years	Lives alone	

Children	*Local*	*Non-Local*	*Occupation*	*Ages*
Son	X		Owns tailoring shop	52

Grandchildren	*Ages*
2 grandsons	12, 16

Siblings	*Local*	*Non-Local*	*Ages*
Ann, Sarah, Miriam	4	1 in Rhodesia	74, 70, 66
Martin, Eva		2 in Scotland	64, 62,
Ben, Margo			59, 56

Length of Residence in Present Neighborhood	*Preceding Neighborhood*
8 years	Roundhay Road (44 years)

Mrs. Aronson

Service or Resource	Self	Children	Grand-children	Sib-lings	Neighbor-Friend	Associational-Friend	Confidant-Friend	Social Service
Assistance								
Transportation	X	X						
Shop for Food or Medicine	X							
Go to Doctor with	X							
Housework or Cooking	X							
Pay Bills	X							
Laundry	X							
Money	X							
Call in Emergency								
Help in Illness								
Emotional Services								
Share Joys & Sorrows					X		X	
Advice & Talk over		X			X		X	
Talk to Daily					X			
Visit at Home		X			X			
Spend Saturdays with		X	X	X	X evening			
Spend Holidays with								
Jewish		X			X 2nd *seyder*			
Secular								
Go on Vacation with							X	
Call when Blue					X			
Invite to a Family Affair					X			
Meet at Clubs & Organizations						X	X	

Mrs. Gottlieb

Age	Health	Marital Status	Household Status
78	Good health, has had recent leg trouble	Widow	Lives alone, daughter, Rose, comes on weekends

Children	Local	Non-Local	Occupation	Ages
Bernice	X Bradford		Homemaker	53
Barney		Los Angeles	Textiles	48

Rose is a factory worker
Spends weekends as housekeeper-companion. She is 56.

(Rose came to work as maid with family at age 15.)

Grandchildren	Ages
6 grandsons	8 to 22 (one lives in America, the others in Bradford)

Siblings	Local	Non-Local	Ages
Sibling		Philadelphia	80
Sister-in-law		London	78
Sister-in-law		London	76

Length of Residence in Present Neighborhood	Preceding Neighborhood
16 years	Downtown Leeds

Service or Resource	Self	Children	Grand-children	Sib-lings (sisters-in-law)	Neighbor-Friend	Associational-Friend	Confidant-Friend	Social Service
Assistance								
Transportation	X	Rose						
Shop for Food or Medicine	X	X			X			
Go to Doctor with							X	
Housework or Cooking	X	X						
Pay Bills	X							
Laundry	X							
Money		X LA son						
Call in Emergency		X		X				
Help in Illness	X	X						
Emotional Services								
Share Joys & Sorrows					X		X	
Advice & Talk over		X LA son			X		X	
Talk to Daily					X	X	X	
Visit at Home		X	X	X	X	X	X	
Spend Saturdays with					X		X	
Spend Holidays with								
Jewish					X High Holidays	X	X Passover *seyder*	
Secular				X			X	
Go on Vacation with				X				
Call when Blue								
Invite to a Family Affair							X	
Meet at Clubs & Organizations						X		

Mrs. Caplan

Age	Health	Marital Status	Household Status
—	Has had a hip operation	Widow	Lives alone

Children	Local	Non-Local	Occupation	Ages
Samuel	X		Tailor at Burton's	53
Florence	X		Nurse	51
Miriam	X		Secretary	45
Leonard		Manchester	Professor	48

Grandchildren	Ages
8	11 to 22

Siblings	Local	Non-Local	Ages
None			

Length of Residence in Present Neighborhood   *Preceding Neighborhood*
Husband was living when they moved to the Estate

Mrs. Caplan

Service or Resource	Self	Children	Grand-children	Sib-lings	Neighbor-Friend	Associational-Friend	Confidant-Friend	Social Service
Assistance								
Transportation	X taxi							
Shop for Food or Medicine	X	X daughter orders	X					
Go to Doctor with	X	X			X			
Housework or Cooking	X							Home-help
Pay Bills	X	X gas bill only						
Laundry	X							
Money		X Manchester son						
Call in Emergency		X			X			
Help in Illness		X			X		X	
Emotional Services								
Share Joys & Sorrows							X	
Advice & Talk over		X			X		X	
Talk to Daily		X			X		X	
Visit at Home		X	X		X	X	X	
Spend Saturdays with		X						
Spend Holidays with								
Jewish		X						
Secular		X						
Go on Vacation with					X		X	
Call when Blue					X	X	X	
Invite to a Family Affair							X	
Meet at Clubs & Organizations					X	X		

Notes

INTRODUCTION

1. R. Paine, "In Search of Friendship: An Exploratory Analysis in 'Middle Class' Culture," *Man*, 4, no. 4 (Dec. 1969), pp.505–524.

2. J.K. Ross, *Old People, New Lives* (Chicago: University of Chicago Press, 1977), p.2.

3. A.R. Hochschild, *The Unexpected Community* (Englewood Cliffs, N.J.: Prentice-Hall, 1973); S.K. Johnson, *Idle Haven: Community Building Among the Working-Class Retired* (Berkeley: University of California Press, 1971); Ross, *Old People, New Lives*.

4. Ross, *Old People, New Lives*; Hochschild, *The Unexpected Community*.

5. The contrast between the elderly in Leeds and Cornell is so striking and the plight of the latter so great that the reader may be tempted to believe that the comparative study depicts the first as a healthy group and the latter as marginal. Yet extensive interviews with elderly people living in the Cornell neighborhood and with contemporaries who chose to move away make it clear that the Cornell sample is representative of the elderly who lived in this Jewish neighborhood in 1960. They are neither a marginal nor an atypical group, and probably also represent many of the 30,000 Jewish immigrants who arrived in Cleveland between 1900 and 1912. Only by understanding the particular difficulties faced by this group can we understand other elderly who adjust to old age better.

6. E. Krausz, *Leeds Jewry* (Cambridge: Heffer, 1964), p.93.

7. For a discussion of the basic method used by anthropologists—participant observation—and the phases of this structured research program, see J. Keith, "Participant Observation," in *New Methods for Old Age Research*, ed. by C.L. Fry and J. Keith (Chicago: Center for Urban Policy, Loyola University of Chicago, 1980) and P. Bohannan, "Unseen Community: The Natural History of a Research Project," in *Anthropologists at Home in North America*, ed. by D.A. Messerschmidt (New York: Cambridge University Press, 1981).

8. E. Shanas, P. Townsend, et al., *Old People in Three Industrial Societies* (New York: Atherton Press, 1968), p.143.

CHAPTER 1

1. Material for this section was drawn from L.P. Gartner, *History of the Jews of Cleveland* (Cleveland: Western Reserve Historical Society and Jewish Theological Seminary of America, 1978); Rabbi A.H. Silver, "One Hundred Years of Temple History: Sermon, The Temple, November 20, 1949," in *A World in its Season* (New York and Cleveland: World Publishing Company, 1972), vol. 2, pp.306–318; and from conversations with Judah Rubinstein, Research Director, Jewish Community Federation of Cleveland.

2. "The Jews of Cleveland are engaged in many different commercial pursuits, being important factors in industrial and commercial enterprises, particularly in the manufacture of cloaks and clothing and all kindred garment industries. They control the chief brass industries and that of making agricultural implements. They conduct the leading department stores and are among the most skillful garment workers. The more recently arrived immigrants are mechanics, such as bricklayers, plumbers, electricians, etc." Quoted in Gartner, *History of the Jews of Cleveland*, p.66, from *Jewish Review and Observer*, Sept. 23, 1910, part 1; cf. *Jewish Review and Observer*, Oct. 9, 1914.

3. The *City Directory* of 1912 for the Woodland and East 55th Street district lists 8 jewelers, 10 bakers, 25 barbers, 6 barrelmakers, 3 bicycle dealers, 21 shoe stores, 30 tobacconists (many of them petty manufacturers), 5 clothiers, 55 candy stores, 16 druggists, 11 furniture stores, 9 saloons, and innumerable grocery stores. All but three of these shops were individually owned, and most by Jews. Gartner, *History of the Jews of Cleveland*, p.127. One informant's father, who emigrated in the 1880s as a young boy from Rumania, owned a used-furniture store in this area.

4. J.J. Grabowski, "A Social Settlement in a Neighborhood in Transition, Hiram House, Cleveland, Ohio, 1896–1926," Ph.D. diss., Case Western Reserve University, 1977, pp.27–28.

5. Although German Jews were prominent in business organizations and philanthropic efforts, they were denied social acceptance and honorific positions in the Museum of Art, the Western Reserve Historical Society, and the Cleveland Orchestra. They did not constitute Howe's group of the "easily and permanently rich," those with money from long-held local land and mining, iron and steel, banking, and public utilities. Jews were in the group of the "equally well-to-do [who] have an uncertain status." None were the associates of Rockefeller or Harkness. Gartner, *History of the Jews of Cleveland*, chap. 3, pp.65–100.

6. Gartner, "Immigration and the Formation of American Jewry, 1840–1925," in M. Sklare, ed., *The Jew in American Society* (New York: Behrman House, 1974), p.50.

7. Ibid., p.42.

8. Quoted in Gartner, *History of the Jews of Cleveland*, p.109.

9. Statistics are taken from Gartner, *History of the Jews of Cleveland*, chap. 4, pp.101–141.

10. Grabowski, "Hiram House," p.28.

11. Ibid., p.118.

12. Ibid., p.35.

13. J. Morgenstern, *Cleveland Fifty Years Ago: Reminiscences of Immigrant Life*, 1949.

14. Documents from Hiram House Records, Western Reserve Historical Society, container 20, folder 4.

15. Gartner, *History of the Jews of Cleveland*, p.128. Material for section on unionism adapted from Gartner, pp.128–135.

16. Grabowski, "Hiram House."

17. Ibid., pp.32–34. On the statistics Grabowski calculated of 3.29 working adults living in each building, he also calculated that each one of these adults was the head of a four-person household, making a density of about fourteen persons in each building.

18. Gartner, *History of the Jews of Cleveland*, p.124.

19. Grabowski, "Hiram House," p.34.

20. Ibid., chap. 3, pp.76–113.

21. Ibid., pp.216–217.

22. Ibid., p.144.

23. "Shin Miller Papers," Western Reserve Historical Society, pp.96–97.

24. Grabowski, "Hiram House," p.255.

25. Gartner, *History of the Jews of Cleveland*, p.123.

26. Of this number, 42.5 percent were under twenty years of age, while only 5.2 percent were sixty and over.

27. Gartner, *History of the Jews of Cleveland*, p.270.

28. Ibid.

29. Ibid., p.297.

30. Ibid.

31. Gartner, "Immigration, 1840–1925," p.39.

32. Material for this section was taken from J. Thomas, "A History of the Leeds Clothing Industry," *Yorkshire Bulletin of Economic and Social Research*, Occasional Paper No. 1, 1953; and J. Buckman, "The Economic and Social History of Alien Immigrants to Leeds, 1880–1914," Ph.D. diss., University of Strathclyde, Scotland, 1968.

33. Buckman, "Alien Immigrants to Leeds," p.195.

34. Thomas, "Leeds Clothing Industry," p.10.

35. L. P. Gartner, *The Jewish Immigrant in England, 1870–1914* (London: Simon, 1973), p.118.

36. Buckman "Alien Immigrants to Leeds," p.317.

37. Thomas, "Leeds Clothing Industry," p.51.

38. Ibid., p.57.

39. A letter from an informant in Leeds told that Burton's shop in Leeds is closing and that workers are being made "redundant." A later letter said that her son, and a few other workers, will be kept on in a special section of the factory.

40. R. O'Brien, "A Jewish Minority in Leeds," Ph.D. diss., University of Bristol, 1973.

41. Material for this section was taken from O'Brien, "A Jewish Minority in Leeds"; and E. Krausz, *Leeds Jewry* (Cambridge: Heffer, 1964).

42. O'Brien, "A Jewish Minority in Leeds," p.20.

43. Ibid., p.17.

44. Krausz, *Leeds Jewry*, p.15.

45. Ibid.

46. O'Brien, "A Jewish Minority in Leeds," p.97.

47. Buckman, "Alien Immigrants to Leeds," p.414.

48. D. Gainer, *The Alien Invasion* (London: Heinerman, 1972), p.42.

49. *Leeds Mercury*, Sept. 10, 1906, quoted in Buckman, "Alien Immigrants to Leeds," p.412.

50. O'Brien, "A Jewish Minority in Leeds," p.119.

51. Krausz, *Leeds Jewry*, p.25.

52. O'Brien, "A Jewish Minority in Leeds," p.3.

53. Krausz, *Leeds Jewry*.

54. O'Brien, "A Jewish Minority in Leeds," p.34.

CHAPTER 2

1. Mrs. Brodsky, who was frequently hungry as a child, recalls going to the home of her brother. His wife, who ran a grocery store, would give her something to eat. She also spent weeks with a brother who owned a cow.

2. In the Eastern European Jewish communities, *kest* made it customary for the bride's father to board her husband while he attended school. Many immigrant husbands thus came to live in the same town with the bride's family. This may account for more intensive contact between them.

3. This memory limitation may be related to the fact that when a man is called up to read from the Torah only his own name and the name of his father are mentioned. Grandfathers are not named.

4. On two occasions these relationships have been extended. Mr. Samuels hired a cousin as an assistant, and Mr. Isenberg gave money to his niece and her husband to buy a delivery truck. He remains "the favorite uncle."

5. Because they emigrated before their younger sisters or brothers married, or before the children of older siblings were wed, informants cannot furnish even minimal information about their nieces and nephews in Europe.

6. In one case, antagonism toward a new stepparent influenced an informant (Mrs. Feingold) to emigrate to America.

7. Frequently it is the sisters-in-law who maintain the contact. They write letters, often enclosing cash. Mrs. Eisner is grateful to her sister-in-law for urging her to see a good surgeon when she needed a hip operation. Although the two women no longer live in the same city, they remain good friends and confidantes.

8. Sixty percent (six of the ten informants) broke contact with their parents when they immigrated to America.

9. *Shive* is the seven solemn days of mourning for the dead, beginning immediately after the funeral, when Jews "sit *shive*" surrounded by family and friends. It is a period encouraging the mourners to vent their grief.

10. Cornell does not require the well-coiffured and well-attired appearance demanded by more affluent areas.

11. A number of the Cornell informants depend on government and social agency assistance to lead the independent lives that relationships with their children seem to demand. Some also receive rent supplements and food stamps. They go to the Jewish Center a few days each week and are picked up by the Center's free minibus. A few pay less than the full 50¢ fee for the Nutrition Program lunch and are also charged less for JC outings. This allows them to manage by themselves on their limited budgets.

12. Two relatively well-to-do women (Mrs. Levi and Mrs. Eisner) continue to help their children financially, helping pay for a house, business, or schooling for grandchildren. This permits them to continue their traditional maternal role and to feel they still have some influence in family affairs.

13. Because of the inherent difficulties and potential strains in the relationship between mother-in-law and daughter-in-law, informants who have only sons rely on social service assistance more than do those with daughters. Social workers and volunteers help them with transportation and shopping. Mrs. Nathan justifies taking this help by saying that her son gives generously to Jewish charities and that her husband paid taxes for many years. (Informants lose status among their peers, however, when they regularly accept help from social service agencies.)

14. Children also pay for permanent waves occasionally.

15. New legislation has eliminated fares during nonrush hours for senior citizens with a pass.

16. Only Mr. Isenberg has his own car.

17. When I observed conversations and visits between Mrs. Nathan and her son and daughter-in-law, they seemed to treat her as a stereotypical "Jewish mother." They joked about her unwillingness to spend money.

18. In the past, two informants (Mrs. Feingold and Mrs. Levitt) were driven to the JC by their sons, but now Mrs. Feingold goes on the pickup bus because her son wishes to spend Sundays with his wife.

19. Orthodox Jews will not travel on the first two days and the final day of Passover.

20. "Leeds was a working town. It was easier to get work in Leeds because there was a lot of factories. I think the main manufacturers, all the clothing manufacturers were in Leeds, mostly" (Mrs. Stein).

21. Mrs. Aronson remembers her mother sewing things to sell. The family, which was very poor after her father died, moved frequently.

22. When Mrs. Perlman showed me her mother's photograph, she said, "There were not many like her then, and no one now at all like her."

23. "The harder we worked, the more money we earned. I earned big money. I was very fast. I used to bring my mother the packet home. . . . I earned more than my brothers" (Mrs. Gottlieb).

24. Mrs. Perlman said of her mother, "We kept my mother marvelous . . . between us, she was never in a hospital. She died at home, in her own bed."

25. Mrs. Gottlieb said, "My mother wanted to come to me [to live]. She wouldn't go with nobody else. She said, 'You are like me, and I am like you.'"

26. Mrs. Cahn and Mrs. Gottlieb each lost a sister at a young age, and each helped raise her sister's surviving child. Others also brought up younger siblings, thereby instilling an even closer bond: "I wasn't the oldest. I had an oldest brother. I were the fourth child. My mother lost two. So I really helped my mother to bring them up, so they were like . . . [my children]. My brother, although he's, bless him, over 70, he's like my child. The love is there and they love me for it" (Mrs. Perlman).

27. Mrs. Pincus says of her relationship with her sisters: "We're not like other families, we don't fall out."

28. Mrs. Pincus says that her sisters helped her with her market stall: "My husband was poorly, he couldn't work, so they started me on markets, our Faye, me sister."

29. Mrs. Gottlieb's sisters-in-law like to visit her: "They love to come here; they all love to come here."

30. "You bought us the fridge and you bought us the lino that's on the floor."

31. When sisters-in-law are no longer able to visit, their company is missed. Mrs. Perlman says of her relationship with her sisters-in-law: "She should try to come. She can see and walk better. . . . We were very close; it's hard now . . . one lives in the Maxboroughs, I can't get there myself and if I can't get down and that one doesn't come up. And so, I don't bother, as long as I hear good news of them, I'm not bothered."

32. Mrs. Perlman answered my question about living with a daughter-in-law: "You're young, you've got a husband, how do you know your husband wants your mother? . . . You've got it in a nutshell! You can't, no one can. You don't mix. You clash. For so long, you can be good, good, good. And then you've got to sit and say nothing."

33. Mrs. Pincus confirmed this view by telling me about her sister: "My sister won't live with her daughters and they're very good. . . . My sister said she won't live with a daughter, as good as they are to her, because it's no good."

34. The Knightsdale Estate was also financed by a loan from the Leeds Corporation.

35. Mrs. Pincus gave her son her market stall: "I gave David the market, so he

can't ask me for anything, can he? So, if I want, I can ask him, because I gave him
the business."

36. Mrs. Gottlieb's son said to her: "Mom, if you can't manage, don't be afraid
to ask, because we can give it to you. Because you don't have to go short of
anything." She commented, "Nothing in the world would be too much for him to
give me. He is fortunate, his wife is the same, she agrees with him."

37. Mrs. Caplan is recovering from a hip operation. She gives her daughter her
weekly fruit, vegetable, and fish list. It is then delivered with the daughter's order
by a friend who owns a greengrocery. Mrs. Caplan takes the food home in a
taxicab after her Saturday visit with this daughter.

38. One late Saturday afternoon when I was visiting Mrs. Pincus, her son
telephoned to say that if I wished to spend the evening with his mother, he would
leave a party to drive me the short distance home at 10:30.

39. Mrs. Pincus said: "David used to call for me from work and then he would
bring me to his home, Tuesdays, Thursdays, and Fridays. . . . I also used to go up
there Friday night, and then she used to send me meal home with me for Saturday."

40. Mrs. Shapiro praised her Edinburgh son for coming to visit her following
her major surgery. "They came four times from Edinburgh to see me and brought
boxes of chocolates and fruit, and all sorts." I think that Cornell parents, in
contrast, would probably complain about how seldom this same son came from
Edinburgh to see his sick mother.

41. Mrs. Caplan says: "It was too cramped. I had my time; now my daughters
are the hostesses."

42. Mrs. Perlman says of her daughter-in-law: "She makes him a wonderful
wife. He does her, they're very much in love with each other. He's a strict boy,
you know. She forgives him a lot because he works hard and a big responsibility,
so sometimes when he gets sharp with her, she forgives him a lot and if not, she'll
just give a shoot at him, like a man and wife do. There's no smoke without fire,
you know. Everyone has, they're very happy."

43. Mrs. Stein talked about her friend's daughter-in-law: "His daughter-in-law
wasn't nice. He could never come on their doorsteps if he hasn't got bags full to
bring them. Then he was welcome. If he brought plenty in, he was welcome. . . . I
said, 'Mr. H., you're not the only one. There is hundreds like you, thousands, I
can't say. Some people are lucky, some people unlucky. You're not the only one.'
He talked about his daughter-in-law, I told about my daughter-in-law. . . . "

44. In situations of strain the daughter-in-law often comes from a family that is
better off financially than that of the son and his mother.

45. Some Leeds informants have home-helps, a few receive rent supplements,
and one recently started getting meals-on-wheels.

46. As noted in some of the quotations, a few Leeds parents feel some dissatisfaction, but not the ambivalence nor the feelings of rejection that Cornell informants mention.

47. Mrs. Stein continued her statement: "You don't know what I've done for
my *kinder*. There isn't another mother in the whole world. I went scrubbing floors
for them. When he moved into his new house, he had a do for all his friends, he
never invited the Mommy. They never invited Mommy for a cup of tea. I went
out and bought them a set, a table and chair set, and I paid 45 pounds for it. Why,
I don't interfere with them, I don't take nothing from them. I don't want to take
him away from his wife. . . . My only prayer, till I close my eyes, shall be that his

son-in-law and his daughter-in-law should give him the same pleasure they give me."

CHAPTER 3

1. Although Mrs. Wexler came to America with her parents in 1911, her life story parallels that of the other informants. Mrs. Levitt was born in New York City, and Mrs. Nathan went there as a teenage immigrant. Since neither woman moved to Cleveland until she was in her sixties, neither biography is discussed before then.

2. The authorized slaughterer of animals, according to the requirements of *kashres*.

3. Mrs. Wexler and her husband first tried living with her family, but this did not work out, so they moved next door.

4. Mrs. Brodsky also gave this woman fruit left over from her husband's peddling.

5. The practice of borrowing and loaning money to relatives was also common among informants. Mr. Isenberg willingly loaned money to his wife's brother. The brother-in-law repaid the debt by giving him a fruit store on 51st and Kinsman. Mr. Isenberg ran this store, at a profit, in the winter off-season when he was not painting.

6. Informants had moved too often to build up trusting friendships and so turned to relatives.

7. Mrs. Samuels remembers how her old friend from the blouse factory left her husband at home and nursed her for a week when she developed leg trouble following the birth of her daughter.

8. Today, informants have purchased cemetery plots and so have arranged to take care of part of the expenses of their own burials.

9. In this voluntary society, each member contributed $1.00 toward the burial expenses of a fellow member.

10. Two boys grew lonely for their fiancées and were married on the army base. When they returned to Cleveland, these sons stayed for a few months with their wives' parents and visited with their mothers frequently.

11. Two fathers—Mr. Samuels and Mr. Isenberg—were housepainters and helped their children by decorating and painting their houses.

12. Mrs. Gottlieb also remembers that when she was small, a neighbor helped her mother bring her home from the hospital: "I remember when I was about seven, and I had my tonsils out and a neighbor went with mother and they took me to the infirmary and then, they were like butchers. They did your tonsils and then they gave you back to your mother. . . . And this lady we came with, she was a tall lady, and she put me over her shoulder, and all the way home, the blood was flowing into the street, from Meanwood Road to the infirmary."

13. The houses were rented from Jewish landlords.

14. "At that time it was the war just finished. We came in 1940 and . . . he started about 1943 and it was booming, and we earned a lot of money."

15. This is a Yorkshire expression.

16. After this informant's husband died, the manufacturers brought her work at home, where she stitched coat lapels.

17. See also the following two statements by Mrs. Perlman:

"I've never been a woman that says I am unhappy. I've gone through life smiling, so really, I could have been unhappy, if I wanted to make it unhappy. You can have plenty and be unhappy and you can be poor and happy. I did it my way. Do you know, twenty-five years I nursed him."

"I've never been a rich woman, I've never known of a lot of money, but that isn't everything. I've been what you call a housewife, a *baleboste*, I've baked, and I've cooked and I've done and I've cleaned myself, I never even had anyone paid and helped—because I didn't have the money."

18. Mrs. Caplan also told me that the son of an old neighbor came to tell her when his mother died. After telling his mother's sister, he went to Mrs. Caplan because he did not want her to read the sad news in the papers.

19. A similar exchange:

"'. . . Danny, have you got money in the house?'

"'How much do you want, Anna?'

"'How much have you got in the house? I'll give you back in two or three weeks time.'

"'I've got thirty-five pounds, you can have it.'

"So he lent me the thirty-five pounds, not a note, I.O.U., nothing. [I told him,] 'You'll give me when you have.'"

20. Mrs. Stein's relationship with a non-Jewish neighbor was different, but also close:

"When he used to be drunk, he'd come home, and she used to come in and say, 'Come on, he's on the floor and we'll empty his pockets.' And I used to go in and we'd empty his pockets, pounds she used to give me. Then when he used to go sober, he'd say, 'I'm sure I had some money in my pockets, I'm sure. Stein, have you been in the house a long time?'

"'No, I don't know nothing about it.'

"'Did Helen go to my pockets?'

"'How dare you say that! Did Helen go to your pockets! You must be daft, you must have drunk the whole lot, or your lady friend must have taken it out of your pockets. Helen wouldn't take it out of your pockets.'

". . . And I knew he had a lot of money in the house in the drawers. I said, 'Helen, I've got a bunch of keys, let's see if we can fit a key to the drawers.' One key fit . . . and she used to take out of every bundle two or three pounds.

"She died from cancer. When she died, her son came for me. He said, 'Mrs. Stein, you must come, I'm sure Mom would have wanted you to come say good-bye to her. You have been a good friend.' The kids knew. We used to laugh."

21. A few informants were friends with people they had gone to school with or worked with before they were married. These friends were invited to one another's weddings, they attended the *bris* and *bar mitsves* of each others' sons, and they helped each other prepare the traditional foods to serve the guests.

22. Every week Mrs. Caplan went to the home of another neighbor, who used to be friendly with her mother, to receive a telephone call from her son in the army. She would then stay for tea. When the mother was ill, Mrs. Caplan returned their kindnesses, preparing the Sabbath dinner for them every Friday. She also comforted the family after the mother died.

CHAPTER 4

1. Mrs. Eisner says: "My son is married thirteen or fourteen years. Originally he was closer but, as the years come in, there's a big rift and he leans to his in-laws and, of course, the wife and the family and her mother and her father, which makes it much nicer—they can go out in a foursome or sixsome with an aunt and uncle—and I'm the odd woman, the odd-woman-out. But I accept it and know it and let it go at that."

2. Mrs. Levi calls her son-in-law's mother to find out what her daughter and husband are planning. Mrs. Samuels described how her son handled a family tragedy without informing her: "When the tragedy happened to my daughter—when her son got killed—I didn't know. She didn't call me, she called my son and he came right away and he was there for almost a week with her. He was to the funeral. . . . I didn't even know, I didn't go, I had a sick man, how could I go? He went and left her some money, I don't know, he left her quite a bit, a few hundred dollars. She didn't want to take it, but he left it on the dresser. My daughter-in-law told me, he didn't tell me. . . ."

3. When I asked informants to include me on the guest list for family affairs, they said they could not invite me themselves but would have to ask their children.

4. Van Gennep discusses the functions of rites of passage in primitive society. See A. Van Gennep, *The Rites of Passage* (London: Routledge & Kegan Paul, 1960).

5. The Gisu in West Africa, in particular, traditionally honor the grand-mother at her granddaughter's wedding. J.S. La Fontaine, "Ritualization of Women's Life Crises in Bugisu," in *The Interpretation of Ritual*, J.S. La Fontaine, ed. (London: Tavistock, 1974), pp.159–186.

6. All informants gave up holding *sdorim* in their homes when their husbands died, when they became too ill to do the cooking, or when their sons moved into larger homes that could better accommodate the whole family. Many were unwilling to abandon sharing this festival with their families, however. Some informants continue their role by preparing the traditional chicken soup, *matse* balls, and gefilte fish.

8. Programs focus on celebrating Jewish holidays and singing Hebrew and Yiddish songs. One favorite song is "Yiddishe Mamme," and many informants cry when it is sung. "I enjoy things that are Jewish and doing things in a Jewish way. The JC is like a second home" (Mrs. Levitt).

9. Mrs. Eisner says: "A neighbor can be an interference if they come while you're eating, tap, tap, and the coffee gets cold and the food no good, so your dinner is ruined. Or they come while you're phoning, or when you want to be comfortable in a housecoat. I don't go for it. Some need it because they don't get out every day, but so far, I'm not at that stage, thank God."

10. Mrs. Feingold says: "No one . . . pays any attention, they think they're bigger than I am, so I leave 'em be. I don't push myself for nobody. I'm just as good as they are."

11. Formal interviews also showed how informants present desired images of self and family. Two women refused to give me their genealogies. One stated that she would tell me personal things about herself, but never about her children. She rarely told me anything in detail except where her children took her for a Sunday trip. Another informant was cross if I wrote down even a brief note about what she told me about her children.

12. There is a Yiddish expression often quoted by informants: "May you have

nakhes [pleasure and pride, especially from the achievement of a child] from your children."

CHAPTER 5

1. Informants chose to move to the Estate because spouses were ill and could no longer climb steps, because their houses were too large, because their homes were scheduled to be torn down by the Corporation, and because their neighborhoods were changing.

2. Mrs. Stein said: "I went on Friday and I made dinner for them. I made chicken soup, *kneydlekh*, *lokshn kugl*, roast potatoes, roast chicken, and everything."

3. The card said, "I'm sending you 5 pounds for your birthday because you're so sweet, kind, and gentle and I love you."

4. Mrs. Gottlieb's sister wrote to her: "I'm glad you were invited out for the two *sdorim*. I was all alone. I used to feel bad, but not anymore—I'm used to it."

5. Mrs. Stein said: "We used to talk about the children. I knew Sam before he were married; I knew Donna before she was married and before her children were born. They knew my children when they were so big. With Mr. H., I could talk to him because he knew my children when they were so big, and I knew his children. I knew Donna and Sam and I remember Donna got married when my Sandy was going on eight. I invited them to come in for a drink, to have the engagement in the house; they wouldn't. I took a whole tray full of stuff and took it into their house—cream cakes and cakes and everything."

6. Another informant defined friendship: "A true friend is very hard to find. A friend is where you can trust 'um, tell 'um your troubles, and you can confide in them."

7. Mrs. Caplan spoke of her neighbor's helpfulness: "She was particularly marvelous at that time—she deserves a medal."

8. Mrs. Gottlieb said: "I don't encourage it . . . ; she's a sick woman as well, you want somebody younger, really."

9. Mrs. Aronson also said: "When you're down in the dumps, you have to pull yourself out of it, what can you do? What can you do when you're by yourself?— You can't. . . . Years ago, you could go out at night, [but] you're not allowed to go out at night, you're told not to go out at night. . . . You've got your television, you make the most of it, and if you're not idle, so you've got plenty of things to occupy your mind with—I have, anyway." For a similar discussion of the mechanisms and network construction for needed assistance in old age, see G.J. Wentowski, "Reciprocity and the Strategies of Older People," *The Gerontologist* 21:600–609 (1981).

10. Informants refer only to those people who live in close proximity to them and with whom they are very friendly as "neighbors." The other residents of the Estate and people from outside, whom they meet at the Day Center or at the Leeds Friendship Club, are associates.

11. Mrs. Pincus says, "They're all widows at the club, very few have got husbands."

12. Mrs. Aronson voiced a similar outlook: "This is a very good life for people who have nobody and are lonely. With the Center they can go every day and spend all their time there. It's not for me. I can always find work to do. I don't do it."

13. Mrs. Caplan and other "leaders" always take the same seats in the front row of the area of the *shul* where the women sit.

14. Mrs. Stein said: "This paper, I pass by and it was on sale, and I say, 'Oh, that will be lovely for my kitchen.' I go in and I buy five rolls. It was a pound a roll. I gave two pounds deposit and I leave it, and next week I go for my pension and I take it out. The window cleaner does all my decorating."

15. Neatness is also important. One evening I was at Mrs. Aronson's flat for two hours. While we talked she ironed doilies, pillowcases, underwear, and nightdresses.

16. The Leeds Friendship Club, under the leadership of Flori Gould, is the largest Friendship Club in Great Britain.

17. The Friendship Club *shnorers* are often people who do not live on the Estate and who seem not to have the values of independence and self-reliance espoused by my informants. There is no implication that they are discontented or have difficult role relationships with their children, as do many Cornell informants, however.

18. Mrs. Pincus said: "You have to be careful. Well, some people are funny, you know. You have to be careful what you do and where you go, and what you say to some people. That's why I don't bother much with anybody. Just good night, good morning, how are you. They ask me how I am, we pass a few words on, and Bob's your uncle."

CHAPTER 7

1. L. Simmons, *The Role of the Aged in Primitive Society* (New Haven: Yale University Press, 1945).

2. In most studies of lineage organizations, anthropologists concentrate on the younger generations, using men who are the fathers of young families as informants. There does not seem to be any particular explanation for this practice.

3. Perhaps this also reflects the general tendency among sociologists to downgrade the significance of kinship in urban settings.

4. The Jewish Community Federation is constructing low-income housing for the elderly in Cleveland Heights and University Heights.

Glossary

baleboste: The mistress of the house, especially a commendable homemaker.

bar mitsve: Literally, "a son of the commandment." A Jewish boy who, having reached the age of thirteen, assumes religious responsibilities of an adult male. The event is marked by inviting the youth to read all or part of the weekly Torah portion on a Sabbath closely following the birthday. In America the event itself has come to be called a *bar mitsve.*

bentshen likht: See *likht bentshen.*

bris: Literally, "covenant." The ceremony of circumcision, normally performed on a male infant on the eighth day following his birth.

bobe: Grandmother.

feter: Uncle.

gefilte fish: Literally, "filled fish," because originally stuffed in the fish skins before cooking. Chopped fish, usually a mixture, as of whitefish, pike, and carp, mixed with chopped onion and egg and seasoning and boiled, now usually in the form of cakes or balls, which are most often served cold.

goy (plural, *goyim*): A non-Jew; gentile.

Hadassah: The women's Zionist organization of America, founded by Henrietta Szold in 1912.

kashres: The complete regimen of the dietary laws of Judaism. (In modern Hebrew, *kashrut.*)

khazer: A pig; also applied to a person who is greedy or a glutton, or to one who is stingy.

kidesh: Literally, "sanctification." The invocation over a cup of wine preceding the festive meal of the Sabbath or a holiday. Also the invocation after a service in the *shul,* followed by the communal sharing of wine, *shnaps,* and something sweet.

kinder: Children or offspring (the singular is *kind*).

kneydlekh: Dumplings.

kvaterin: Godmother.

landsman (plural, *landslayt*): A countryman or compatriot, especially someone who comes from the same hometown as oneself.

likht bentshen: To light the Sabbath or holiday candles and recite the appropriate blessing.

lokshn kugl: Noodle pudding.

mekhuteneste: The mother-in-law of one's daughter or son, in her relationship to oneself.

mekhutonim: The in-laws of one's daughter or son, in their relationship to oneself.

mekhutn: The father-in-law of one's daughter or son, in his relationship to oneself.

mikve: The ritual bath prescribed variously in Judaism, as for married women following each menstrual period or as a purification rite for converts to Judaism.

241

mitsve: Literally, "a commandment." A good, kind, considerate, ethical deed, viewed as fulfilling the spirit of biblical or rabbinic commandments.

mume: Aunt.

nakhes: Pleasure and pride that one derives from the achievements of others, especially of one's children or grandchildren.

olevasholem: Literally, "On him peace." A conventional expression used in referring to someone who is dead, equivalent to English "May he rest in peace." (The Yiddish equivalent of "of blessed memory" is *zikhroyne-livrokhe.*)

Passover (Yiddish, *pesakh*): The festival celebrating the liberation of the ancient Hebrews from slavery in Egypt over 3200 years ago, as recounted in Exodus. It is observed for eight days in the spring, with special dietary restrictions on the use of any food containing leaven. On the first and second evenings of *pesakh,* a family feast is called a *seyder* (plural, *sdorim*), at which the story of the exodus is told in songs, readings, and prayers, and unleavened bread *(matse)* is eaten.

Purim: The Feast of Lots, commemorating the rescue of the Jews of Persia from Haman's plot to exterminate every man, woman, and child of them.

rosheshone (in Hebrew, *rosh hashana,* literally, the head of the year): The Jewish New Year, observed with special prayers in the fall.

seyder: See Passover.

shabes goy: The non-Jew who may be asked to light the fire or perform other chores on the Sabbath that are forbidden to Sabbath-observing Jews.

sheeny: A term of opprobrium and contempt for a Jew, especially formerly, used by anti-Semites.

shive: The seven days of mourning for the dead, beginning immediately after burial, and observed by the family of the deceased. Friends come to extend condolences.

shnaps: Brandy, whiskey, or other alcoholic drink.

shnorer: A beggar or panhandler; also, anyone who lives by sponging on others, a moocher.

shoykhet: A man certified as a slaughterer of animals, in accordance with the requirements of *kashres.*

shul: Synagogue.

shvartser: A black. A neutral term in Yiddish, but when used in English, it may have patronizing or contemptuous connotations.

simkhe: A joyous event or celebration, such as a wedding or *bris.*

yakhne: A busybody or gossip, especially a shrewish woman who delights in spreading rumors.

yom kiper (in Hebrew, *yom kipur*): The Day of Atonement, the last of the annual Ten Days of Penitence that begin with the first day of *rosheshone.* It is observed by day-long prayer in the synagogue and total abstinence from food and drink.

yortsayt: The anniversary of someone's death, observed by the lighting of a memorial candle and the recitation of a special doxology (the mourner's *kadish*) at prayer services.

Bibliography

Adams, B.N. *Kinship in an Urban Setting*. Chicago: Markham, 1968.

Atchley, R.C. *The Social Forces in Later Life*. California: Wadsworth, 1977.

Banton, M.P. *Roles: An Introduction to the Study of Social Relations*. New York: Basic Books, 1965.

Becker, G. *Growing Old in Silence*. Berkeley: University of California Press, 1980.

Bengtson, V.L., and N.E. Cutler, "Generations and Intergenerational Relations: Perspective on Age Groups and Social Change," in *Handbook of Aging and the Social Sciences*, R.H. Binstock and E. Shanas, eds. New York: Van Nostrand Reinhold, 1976.

Binstock, R.H., and E. Shanas, eds. *Handbook of Aging and the Social Sciences*. New York: Van Nostrand Reinhold, 1976.

Blau, P. *Exchange and Power in Social Life*. New York: Wiley, 1964.

Bohannan, P. "Unseen Community: The Natural History of a Research Project," in *Anthropologists at Home in North America: Methods and Issues in the Study of One's Own Society*, D.A. Messerschmidt, ed. New York: Cambridge University Press, 1981.

Bott, E. *Family and Social Network*. London: Tavistock, 1964.

Buckman, J. "The Economic and Social History of Alien Immigrants, 1880–1914." Unpublished Ph.D. diss., University of Strathclyde, Scotland, 1968.

Campbell, J. *Honour, Family, and Patronage*. Oxford: Clarendon Press, 1964.

Carp. F.M. *A Future for the Aged*. Austin: University of Texas Press, 1966.

Clark, M., and B.G. Anderson. *Culture and Aging: An Anthropological Study of Older Americans*. Springfield, Illinois: Charles C. Thomas, 1967.

Clark, M.M. Cultural Values and Dependency in Later Life," in *Aging and Modernization*, D.O. Cowgill and Lowell D. Holmes, eds. New York: Appleton-Century-Crofts, 1972.

——. "Contributions of Cultural Anthropology to the Study of the Aged," in *Cultural Illness and Health*, L. Nader and T. Maretzki, eds. Washington, D.C.: American Anthropological Association, 1973.

Cowgill, D.O., and Lowell D. Holmes, eds. *Aging and Modernization*. New York: Appleton-Century-Crofts, 1972.

Cumming, E., and W.E. Henry. *Growing Old: The Process of Disengagement*. New York: Basic Books, 1961.

——, and D.M. Schneider. "Sibling Solidarity: A Property of American Kinship." *American Anthropologist* 63:498–507 (1961).

Curtin, S.R. *Nobody Ever Died of Old Age*. Boston: Little, Brown and Company, 1972.

Dyson-Hudson, N. *Karimojong Politics*. Oxford: Clarendon, 1966.

Eckert, J.K. *The Unseen Elderly*. San Diego: Campanile Press, 1980.

Fennell, V. "Friendship and Kinship in Older Women's Organizations: Curlew Point, 1973," in *Dimensions: Aging, Culture, and Health*, C.L. Fry, ed. New York: Praeger (a James Bergin Book), 1981.

Firth, R.W. *We, the Tikopia*. London: Allen and Unwin, 1936.
———. *Two Studies of Kinship in London*. London: The Athlone Press, 1956.
———, J. Hubert, and A. Forge. *Families and their Relatives: Kinship in a Middle-Class Sector of London*. New York: Humanities Press, 1970.
Foner, A., and D.I. Kertzer. "Transitions over the Life Course: Lessons from Age-Set Societies." *American Journal of Sociology* 83:1081–1104 (1978).
Fortes, M. "Oedipus and Job in West African Religion," in *Anthropology of Folk Religion*, Charles Leslie, ed. New York: Vintage, 1960.
Francis, D. "Adaptive Strategies of the Elderly in England and Ohio," in *Dimensions: Aging, Culture, and Health*, C.L. Fry, ed. New York: Praeger (a James Bergin Book), 1981.
Frank, G. "Life Histories in Gerontology: The Subjective Side of Aging," in *New Methods for Old Age Research*, C.L. Fry and J. Keith, eds. Chicago: Center for Urban Policy, Loyola University of Chicago, 1980.
Freedman, M. *A Minority in Britain: Social Studies of the Anglo-Jewish Community*. London: Vallentine Mitchell, 1955.
Fry, C.L. "Structural Conditions Affecting Community Foundation among the Aged," in *The Ethnography of Old Age*, J. Keith, ed. Special issue of *Anthropological Quarterly* 52(1):7–18 (1979).
———. "Toward an Anthropology of Aging," in *Aging in Culture and Society*, C.L. Fry, ed. New York: Praeger (a James Bergin Book), 1980.
———, ed. *Aging in Culture and Society: Comparative Viewpoints and Strategies*. New York: Praeger (a James Bergin Book), 1980.
———. *Dimensions: Aging, Culture, and Health*. New York: Praeger (a James Bergin Book), 1981.
Gainer, B. *The Alien Invasion*. London: Heinemann, 1972.
Gans, H.J. "The Origin and Growth of a Jewish Community in the Suburbs: A Study of the Jews of Park Forest," in *The Jews: Social Patterns of an American Group*. M. Sklare, ed. Glencoe: Free Press, 1958.
Gartner, L.P. *The Jewish Immigrant in England, 1870–1914*. London: Simon, 1973.
———. "Immigration and the Formation of American Jewry, 1840–1925," in *The Jew in American Society*, M. Sklare, ed. New York: Behrman House, 1974.
———. *History of the Jews of Cleveland*. Cleveland: Western Reserve Historical Society and Jewish Theological Seminary of America, 1978.
Glazer, N. "The American Jew and the Attainment of Middle-Class Rank: Some Trends and Explanations," in *The Jews: Social Patterns of an American Group*. M. Sklare, ed. Glencoe: Free Press, 1958.
Gluckman, M. "Les Rites de Passage," in *The Ritual of Social Relations*, M. Gluckman, ed. Manchester: University Press, 1962.
Goffman, E. *The Presentation of Self in Everyday Life*. Edinburgh: University of Edinburgh Social Sciences Research Centre, 1959.
Goody, J. "Aging in Nonindustrial Societies," in *Handbook of Aging and the Social Sciences*, R.H. Binstock and E. Shanas, eds. New York: Van Nostrand Reinhold, 1976.
Gordon, A.I. *Jews in Suburbia*. Boston: Beacon Press, 1959.
Gouldner, A.W. "The Norm of Reciprocity: A Preliminary Statement." *American Sociological Review* 25:161–178 (1960).
Grabowski, J.J. "A Social Settlement in a Neighborhood in Transition, Hiram House, Cleveland, Ohio, 1896–1926." Unpublished Ph.D. diss., Case Western Reserve University, 1977.

Gulliver, P.H. *Social Control in an African Society*. Boston: Boston University Press, 1963.

Hapgood, H. *The Spirit of the Ghetto*. Cambridge: Harvard University Press, 1967.

Harris, G.G. *Casting Out Anger: Religion among the Taita of Kenya*. Cambridge: Cambridge University Press, 1978.

Hess, B. "Friendship," in *Aging and Society, Vol. 3: A Sociology of Age Stratification*. M.W. Riley et al., eds. New York: Russell Sage Foundation, 1972.

Hochschild, A.R. *The Unexpected Community*. Englewood Cliffs, New Jersey: Prentice-Hall, 1973.

Homans, G. "Social Behavior as Exchange." *American Journal of Sociology* 63 (1958).

Howe, I. *World of Our Fathers*. New York: Simon and Schuster, 1976.

Hubert, J., A. Forge, and R. Firth. *Methods of Study of Middle-class Kinship in London: A Working Paper on the History of an Anthropological Project, 1960–65*. London: Occasional Papers of the Department of Anthropology, London School of Economics and Political Science, 1968.

Jacobs, J. *Fun City: An Ethnographic Study of a Retirement Community*. New York: Holt, Rinehart and Winston, 1974.

Johnson, S.K. *Idle Haven: Community Building Among the Working Class Retired*. Berkeley: University of California Press, 1971.

Jonas, K. "Factors in Development of Community Among Elderly Persons in Age-Segregated Housing: Relationships between Involvement in Friendship Roles within the Community and External Social Roles," in *The Ethnography of Old Age*, J. Keith, ed. Special issue of *Anthropological Quarterly* 52(1):29–38 (1979).

Kayser-Jones, J.S. *Old, Alone and Neglected: Care of the Aged in Scotland and the United States*. Berkeley: University of California Press, 1981.

——. "Quality of Care for the Institutionalized Aged: A Scottish-American Comparison," in *Dimensions: Aging, Culture and Health*, C.L. Fry, ed. New York: Praeger (a James Bergin Book), 1981.

Keith, J. "Participant Observation," in *New Methods for Old Age Research*, C.L. Fry and J. Keith, eds. Chicago: Center for Urban Policy, Loyola University of Chicago, 1980.

——. *Old People as People—Social and Cultural Influences on Aging and Old Age*. Boston: Little, Brown & Company, 1982.

Kertzer, D., and O. Madison. "Women's Age-Set Systems in Africa: The Latuka of Southern Sudan," in *Dimensions: Aging, Culture and Health*, C.L. Fry, ed. New York: Praeger (a James Bergin Book), 1981.

Kleemeier, R. "Moosehaven: Congregate Living in a Community of the Retired." *American Journal of Sociology* 59:347–351 (1954).

Kramer, J.R., and S. Leventman. *Children of the Gilded Ghetto*. New Haven: Yale University Press, 1961.

Kramer, S., and J. Masur. *Jewish Grandmothers*. Boston: Beacon Press, 1976.

Krausz, E. *Leeds Jewry*. Cambridge: Heffer, 1964.

La Fontaine, J.S. "Ritualization of Women's Life-Crises in Bugisu," in *The Interpretation of Ritual*, J.S. La Fontaine, ed. London: Tavistock, 1974.

Lancaster, L. "Some Conceptual Problems in the Study of Family and Kin Ties in the British Isles." *British Journal of Sociology* 12:317–333 (1961).

Landes, R., and M. Zborowski, "Hypothesis Concerning the Eastern European Jewish Family." *Psychiatry* 13:447–464 (1950).

Lawton, M.P. *Environment and Aging*. Belmont, California: Wadsworth (a Brooks/Cole Book), 1980.

———, M. Kleban, and M. Singer. "The Aged Jewish Person and the Slum Environment." *Journal of Gerontology* 26:231–239 (1971).

Leichter, H.J., and W.E. Mitchell. *Kinship and Casework.* New York: Russell Sage Foundation, 1967.

Litwak, E. "Occupational Mobility and Extended Family Cohesion." *American Sociological Review* 25:9–21 (1960).

———. "Geographic Mobility and Extended Family Cohesion." *American Sociological Review* 25:385–394 (1960).

Malinowski, B. *Argonauts of the Western Pacific.* London: G. Routledge & Sons, 1922.

Matthews, S.H. *The Social World of Old Women: Management of Self-Identity.* Beverly Hills: Sage, 1979.

Mauss, M. *The Gift.* New York: Norton, 1925.

Middleton, J. *The Lugbara of Uganda.* New York: Holt, Rinehart, and Winston, 1965.

Mitchell, W.E. "Proximity Patterns of the Urban Jewish Kindred," *Man* 65:137–140 (1965).

———. *Mishpokhe: A Study of New York City Jewish Family Clubs.* The Hague: Mouton, 1978.

Mogey, J.M. *Family and Neighborhood: Two Studies in Oxford.* London: Oxford University Press, 1956.

Moore, S.F. "Old Age in a Life-Term Social Arena," in *Life's Career—Aging: Cultural Variations in Growing Old,* B. Myerhoff and A. Simić, eds. Beverly Hills: Sage, 1977.

Morgenstern, J. *Cleveland Fifty Years Ago: Reminiscences of Immigrant Life.* 1949.

Myerhoff, B.G. *Number Our Days.* New York: E.P. Dutton, 1978.

———, and A. Simić, eds. *Life's Career—Aging: Cultural Variations on Growing Old.* Beverly Hills: Sage, 1977.

Needham, R. "Introduction," in *Rethinking Kinship and Marriage,* R. Needham, ed. London: Tavistock Publications, 1971.

Neugarten, B.L., ed. *Middle Age and Aging: A Reader in Social Psychology.* Chicago: The University of Chicago Press, 1968.

———, and G.O. Hagestad. "Age and the Life Course," in *Handbook of Aging and the Social Sciences,* R.H. Binstock and E. Shanas, eds. New York: Van Nostrand Reinhold, 1976.

O'Brien, R. "A Jewish Minority in Leeds." Unpublished Ph.D. diss., University of Bristol, 1973.

Paine, R. "In Search of Friendship: An Exploratory Analysis in 'Middle Class' Culture." *Man,* Vol. 4, No. 4, December 1969.

Rosenberg, G.S., and D.F. Anspach, *Working Class Kinship.* Lexington, MA: D.C. Heath, 1973.

Rosow, I. *Social Integration of the Aged.* New York: Free Press, 1967.

———. *Socialization to Old Age.* Berkeley: University of California Press, 1974.

Ross, J.K. *Old People, New Lives.* Chicago: University of Chicago Press, 1977.

Rosten, L. *The Joys of Yiddish.* New York: McGraw-Hill, 1968.

Schneider, D.M. *American Kinship: A Cultural Account.* Englewood Cliff, N.J.: Prentice-Hall, 1968.

———, and G.C. Homans. "Kinship Terminology and the American Kinship System," *American Anthropologist* 57:1194–1208 (1955).

———, and R. Smith. *Class Differences and Sex Roles in American Kinship and Family Structure.* New York: Prentice-Hall, 1973.

Schneider, H.K. *Economic Man*. New York: Free Press, 1974.

Simmons, L. *The Role of the Aged in Primitive Society*. New Haven: Yale University Press, 1945.

Silver, Rabbi A.H. *A Word In Its Season*. Vol. 2. World Publishing Company.

Simić, A. "Winners and Losers: Aging Yugoslavs in a Changing World," in *Life's Career—Aging: Cultural Variations on Growing Old*, B. Myerhoff and A. Simić, eds. Beverly Hills: Sage Publications, 1977.

Sklare, M., ed. *The Jews: Social Patterns of An American Group*. New York: Free Press, 1958.

——, ed. *The Jew in American Society*. New York: Behrman House, 1974.

Sokolovsky, J. "Interactional Dimensions of the Aged: Social Network Overlapping," in *New Methods for Old Age Research*, C.L. Fry and J. Keith, eds. Chicago: Center for Urban Policy, Loyola University of Chicago, 1980.

——. *Growing Old in Different Societies: Cross-Cultural Perspectives*. Belmont: Wadsworth, 1983.

——, and C. Cohen. "The Cultural Meaning of Personal Networks for the Inner City Elderly." *Urban Anthropology* 7:323–343 (1978).

——. "Being Old in the Inner City: Support Systems of the SRO Aged," in *Dimensions: Aging, Culture and Health*, C.L. Fry, ed. New York: Praeger (a James Bergin Book), 1981.

Spencer, P. *The Samburu: A Study of Gerontocracy in a Nomadic Tribe*. London: Routledge & Kegan Paul, 1965.

——. "Opposing Streams and the Gerontocratic Ladder: Two Models of Age Organization." *Man* 2:153–174 (1976).

Spevack, V. "More Memories of 'Kinsman Cowboys,'" *The Cleveland Jewish News*. Friday, January 21, 1972.

Thomas, J. "A History of the Leeds Clothing Industry." *Yorkshire Bulletin of Economic and Social Research*, Occasional Paper, No. 1, 1953.

Townsend, P. *The Family Life of Old People*. Glencoe: Free Press, 1957.

Van Gennep, A. *The Rites of Passage*. London: Routledge & Kegan Paul, 1960.

Wax, J. "It's Like Your Own Home Here," *The New York Times Magazine*. November 21, 1976.

Weatherford, J.M. "Labor and Domestic Cycles in a German Community," in *Dimensions: Aging, Culture and Health*, C.L. Fry, ed. New York: Praeger (a James Bergin Book), 1981.

Wentowski, G.J. "Reciprocity and the Coping Strategies of Older People: Cultural Dimensions and Network Building." *The Gerontologist* 21 (no. 6):600–609 (1981).

Willmott, P., and M.D. Young. *Family and Class in a London Suburb*. London: Routledge and K. Paul, 1960.

Wirth, L. *The Ghetto*. Chicago: University of Chicago Press, 1956.

Young, M.D., and H. Geertz. "Old Age in London and San Francisco: Some Families Compared," *British Journal of Sociology* 12:124–141 (1961).

——, and P. Willmott. *Family and Kinship in East London*. Rev. ed. Baltimore: Penguin Books, 1962.

Zborowski, M., and E. Herzog. *Life Is With People: The Jewish Little-Town of Eastern Europe*. New York: International Universities Press, 1952.

Index